# Using the Internet for Active Teaching and Learning

## STEVEN C. MILLS

*The University Center of Southern Oklahoma*

**PEARSON**

Merrill
Prentice Hall

Upper Saddle River, New Jersey
Columbus, Ohio

**Library of Congress Cataloging-in-Publication Data**

Mills, Steven C.
   Using the internet for active teaching and learning / Steven C. Mills.—1st ed.
     p. cm.
   Includes bibliographical references and index.
   ISBN 0-13-110546-9
   1. Internet in education. 2. Computer-assisted instruction.  I. Title.
   LB1044.87.M55 2006
   371.33′44678–dc22

                        2005023786

**Vice President and Executive Publisher:** Jeffery W. Johnston
**Executive Editor:** Debra A. Stollenwerk
**Assistant Development Editor:** Elisa Rogers
**Editorial Assistant:** Mary Morrill
**Production Editor:** Alexandrina Benedicto Wolf
**Production Coordination:** The GTS Companies/York, PA Campus
**Design Coordinator:** Diane C. Lorenzo
**Cover Designer:** Bryan Huber
**Cover Image:** Corbis
**Production Manager:** Susan Hannahs
**Senior Marketing Manager:** Darcy Betts Prybella
**Marketing Coordinator:** Brian Mounts

This book was set in Garamond by The GTS Companies/York, PA Campus. It was printed and bound by Banta Book Group. The cover was printed by Phoenix Color Corp.

Microsoft® and Windows® are registered trademarks of the Microsoft Corporation in the U.S.A. and other countries. Screen shots and icons reprinted with permission from the Microsoft Corporation. This book is not sponsored or endorsed by or affiliated with the Microsoft Corporation.

Pearson Education Ltd.                    Pearson Education Australia Pty, Limited
Pearson Education Singapore, Pte. Ltd.     Pearson Education North Asia Ltd.
Pearson Education, Canada, Ltd.          Pearson Educación de Mexico, S.A. de C.V.
Pearson Education—Japan                Pearson Education Malaysia, Pte. Ltd.

10 9 8 7 6 5 4 3 2 1
ISBN 0-13-110546-9

FOR JOSEPH WYATT HILL AND ABIGAIL ELIZABETH LANGWELL,
*a new generation of active learners*

AND FOR ABIODUN ADEFERATI,
*a friendship formed by the Internet*

# PREFACE

There is no doubt that things are changing in the modern classroom as teachers find more ways to leverage technology for learning. As the Internet grows at exponential rates, its associated technologies provide a toolbox of educational and informational resources for enhancing teaching and learning in the classroom. The Internet is affecting, if not instigating, many of the changes that are occurring in classrooms today because of its capacity to connect learners to an almost unlimited supply of information, while providing an interface that allows flexible, multimodal, and interactive knowledge acquisition and exploration.

Computer technology and the Internet can have a significant impact on educational effectiveness. These technologies can enable teachers to deploy complex learning tasks in the classroom, using powerful instructional methodologies. In addition, certain features and capabilities of the Internet enable active learning environments, which prompt learners to become problem solvers, decision makers, communicators, and collaborators.

## ■ LEVERAGING TECHNOLOGY FOR TEACHING AND LEARNING

This textbook provides both a theoretical and a practical guide to help teachers implement active learning environments that exploit Internet technologies. The focus is on using Internet technologies to support project-based learning in the classroom. This instructional presentation has several components:

- An educational approach to using the information and communication features of Internet technologies in the classroom
- Instructional strategies for deploying those technologies in the classroom
- Tutorials and learning activities that present Internet tools and resources for use in the classroom.

*Web-enhanced learning* describes this approach to leveraging technology in the classroom. Web-enhanced learning is flexible, interactive, and media rich, and it supports both collaborative and individualized instruction. The focus of Web-enhanced learning is not so much on using the Web for content delivery as it is on using Web resources to enable project-based learning in the classroom. The use of information and Internet technologies can promote active learning environments, which empower students to exercise greater autonomy in their own learning.

## ■ SOME ASSUMPTIONS ABOUT TECHNOLOGY AND LEARNING

The integration of technology into instructional activities increases the need for well-trained teachers. Currently, however, there is a lack of reliable research on using the Internet to enhance pedagogy. The teaching and learning activities presented in this text are designed to support theory-based, effective practices; they are based on the premise that learning can be facilitated by tasks that require students to acquire information and leverage it into useful knowledge. The Internet technologies that are included here rely on several assumptions about learners and the learning process:

1. *Learning is an active, constructive process.* To learn new information, ideas, or skills, students must actively engage the lesson content in meaningful and purposeful ways. Students need to integrate new material with what they already know or use it to restructure what they thought they knew. The tools and resources of the Internet can be used to create instructional situations or environments that maximize the potential for learning.

2. *Resource-rich contexts can support learning.* Resource-rich learning environments or contexts can immerse students in challenging tasks. Resource-rich learning activities frequently begin with problems in which students can become immediate participants. The information resources of the Internet make it possible to establish learning contexts in the classroom that are connected to the real world.

3. *Learners have diverse learning needs.* Students bring multiple perspectives to the classroom—that is, diverse backgrounds, learning needs, experiences, beliefs, values, and aspirations. Internet technologies provide teachers with an alternative to the one-size-fits-all approach to teaching and learning.

4. *Learning is inherently social.* Cooperative or collaborative learning processes can produce an intellectual synergy when several minds address problems from varying perspectives and with varying abilities. Classrooms can be transformed into communities of learning when the communication features and tools of the Internet are used for mutual exploration and meaning making.

## ■ ORGANIZATION OF THE TEXT

This text presents an instructional model called Web-enhanced learning. Chapters 1 through 6 provide explanations and examples of Internet communication technologies and information resources, including theories and strategies supporting Web-enhanced learning. Chapters 7 through 10 demonstrate the use of specific strategies, including information problem solving, cooperative problem solving, inquiry and discovery, and online collaborations.

The instructional approach demonstrated here focuses on projects that bring real-world problems into the classroom for students to interpret and solve. Information collection and publication are fundamental to most Web-enhanced learning activities; students compile, analyze, synthesize, compare, validate, and publish information located on and collected from the Internet. Information searches can be conducted as individual, team, or collaborative activities. Internet synchronous and asynchronous communication features can facilitate collaboration among peers, groups, and experts to solve problems or complete projects. The Internet can also enable teachers to create highly motivating and intellectually challenging exploratory learning environments for students. WebQuests are inquiry-oriented activities in which most or all of the information used by learners is drawn from the Web. These are usually group activities designed to support the analysis, synthesis, and evaluation of information.

As teachers become more familiar with Internet technologies and information resources and the ways to incorporate them in learning activities, their use will become embedded in teaching practices. And as their expertise develops, the focus will be less on the use of technology to do a task and more on the task itself with technology in a supportive role.

# ■ FEATURES OF EACH CHAPTER

Each chapter contains similar features and learning activities:

- *Real-world scenarios*—Each chapter is introduced by a story or a scenario based on real-world events and actual case studies of persons, schools, and colleges that are integrating technology into classrooms. Additional scenarios are sometimes presented throughout a chapter.

- *New Terms*—New terms are presented near the beginning of each chapter and their definitions are provided in the Glossary.

- *National Educational Technology Standards*—Each chapter identifies the standards for students and for teachers that correspond to the learning activities presented in the chapter.

- *Overview*—This section highlights the major concepts of the chapter.

- *Focus Questions*—Each lesson begins with a set of questions that focus on essential concepts, providing an advance organizer for the lesson's activities.

- *Lesson Links*—In-depth examinations of special topics related to chapter content are located on the Companion Website (www. prenhall.com/mills).

- *Building Your Toolkit*—Each lesson contains one or more step-by-step exercises or tutorials to demonstrate various Internet tools and resources.

- *Enrichment Activities*—Immediately following most toolkit activities is a reference to a practice exercise located on the Companion Website, which extends and expands the skills demonstrated in the previous activity.

- *Reflections*—Remarks at the end of each chapter motivate students to reflect on the concepts and skills just presented.

- *End-of-chapter exercises*—At the end of each chapter are four sets of exercises:

  1. *Reflecting on Practice*—Information presented is used as a basis for reflection. This section includes a *Closing the Case* activity for each real-world scenario presented, and integrates thought and action—that is, thinking about and critically analyzing one's actions to improve professional practice.

  2. *Expanding Your Skills*—These exercises or activities extend what has been learned in the chapter.

  3. *Using Productivity and Web-Authoring Tools*—These exercises suggest ways to use productivity and Web-authoring software for related learning activities.

  4. *Creating Your Own Web-Enhanced Project Lesson*—These activities provide opportunities to develop a project or a lesson that makes effective use of the Internet features presented in the chapter. These ideas can be turned into Web-enhanced lesson plans for the classroom.

# ■ CREDITS

Numerous examples of Internet tools and programs are cited in this text:

Big6™ is a product of Michael B. Eisenberg and Robert E. Berkowitz, copyright 1987. For more information visit www.big6.com.

Blackboard® is a registered trademark of Blackboard, Inc.

Dreamweaver® is a registered trademark of Macromedia.

Entourage®, FrontPage®, Hotmail®, Microsoft®, MSN®, Outlook®, PowerPoint®, and Windows® are registered trademarks of Microsoft Corporation.

Google™ is a trademark of Google, Inc.

Inspiration® and Inspiration Software® are registered trademarks of Inspiration Software, Inc.

Mac® and Macintosh® are registered trademarks of Apple Computer, Inc.

Tapped In® is a registered trademark of SRI International.

WebCT™ is a trademark of WebCT, Inc.

# ■ ACKNOWLEDGMENTS

I would like to acknowledge some of the people who have made it possible for me to write and to publish. My thanks to my editor, Debbie Stollenwerk, who patiently guided the development of this textbook. Debbie diligently worked me through numerous versions before this book took its final form.

I am also grateful to my family, who supported my efforts during the long process of writing and revising: my wife, Diane Mills, who has always encouraged me to write, and my son, Eddy Mills, whose shoulder massages and backrubs sustained me during the long hours spent in front of the computer. And thanks to Cynthia Huebner, my former assistant at the University of Kansas, for her long hours of labor acquiring permissions and proofing manuscripts.

Special thanks go to the reviewers, who provided many useful suggestions that were incorporated into the manuscript.

They are Ronald J. Anderson, Texas A&M International University; Donna J. Baumbach, University of Central Florida; J. Michael Blocher, Northern Arizona University; Janet Buckenmeyer, Lourdes College; Cathy Cavanaugh, University of North Florida; Charles D. Dickens, Tennessee State University; Abigail Garthwait, University of Maine; Debra L. Hollister, Valencia Community College; Michael Jackson, Southern Illinois University, Carbondale; Virginia R. Jewell, Columbus State University; Lorana A. Jinkerson, Northern Michigan University; Mary Juliano, Caldwell College; Sara McNeil, University of Houston; Ronghua Ouyang, Kennesaw State University; Brenda S. Peters, College of Saint Rose; Lynne Schrum, University of Utah; Steven B. Smith, University of Kansas; Lawerence A. Tomei, Duquesne University; and David VanEsselstyn, Long Island University, C. W. Post.

# BRIEF CONTENTS

# CONTENTS

*Note: Every effort has been made to provide accurate and current Internet information in this book. However, the Internet and information posted on it are constantly changing, so it is inevitable that some of the Internet addresses listed in this textbook will change.*

# Before You Begin

Integrating technology into the classroom is not so much about technology—it's about teaching and it's about learning! Before you can integrate technology into your teaching, however, you need to be proficient in using the teaching tools that computer technology makes available. Although this textbook is intended as a tutorial, it also focuses on applying technology skills to create interesting and engaging learning experiences in classrooms. The tutorials and practice exercises in this text are loaded with instructional activities and lesson plan examples that will enable you to quickly add the various tools to your teaching toolbox and incorporate your new skills into your teaching. Even though it takes some hard work to acquire these new skills, you will be making a good investment of time and effort.

## ■ RESOURCES NEEDED TO USE THIS TEXT

You will need three kinds of resources to take advantage of this text.

1. *Computer requirements.* You will need a personal computer (a Windows PC or a Macintosh) with a monitor, keyboard, mouse, and Internet access.

2. *Software requirements.* You will need a Web browser program, an e-mail account, productivity software, and an optional Web page authoring program for a few activities. Although most of the activities simply require a Web browser, such as Internet Explorer, running on a computer connected to the Internet, additional exercises are offered that integrate Web-enhanced learning with other technology tools to form a comprehensive approach to technology-enhanced learning and teaching. Many learning activities extend the skills presented through the use of word processing, electronic spreadsheet, database management, multimedia presentation, concept mapping, and Web-authoring programs.

3. *Prerequisite skills.* You should know the hardware and software specifications and the configuration of the computer you are using. You should be able to identify the hard disk, CD, and DVD drives on your computer; and you should know what version of the operating system your computer uses. You should also know some basic information about your computer network and the way your computer is connected to the Internet. In addition, you should know how to set the resolution and other settings of your monitor; you should be able to turn all the devices of your computer on and off properly; and you should know how to use a mouse and a keyboard. Finally, you should know how to locate and retrieve files on your computer and how to copy them from one location on your computer to another.

# ■ CONSIDERATIONS IN USING THE INTERNET

### Free or Fee-Based Web Tools

Websites and tools that are appropriate for classrooms and do not have a cost or fee associated with their use are used in this text. Although some tools and resources may require registration for a free account, users should be careful not to inadvertently register for tools or resources that charge a fee.

Some free websites use advertising in the form of banners and pop-up windows to generate revenue to maintain the website. Even though banner advertising is acceptable when it is appropriate to the content of the website, the author does not approve of browser windows that are opened without the user's request. Such features may have been added to a website after the printing of this textbook.

### The Volatility of the Web

Because the Web is always changing, the location of some tools or resources mentioned in this text may have changed by the time you read about them. When websites are relocated to a different folder or a different server, most responsible Webmasters will direct you to the new location. If you encounter a URL with a broken link and a forwarding feature does not appear, you should try a simple search to see whether you can locate the website yourself. If you cannot locate it, it may have been removed from the Web.

### Open-Source Software Tools

*Open-source software* has released its source code to the public domain or is copyrighted and distributed under an open-source license. An open-source license may require that the source code be distributed along with the software and be freely modifiable with only minor restrictions. An open-source license does not require the software to be available for free, but most popular open-source software can be freely downloaded on the Internet.

In 1998 Netscape Communications announced that the Netscape Communicator, a Web browser program, would be available free of charge and that its source code would also be free. Mozilla was the original code name for the product that came to be known as Netscape Navigator and then Netscape Communicator. Mozilla technologies were developed through the Mozilla.org open-source project, which serves as the virtual meeting place for those interested in using or improving the Mozilla source code.

Even though some of the examples in this textbook use Microsoft's Internet Explorer, educators may choose to use open-source products in the classroom. Although some websites work correctly only with Internet Explorer, open-source products often provide a high-quality alternative to proprietary software. For example, with Mozilla, educators can create tabs that display a Web page within a single window (without the need to open multiple browser windows) and perform HTML editing.

The term *Mozilla* is often used to refer to the open-source Web browser even though Mozilla.org currently has three main open-source products. Firefox is Mozilla's Web browser; Thunderbird is Mozilla's e-mail program, or client; and the Mozilla Suite is a Web browser, advanced e-mail and newsgroup program, chat program, and HTML editor. These products can be downloaded from the Mozilla project website at http://www.mozilla.org.

Whereas Mozilla Firefox is a Web browser for computers using the Windows operating system, Safari is the Mac OS X default Web browser. Safari uses open-source software, and Apple shares its enhancements with the open-source community. Safari can be downloaded from Apple's website at http://www.apple.com/safari/.

# ■ CONVENTIONS USED IN THIS TEXTBOOK

Several conventions are used here to standardize the explanation of tutorial steps.

- ■ The first step in selecting a command from the command menu bar is expressed by stating the menu command, followed by the option from the pull-down menu. For example, the action of selecting Open from the File menu would be expressed as **File > Open.**

- ■ Capital letters are used for keyboard key names—for example, the DELETE key.

- ■ When the tutorial steps refer to the ENTER key, Macintosh users should press the RETURN key.

- ■ Most dialog boxes have an OK button to complete an action. The tutorial step will say, "Click **OK**."

- ■ All specific user actions required to perform the tutorial steps are listed in **bold** print.

- ■ For some tasks screen shots are provided to assist the learner in visualizing the corresponding task. Even though most screen shots depict the Windows version of the program, some differences may appear. These may result from differences in browser or operating system versions or differences in hardware platforms.

- ■ If you download or save a file, you should be sure to navigate to an appropriate location on your hard disk or other media and then note the location of the file. It is best to create a folder or subdirectory to contain the files you save from lessons in this text.

# ■ BEST PRACTICES AND TEACHING STANDARDS FOR TECHNOLOGY INTEGRATION IN THE CLASSROOM

Standards identify and describe those things that are important to know and do. The National Educational Technology Standards (NETS) is an ongoing initiative of the International Society for Technology in Education (ISTE). The primary goal of the NETS project is to facilitate school improvement in the United States through educational use of technology.

The ISTE NETS project has defined standards for students (NETS•S), teachers (NETS•T), and school administrators (TSSA). These standards are useful for teachers in planning classroom learning activities as well as in developing their own technology skills. Each chapter in this textbook identifies the NETS•S and NETS•T addressed by the learning activities in the chapter.

## National Educational Technology Standards for Teachers[*]

The NETS•T build on the NETS•S to define the fundamental concepts, knowledge, skills, and attitudes teachers need for applying technology in educational settings. All current teachers as well as candidates seeking certification or endorsement in teacher preparation should meet these educational technology standards, which are designed to be general enough to fit state, university, or district guidelines and yet specific enough to define the scope of the topic. The performance indicators for each standard provide specific outcomes that can be used for evaluation and assessment of technology proficiency.

---

[*]Reprinted with permission from *National Educational Technology Standards for Teachers: Preparing Teachers to Use Technology.* Copyright © 2002, ISTE, *iste@iste.org, www.iste.org*. All rights reserved. Permission does not constitute an endorsement by ISTE.

### I. Technology operations and concepts

Teachers demonstrate a sound understanding of technology operations and concepts. Teachers

    **A.** demonstrate introductory knowledge, skills, and understanding of concepts related to technology (as described in the ISTE NETS•S).

    **B.** demonstrate continual growth in technology knowledge and skills to stay abreast of current and emerging technologies.

### II. Planning and designing learning environments and experiences

Teachers plan and design effective learning environments and experiences supported by technology. Teachers

    **A.** design developmentally appropriate learning opportunities that apply technology-enhanced instructional strategies to support the diverse needs of learners.

    **B.** apply current research on teaching and learning with technology when planning learning environments and experiences.

    **C.** identify and locate technology resources and evaluate them for accuracy and suitability.

    **D.** plan for the management of technology resources within the context of learning activities.

    **E.** plan strategies to manage student learning in a technology-enhanced environment.

### III. Teaching, learning, and the curriculum

Teachers implement curriculum plans that include methods and strategies for applying technology to maximize student learning. Teachers

    **A.** facilitate technology-enhanced experiences that address content standards and student technology standards.

    **B.** use technology to support learner-centered strategies that address the diverse needs of students.

    **C.** apply technology to develop students' higher order skills and creativity.

    **D.** manage student learning activities in a technology-enhanced environment.

### IV. Assessment and evaluation

Teachers apply technology to facilitate a variety of effective assessment and evaluation strategies. Teachers

    **A.** apply technology in assessing student learning of subject matter using a variety of assessment techniques.

    **B.** use technology resources to collect and analyze data, interpret results, and communicate findings to improve instructional practice and maximize student learning.

    **C.** apply multiple methods of evaluation to determine students' appropriate use of technology resources for learning, communication, and productivity.

### V. Productivity and professional practice

Teachers use technology to enhance their productivity and professional practice. Teachers

    **A.** use technology resources to engage in ongoing professional development and life-long learning.

    **B.** continually evaluate and reflect on professional practice to make informed decisions regarding the use of technology in support of student learning.

    **C.** apply technology to increase productivity.

    **D.** use technology to communicate and collaborate with peers, parents, and the larger community in order to nurture student learning.

## VI. Social, ethical, legal, and human issues

Teachers understand the social, ethical, legal, and human issues surrounding the use of technology in PK–12 schools and apply those principles in practice. Teachers

**A.** model and teach legal and ethical practice related to technology use.

**B.** apply technology resources to enable and empower learners with diverse backgrounds, characteristics, and abilities.

**C.** identify and use technology resources that affirm diversity.

**D.** promote safe and healthy use of technology resources.

**E.** facilitate equitable access to technology resources for all students.

# National Educational Technology Standards for Students*

The technology standards for students are divided into six broad categories, which provide a framework for linking performance indicators to the standards. Teachers can use these standards as guidelines for planning technology-based activities.

1. *Basic operations and concepts*
   - Students demonstrate a sound understanding of the nature and operation of technology systems.
   - Students are proficient in the use of technology.
2. *Social, ethical, and human issues*
   - Students understand the ethical, cultural, and societal issues related to technology.
   - Students practice responsible use of technology systems, information, and software.
   - Students develop positive attitudes toward technology uses that support lifelong learning, collaboration, personal pursuits, and productivity.
3. *Technology productivity tools*
   - Students use technology tools to enhance learning, increase productivity, and promote creativity.
   - Students use productivity tools to collaborate in constructing technology-enhanced models, prepare publications, and produce other creative works.
4. *Technology communications tools*
   - Students use telecommunications to collaborate, publish, and interact with peers, experts, and other audiences.
   - Students use a variety of media and formats to communicate information and ideas effectively to multiple audiences.
5. *Technology research tools*
   - Students use technology to locate, evaluate, and collect information from a variety of sources.
   - Students use technology tools to process data and report results.
   - Students evaluate and select new information resources and technological innovations based on their appropriateness for specific tasks.
6. *Technology problem-solving and decision-making tools*
   - Students use technology resources for solving problems and making informed decisions.
   - Students employ technology in the development of strategies for solving problems in the real world.

---

*Reprinted with permission from *National Educational Technology Standards for Students: Connecting Curriculum and Technology*. Copyright © 2002, ISTE, *iste@iste.org*, *www.iste.org*. All rights reserved. Permission does not constitute an endorsement by ISTE.

# CHAPTER 1

# Active Learning Using the Internet
## *An Introduction*

Diane Cunningham has been teaching fourth grade for 8 years. She has always maintained a structured, organized class and is proud of the fact that she makes it through all the curriculum objectives for her class each school year. Her school recently received a grant from the state department of education for a project to create technology-rich classrooms in selected fourth- and fifth-grade classrooms. As a result, the school district will place 10 computers with software and Internet connections in each of two classrooms in her school.

Ms. Cunningham was recently selected by her principal to be one of the teachers in the pilot project during the following school year. Although she is excited about getting the new technology resources in her classroom, she is not sure how she will integrate technology into her regular teaching routine. She is concerned both about getting sidetracked from the curriculum objectives by the presence of so much technology and about providing evidence that the use of technology has impacted student learning.

In discussions with the district technology coordinator, her principal, and several of her technology-savvy colleagues, Ms. Cunningham learns that in a technology-rich classroom the technology should facilitate student learning but should not be the focus of it. Her colleagues tell her that she will begin to have new expectations for her students as they assume responsibility for their own learning.

Ms. Cunningham realizes that with students using technology tools and information resources to accomplish learning activities, her technology-rich classroom may not be as well organized and structured as it was before. She now recognizes, however, that a classroom where students assume responsibility for learning and are motivated to pursue deeper understanding of curriculum content is better than a classroom focused solely on accomplishing curriculum objectives. Ms. Cunningham is looking forward to using the technology tools in her technology-rich classroom to develop a new understanding of teaching and learning.

## NEW TERMS

| | |
|---|---|
| blackboard | course management software |
| cognitive tools | courseware |

e-learning
pedagogical content knowledge
plagiarism
student-centered learning
TEACH Act
universal design

Web accessibility
Web-based instruction
Web-enhanced learning
Web portal
WebCT

## National Educational Technology Standards for Teachers

The following NETS•T are addressed by the lesson content and learning activities in this chapter:

### II. Planning and Designing

**A.** Design technology-enhanced learning opportunities to support diverse needs
**B.** Apply current research on teaching and learning with technology
**C.** Identify, locate, and evaluate technology resources
**D.** Plan for the management of technology resources
**E.** Manage student learning in a technology-enhanced environment

### III. Teaching, Learning, and the Curriculum

**A.** Facilitate technology-enhanced experiences to address standards
**B.** Use technology to support learner-centered strategies
**C.** Apply technology to develop students' higher order skills
**D.** Manage student learning activities

## National Educational Technology Standards for Students

The following NETS•S are addressed by the lesson content and learning activities in this chapter:

### 1. Basic Operations and Concepts

• Demonstrate sound understanding of technology
• Be proficient in the use of technology

### 2. Social, Ethical, and Human Issues

• Understand ethical, cultural, and societal issues related to technology
• Practice responsible use of technology
• Develop positive attitudes toward technology

### 3. Technology Productivity Tools

• Use technology to enhance learning, increase productivity, and promote creativity
• Use tools to collaborate, prepare publications, and produce creative works

## OVERVIEW

Today's classrooms must teach students to think critically; analyze and synthesize information to solve technical, social, economic, political, and scientific problems; and work productively in groups. The real power of educational technology is its ability to support the development of these skills by facilitating basic changes in the way teaching and learning occur in the classroom. The information resources and processing features of the Internet have great potential for creating active, student-centered learning environments.

In student-centered classrooms teachers, students, and instructional resources assume roles that are fundamentally different from those in teacher-directed classrooms. Today's teacher must be a technologist, instructional designer, facilitator, evaluator, and colearner. And students must begin to manage their own learning and work in teams with other students to accomplish learning tasks.

Integrating technology into the curriculum of the classroom is becoming an inseparable part of good teaching. The use of technology should foster learning that goes beyond information retrieval to problem solving and should promote the deep processing of ideas, increase student engagement with the subject matter, promote teacher and student motivation for learning, and increase student-to-student and student-to-teacher interactions.

Tools for planning and designing learning activities using the Internet are introduced in this chapter. These lesson planning tools will help you develop project-based lessons using Internet technologies and resources.

## Lesson 1.1    Using the Internet to Support Active Learning in the Classroom

### FOCUS QUESTIONS

- How can Internet technologies be used as cognitive tools for learning?
- How does the use of Internet technologies in the classroom change the roles of teachers and students?
- What is Web-enhanced learning?
- What are the differences between Web-enhanced learning and Web-based instruction?

## ■ USING INTERNET TECHNOLOGIES AS COGNITIVE TOOLS FOR STUDENT-CENTERED LEARNING

The world is changing from an industrialized society to a knowledge-based society. Unlike workers of the industrial age, who were expected to acquire most of the necessary knowledge prior to performing a job, information-age workers are expected to process large amounts of information on the job and develop the knowledge needed to solve problems or make decisions. The complex skills that define success for workers of the information age include critical thinking and doing, creativity, collaboration and teamwork, cross-cultural understanding, communication using a variety of media, technological fluency, and continuous learning of new skills (Trilling & Hood, 1999).

One way for schools and classrooms to address complex skills is by deploying technology in the classroom to support active, **student-centered learning.** In student-centered classrooms the goal of education is to create independent, autonomous learners who assume the responsibility for their own learning (Weimer, 2002). Weimer identified seven principles of teacher behavior in classrooms that are student-centered (see Figure 1-1).

Current research on learning suggests that the real power of technology in the classroom is its potential to facilitate basic changes in the way teaching and learning occur. Based on teaching and learning theories that focus on students exploring, manipulating, and generating knowledge, teachers can build student-centered learning environments supported and enabled by the information and communication technology resources available through the Internet.

What makes the Internet advantageous for supporting teaching and learning in the classroom is not only its capability of supporting a number of media features—such as text, graphics, animation, audio, video, or hyperlinks—but also its support of a number of pedagogical methodologies that can provide teachers with valuable and necessary tools for teaching and learning (Reeves & Reeves, 1997). Principally, Internet technologies can function as cognitive tools for researching and representing knowledge. **Cognitive tools** are both mental mechanisms and digital devices that support, guide, and extend the thinking processes of users (Derry, 1990). Cognitive tools function as intellectual partners to stimulate and facilitate critical thinking and higher order learning in students (Jonassen, 2000). Some examples of computer-based cognitive tools include databases, spreadsheets, multimedia software, graphic organizers, graphing and charting programs, and computer programming languages. Using Internet technologies as cognitive tools has the potential to augment teaching and learning in several ways (Oliver, Omari, Herrington, & Herrington, 2000):

- *Student-centered learning*—Learning activities enhanced by Internet technologies can create powerful learning environments that facilitate independent and collaborative student-centered learning.

| FIGURE 1–1 | Principles of Learner-Centered Teaching |
| --- | --- |
| **PRINCIPLE 1:** | **Teachers do learning tasks less.** Teachers must stop always doing the learning tasks of organizing content, generating examples, asking and answering questions, summarizing discussion, solving problems, constructing diagrams, and others. |
| **PRINCIPLE 2:** | **Teachers do less telling; students do more discovering.** Teachers should stop telling students everything they need to know and begin to permit students to find out for themselves what they need to know. |
| **PRINCIPLE 3:** | **Teachers do more design work.** With student-centered learning the instructional design functions of the teacher are more important because learning activities become the vehicles by which learning occurs. |
| **PRINCIPLE 4:** | **Teachers do more modeling.** Teachers must assume the role of master learner and demonstrate for students how expert learners approach learning tasks. |
| **PRINCIPLE 5:** | **Teachers do more to get students learning from and with each other.** Teachers often underestimate the potential of students working together collaboratively and cooperatively on learning tasks. |
| **PRINCIPLE 6:** | **Teachers work to create climates for learning.** With student-centered learning teachers are much more involved in designing and implementing activities that create conditions conducive to learning. |
| **PRINCIPLE 7:** | **Teachers do more with feedback.** Evaluation and assessment are used to maximize learning through the constructive delivery of feedback to students. |

*Source:* From *Learner-Centered Teaching: Five Key Changes to Practice* by M. Weimer, 2002, San Francisco: Jossey-Bass. Copyright 2002 by John Wiley & Sons. Reprinted with permission of John Wiley & Sons, Inc.

- *Collaborative learning*—The communication features of the Internet provide meaningful ways for students to learn with and from one another.
- *Student engagement*—The multimedia features of the World Wide Web motivate students to work with information and content, to reflect on the material, and to articulate their knowledge and understanding.
- *Scaffolding*—Web-enhanced learning activities provide multiple methods for teachers to support student learning without relying primarily on direct instruction.
- *Authentic settings*—The information features of the World Wide Web provide authentic or real-world contexts to support transfer of knowledge to other contexts.
- *Lifelong learning*—Learning activities that utilize Internet technologies can motivate students and help them learn to manage their own learning.

Many of the features of the Internet have great potential for educational and instructional use that make the Internet more than just another medium for the delivery of instruction. Internet technologies and resources can support teaching and learning through interactive communication, learner control, collaboration, authentic contexts, and access to varied expertise. Using these features in the classroom, however, may require a fundamental change in the way teaching and learning take place.

## ■ CREATING ACTIVE LEARNING ENVIRONMENTS

For students to learn, they must do more than just listen to a lecture or a presentation from a teacher—they must *do* something. And then they must think about what they are doing. Active learning occurs when instructional activities involve students in doing things and thinking about what they are doing.

| TABLE 1–1 | A Comparison of Traditional and Active Learning Environments |
|---|---|
| **Traditional learning environment** | **Active learning environment** |
| Teacher-centered instruction | Student-centered learning |
| Single-sense stimulation | Multisensory stimulation |
| Single-path progression | Multipath progression |
| Single media | Multimedia |
| Isolated work | Collaborative work |
| Information delivery | Information exchange |
| Passive | Active/exploratory/inquiry-based |
| Factual, knowledge-based | Critical thinking/informed decision making |
| Reactive response | Proactive, planned action |
| Isolated, artificial context | Authentic real-world context |

*Source:* Reprinted with permission from *National Educational Technology Standards for Students; Connecting Curriculum and Technology.* Copyright © 2000, ISTE, iste@iste.org, www.iste.org. All rights reserved. Permission does not constitute an endorsement by ISTE.

A highly active (and interactive) learning environment has always been one aspect of the classroom of effective teachers. Technology can enhance and extend instructional activity (and interactivity) to stimulate students to engage in learning even as it makes teaching a more enjoyable experience. Table 1–1 compares the attributes of new, active learning environments facilitated by technology with the traditional classroom learning environment.

Active learning environments are characterized by meaningful or relevant activity that is directly related to the curriculum and supported by knowledge-building collaboration with peers and tutors and by the expert guidance of a teacher (see also Bruce & Levin, 1997; Collis, 1997). For example, a teacher elicits prior knowledge from students through discussions about the content and then legitimizes the content and related concepts by making it relevant to the lives of the students. Discussion is a common strategy for promoting active learning, as are approaches based on a problem-solving model, such as role playing, simulations, debates, and dramatic presentations. In active learning environments, teachers and students assume roles that are fundamentally different from those in traditional learning environments.

## New Roles for Teachers

As Ms. Cunningham worked to implement her technology-rich classroom, she discovered that using technology as a tool for teaching and learning changed her role as a teacher. The implementation of technology-enhanced, student-centered learning environments requires teachers to change their beliefs about classroom practices and, in some cases, change their actual classroom practices (Pedersen & Liu, 2003). In a student-centered learning environment, the role of the teacher shifts from directing decisions about learning to guiding, facilitating, and supplementing instruction. In the new learning environments facilitated by technology, the role of the teacher becomes much more diverse and multifaceted.

- *The teacher as learner*—In a student-centered learning environment it is no longer necessary for the teacher to know all there is to know about a particular subject or topic being discussed, studied, or researched. Instead, teachers shift from teaching their students to learning *with* their students and sometimes learning *from* their students (McCain & Jukes, 2001). Teachers maintain relevance in the classroom by modeling the process of learning that they are asking their students to perform.

■ *The teacher as instructional designer*—Proficiency in instructional design methodologies is necessary to effectively apply student-centered learning principles in learning environments using the Internet (Tennyson, 2001). The usual approach is based on principles of knowledge transmission (Vermunt & Verloop, 1999) and focuses on the elaboration and structuring of domain content (Hoogveld, Paas, Jochems, & van Merrienboer, 2001). The instructional strategies that support student-centered learning require teachers to design activities that enable students to master complex cognitive skills used to construct knowledge. Thus, teachers must learn *how* to teach their particular content or subject matter—something Shulman (1986) calls **pedagogical content knowledge** (PCK)—so that students understand the way that knowledge develops and can apply that knowledge flexibly and in multiple contexts (Davis & Krajcik, 2005).

■ *The teacher as instructional facilitator and coach*—In a student-centered classroom students are actively engaged in aspects of learning that are generally performed by the teacher in a conventional classroom (Brush & Saye, 2000). Instilling in students the responsibility for their own learning is probably one of the most important lessons a teacher can impart. The teacher should model the interpretation and extrapolation of information by guiding, consulting, providing feedback, and even colearning with the student.

■ *The teacher as evaluator*—In a student-centered learning environment product and process are both important aspects of learning. Therefore, the teacher not only evaluates final student performance on a central task or problem but also designs measures to evaluate the underlying activities and procedures (Brush & Saye, 2000). These process measures can be derived from observations, interviews, student logs, outlines, presentations, and ratings from team or group members.

■ *The teacher as technologist*—For students to become knowledge constructors, problem solvers, and critical thinkers, technology must be an integral part of the learning process. In student-centered learning environments, technology is a tool the teacher uses for teaching and learning. The teacher does not have to be a technology expert but must be confident in using technology and in supporting student use of technology.

## New Expectations for Students

As Ms. Cunningham began to deploy technology resources in her classroom, she found that her expectations for her students were changing. Technology helps to create an environment in which students take on more of the responsibility for their own learning.

■ *The student as active learner*—Classrooms that are conducive to learning are characterized by action; learning is enhanced when students are engaged in processing personally relevant content and are reflective during the learning process. Active learners are involved in setting meaningful goals for learning and then using, experiencing, or otherwise manipulating lesson content. Advanced reasoning, comprehension, and composition skills are more likely to be acquired through an interaction with content rather than through the transmission of facts.

■ *The student as intentional learner*—In student-centered learning environments students should view learning as a goal and not an incidental outcome. Students must be purposeful about learning not only through the acquisition of information, but through the use of techniques and strategies that help them learn. Students must learn how to learn like experts before they can learn to think like experts. Learning to learn is a particularly valuable skill for an intentional learner and may have a lasting influence on student achievement.

- *The student as learning manager*—Students must manage, monitor, and evaluate their own progress in completing learning activities. For example, because student-centered learning activities often involve cooperative or collaborative learning, students must practice team-building and management skills. Students who do not have appropriate skills or strategies to manage their own learning may become overwhelmed by the scope of student-centered learning activities (Brush & Saye, 2000).

- *The student as collaborator*—Students are encouraged to discuss and interact with other participants, peers, or experts inside or outside the classroom. Learning activities should create opportunities for learners to receive feedback from peers and experts, to engage in reflection on their own learning processes, and to receive guidance from teachers or peers in revising and improving their own learning and reasoning.

## ■ WEB-ENHANCED LEARNING

Although technology can support teachers and students in accessing, managing, analyzing, and sharing information (Riel & Fulton, 2001), a well-developed understanding of how to fully exploit the features and resources of the Internet in an educational context has not fully emerged (Jukes, Dosaj, & Macdonald, 2000). It is important not to decontextualize Internet technologies in the classroom by using them in isolation from the curriculum. Students must be helped to transform free-standing information into personally relevant knowledge (Hannafin, Hill, & Land, 1997).

This textbook uses the term *Web enhanced* to describe classrooms that use the Internet to create active learning environments. (Even though the World Wide Web is one of several technologies available on the Internet, the term *Web* is often used synonymously with *Internet* to refer to all the communication technologies and information resources of the Internet.) For a Web-enhanced learning approach to be effective in the classroom, it should be based on established instructional theories, teaching practices, and learning principles.

### Educational Models

A few models have been proposed that identify categories of learning activities supported by Web-based or Web-enhanced learning. For example, Oliver, Omari, Herrington, and Herrington (2000) identified four forms that Web-based learning environments and materials can assume:

1. *Information access.* The Web is used only to convey information to the learner
2. *Networked instruction.* The Web is used to present instructional elements that engage the learner
3. *Interactive learning.* The Web is used as a means to communicate and exchange ideas among learners, teachers, and experts
4. *Materials development.* The Web is used as a means for learners to create and publish materials.

Web-enhanced learning generally includes activities to access the information resources of the Web, communicate and exchange information with experts and peers, and publish products of learning.

Two educational models that have informed the approach to Web-enhanced learning presented in this textbook are worth noting. Grabowski, Koszalka, and McCarthy (2000) matched the features of the Web with six current methods of teaching to formulate four Web-enhanced learning environment strategies (WELES): (a) frame learning activities within current and meaningful realities, (b) inform learners about lesson content, (c) explore information and knowledge, and (d) try out new knowledge.

Judi Harris (1998a, 1998b) used the term *activity structures* to describe a flexible framework teachers can use to capture the most important elements of a learning activity and create contextualized environments for using Internet tools and resources. Harris identified the two primary educational applications as either collaboration with peers and/or experts at a distance (telecollaboration) or research using information resources on distant computers (teleresearch). She designated the teaching and learning activities that use these applications as curriculum-based educational telecomputing. According to Harris (1998b), telecomputing activities can be classified according to one of three primary learning processes: (a) interpersonal exchanges, (b) information collection and analysis, and (c) problem solving. She has identified 18 telecomputing structures for these three process categories, including keypals, global classrooms, telementoring, information exchanges, electronic publishing, telefieldtrips, information searches, simulations, and social action projects. These structures are intended to focus on curriculum-integrated learning rather than the telecommunications technologies used.

## Educational Dimensions: Information and Interaction

Internet technologies provide access to information that would have been impossible to access just a few years ago, including virtual libraries, electronic databases, and powerful search engines. This information can be manipulated to generate knowledge for solving problems or making decisions. The Internet also permits communication and interaction that facilitate information exchanges among peers and with experts outside the local classroom, allowing students to share ideas, ask questions, and discuss classroom projects.

These two salient features of the Internet, access to information and interaction, can be used as a basis for an educational approach to Web-enhanced learning. The information features of the Internet allow locating, organizing, and structuring information in ways that augment new knowledge and understandings. The interaction features support communication and exchanges of information in ways that augment new knowledge and understandings. These features can be combined and used to support Web-enhanced learning.

## Web-Enhanced Learning Versus Web-Based Instruction

There are two primary educational models for using the Internet and the World Wide Web for teaching and learning: Web-based instruction and Web-enhanced learning. The main distinction between them is that Web-based instruction uses the Web and Internet technologies as the primary delivery medium, whereas Web-enhanced learning uses the technologies, tools, and resources of the Internet and the World Wide Web to support teaching and learning in the classroom.

### Web-Based Instruction

Web-based instruction is also called Web-based training, Web-based learning, or simply **e-learning. Web-based instruction** is a form of distance learning that delivers instruction to the learner through a computer, using standard Internet technologies, especially the World Wide Web (Rosenberg, 2001). Online courses delivered through the Internet are examples of Web-based instruction. **Blackboard** and **WebCT** are examples of popular →**course management software** used to develop Web-based instruction, or courseware.

With Web-based instruction Web pages are structured to guide learners through a sequence of instructional activities that present information,

*Go to the Companion Website and browse Chapter 1 Lesson Links: Course Management Software to learn more about this topic.*

allow practice, provide feedback, and may even assess learning. Web-based instruction is often used for the delivery of educational content, tutoring, or drill-and-practice activities, the teacher's role is primarily supportive because the computer assumes the primary teaching load. Web-based instruction works best in classrooms or a computer lab in which each student has access to a computer.

Web-based instruction has several advantages over other forms of distance education, such as satellite broadcasts, broadband broadcasts, and compressed video broadcasts. These forms of distance education are time and place bound and, therefore, allow only synchronous delivery of instruction, with student and teacher both in a specialized classroom (albeit in different places) at the same time.

Because the Internet is widely available and relatively easy to access through a computer, Web-based instruction is a less costly form of distance education. The Internet allows for asynchronous delivery of instruction, providing anytime-anywhere communication between teacher and student. With the distinct advantages of the Internet, many universities and some K–12 schools are developing Web-based instruction to provide universal access to their courses.

### Web-Enhanced Learning

**Web-enhanced learning** is a classroom-based educational approach that allows students to use Internet technologies, especially the Web, to access information and human resources purposefully and intentionally in ways that are conducive to learning (Grabowski, Koszalka, & McCarthy, 2000). Web-enhanced learning increases the potential for learning that can be offered by a single teacher in a classroom situation.

Web-enhanced learning makes it possible to extend teaching and learning beyond mere information retrieval to problem solving and knowledge building. Web-enhanced learning has the potential to provide multiple learning contexts for both student learners and teacher learners. Web-enhanced learning can promote independent learning as well as facilitate collaborative communities of learners. This textbook presents three primary forms in which Web-enhanced learning can be used in the classroom: problem solving, inquiry and exploration, and collaborative learning.

Web-enhanced learning depends on the features of Internet technologies, such as asynchronous communication, and information access and searching. These features offer teachers powerful tools for more efficient and flexible instruction and, hopefully, more effective learning (Collis, 1997). Web-enhanced learning can work well even in classrooms that do not have a computer for each student.

---

### Building Your Toolkit:
### Educational Resources for Web-Enhanced Learning Activities

MarcoPolo is a website dedicated to providing high-quality Internet content and professional development for teachers and students throughout the United States. Its resources include standards-based, classroom-ready lesson plans, student materials, interactive learning activities, primary source materials, and assessments developed and reviewed by experts in their respective fields. MarcoPolo content covers arts and humanities, economics, geography, mathematics, reading, language arts, and science. MarcoPolo is a great off-the-shelf resource for Web-enhanced learning activities.

| STEP | PROCEDURE |
|------|-----------|
| 1. | Open your Web browser and then the website MarcoPolo: Internet Content for the Classroom at **http://www.marcopolo-education.org**. |
| 2. | To locate lesson plans and resources for a specific topic, click on the **Search MarcoPolo** button in the top right-hand corner of the home page. Your browser should display a Web page similar to Figure 1–2. |

*(Continued)*

### ▰▰ Building Your Toolkit:
### Educational Resources for Web-Enhanced Learning Activities (Continued)

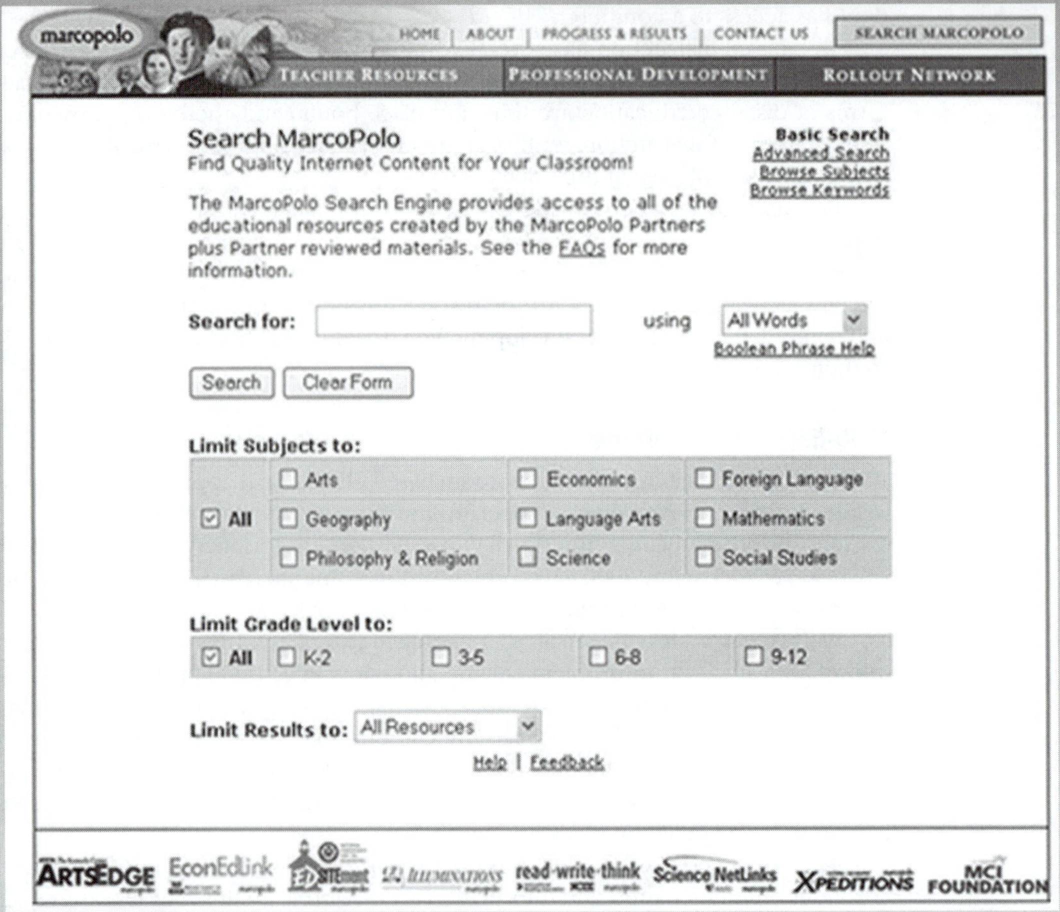

**FIGURE 1-2:   The MarcoPolo Search Page**

*Source:* Retrieved from http:www.marcopolo-education.com. © Copyright 2005 MCI Education. All rights reserved. Reproduced with permission.

| STEP | PROCEDURE |
|------|-----------|
| 3. | In the **Search for:** field, enter a subject or a topic that you teach (e.g., algebra, biology, poetry, U.S. presidents, nutrition). Then check a subject area and a grade level appropriate for your own teaching. Select **Lesson Plans Only** from the drop-down menu near the bottom of the web page. Click on the **Search** button to locate lesson plans related to your subject or topic. |
| 4. | Results appear in two tiers: first, the resources developed by MarcoPolo partners and second, the resources reviewed by the partners. The logos at the left identify the associated partner. From the search results list, select two or three lesson plans to view and/or print (there may be a link to a printable version of the lesson). What elements (objectives, procedures, assessment, etc.) are included in these lesson plans? What components are common across lesson plans from different sources? What components do you think need to be included in lesson plans? |
| 5. | For each of the lesson plans you selected, consider the teaching and learning strategies, procedures, and assessments used in the lesson. What is the teacher's role in this lesson? What is the student's role? Would this lesson be suitable to use for Web-enhanced learning? Explain. |
| 6. | MarcoPolo's lessons are aligned with national education standards. Many states have also aligned MarcoPolo with state standards. From the MarcoPolo home page, select the **Rollout Network** button and then the **Rollout Progress** and **Content & Web Projects** links on the left. Review the information for your state for each of the links. |

*(Continued)*

## Building Your Toolkit:
## Educational Resources for Web-Enhanced Learning Activities (Continued)

| STEP | PROCEDURE |
| --- | --- |
| **7.** | MarcoPolo is a Web portal to the educational resources of a number of organizations providing curriculum standards and content. A **Web portal** is a website or service that offers a broad array of resources and services, such as e-mail, forums, search engines, and related contents. The first Web portals were online services such as America OnLine. Now Web portals can also be theme or topic specific, like MarcoPolo, providing educational content for teachers and students. A Web portal may also be called a *portal*. |

Return to the MarcoPolo home page. On the right side you will see a list of partners. Move your mouse pointer over each of the partner icons to view the type of content each provides. Select one or more of the partner websites, and review the information featured. When you select a partner website, a new browser window is opened, so you can simply close the new browser window to return to the MarcoPolo Website.

**Go** to the Companion Website and browse *1.1 Building Your Toolkit Enrichment Activity: More Educational Resources for Teachers.* Use the Internet resources in the enrichment activity to locate more activities for Web-enhanced learning.

## Lesson 1.2    Planning Web-Enhanced Learning Activities

### FOCUS QUESTIONS

- What cognitive processes do students perform when learning with multimedia?
- What strategy should be used in planning and developing Web-enhanced learning projects?
- What is a Web-enhanced learning lesson plan? What is a project sample? How is each of these tools used in developing Web-enhanced projects?
- What practical considerations should be given to planning and designing Web-enhanced learning activities?

### ■ DESIGN OF WEB-ENHANCED LEARNING ACTIVITIES

The instructional tasks a teacher assigns have a lot to say about that teacher's theories and beliefs about teaching and learning (Christie, 2002). Different approaches to teaching the same content can represent very different theories. For example, paper-and-pencil activities in which students choose a correct answer or solution may indicate that getting the right answer is what matters most, whereas instructional activities that have students construct a solution may indicate that learning how to solve a problem is just as important as getting the right answer.

Changes in the roles of teachers and students in active, student-centered classrooms can also influence the way instructional materials are designed, developed, and delivered. This lesson will provide you with some basic tools to help you determine the appropriate Internet technologies for particular subject matter and learning goals. These tools will also help you select teaching methodologies that are appropriate to meet the multiple learning needs of students.

Designing learning activities that use Internet information resources and communication technologies is a complex process. Web-enhanced learning activities require enough structure and organization that students have a clear understanding of what they are to accomplish. Yet the learning process should be open-ended so that students can follow their interests while completing the project.

Oliver (2000) specified a set of design strategies for learning activities in Web-based learning environments:

1. *Choose meaningful contexts for learning.* Create settings that provide a connection between learning and the purposes for which the learning is intended.

2. *Choose learning activities ahead of the content.* First, establish the goals and outcomes of learning, and then decide what resources and content are needed to support the learning activities.

3. *Choose open-ended and unstructured tasks.* Process is often as much a part of the solution as the exhibits created.

4. *Make resources plentiful.* Learning activities should grow and evolve over time as students contribute to the knowledge base of the activities.

5. *Provide supports for learning.* In Web-based learning environments, scaffolds to support learning can take many forms, including explanations, feedback, examples, and demonstrations.

6. *Use authentic assessment activities.* Students are motivated to learn when learning activities are related to the planned assessment.

## ■ THE PLANNING PROCESS

As Ms. Cunningham began planning and developing technology-based learning activities, she formulated a process for developing classroom projects that used Internet technologies and resources (see Figure 1–3). This planning process allowed her to develop high-quality, curriculum-based Web-enhanced learning activities and minimize technology-related problems and issues when students performed the activities.

The first step in designing Web-enhanced learning projects is to determine the learning objectives, which should always support the classroom curriculum. Then the assessment protocols should be established. Assessment should be based on the learning objectives and should take into consideration the processes of learning as well as the products of learning. Assessment should identify a final student exhibit, such as a Web page, an oral presentation, a written report, or some other artifact of learning. Rubrics are often used to establish an objective basis for evaluating both process and product learning.

Once learning objectives and assessment plans are established, teachers should identify and define the learning tasks that will accomplish the learning objectives and permit students to complete the assessment process. Internet information resources that support the learning tasks should also be identified and their use described. The learning tasks should then be structured and sequenced to keep students on task while allowing them the flexibility to pursue related questions and issues.

Once the plan for a project is complete, the learning tasks should be rehearsed to ensure that their sequence and associated information resources will lead students to accomplish the learning objectives. Links to information resources should always be verified as accurate and appropriate. After any necessary revisions the project is ready for implementation in the classroom, although there will be additional revisions and improvements when it is actually used by students.

| FIGURE 1–3 | Steps for Building Web-Enhanced Learning Activities |
|---|---|

1. Identify curriculum-based goals for student learning.
2. Establish learning objectives that indicate accomplishment of curriculum goals.
3. Plan for assessment of student process and product learning.
4. Define learning tasks and identify information resources that accomplish learning objectives.
5. Structure and sequence learning tasks to work with corresponding Internet technologies.
6. Rehearse and revise learning tasks before presenting to students.

# ■ ORGANIZATIONAL TOOLS

Because the use of Internet technologies to enhance teaching and learning in the classroom is a complex instructional process, this textbook uses two organizational tools for planning and structuring Web-enhanced learning activities. The Web-enhanced learning (WEL) lesson plan is a project development tool for documenting the learning goals and objectives and the Internet technologies and information resources associated with the learning activity. The WEL project sample is a planning tool for recording the essential elements of a learning activity, including its instructional purposes and the procedures for later adaptation to a Web-enhanced learning project.

## WEL Lesson Plans

For meaningful learning to occur in Web-enhanced learning environments, learners must engage in several cognitive processes. According to Mayer (2001), the processes that are essential for active learning with multimedia are (a) selecting relevant information, (b) organizing selected information, and (c) integrating selected information with existing knowledge. The components of the WEL lesson plan are designed to support these processes (see Table 1–2).

The WEL lesson plan is intended to be a flexible tool for planning and designing projects for Web-enhanced learning (see Figure 1–4); it provides a road map for achieving curriculum-related learning goals with specific activities. WEL lesson plans can be adapted to the content, instructional strategies, and supporting Web resources of a project. For example, a teacher might select a lesson plan from MarcoPolo or another lesson plan website and adapt its content to the WEL lesson plan. Thus, the structure of the plan may differ from project to project, based on the learning environment or the setting of the project.

Teachers can use elements of the lesson plan for student handouts or project Web pages. For example, the teacher could create a student syllabus for a project using the title, objectives, background, scenario, problem statement, procedures, resources, and assessment components.

| TABLE 1–2 | Cognitive Processes Supported by a WEL Lesson Plan | | |
|---|---|---|---|
| **Cognitive process for multimedia learning** | **Description of cognitive process** | **Example of cognitive process** | **Components of WEL lesson plan** |
| Selecting: bringing information into working memory | Learner pays attention to relevant words and pictures to create a word base and an image base. | In viewing a narrated animation on lightning formation, learner pays attention to words and pictures describing each of the main steps. | • Background information<br>• Resources<br>• Credits/references |
| Organizing: building structural relations among information elements | Learner builds internal connections among selected words to create a coherent verbal model and among pictures to create a coherent pictorial model. | Learner organizes the steps into a cause-and-effect chain for the words and for the pictures. | • Title/topic<br>• Curriculum area<br>• Grade level<br>• Scenario<br>• Procedures<br>• Teaching/learning strategies |
| Integrating: building connections between incoming information and relevant prior knowledge | Learner builds external connections between the verbal and the pictorial models and with prior knowledge. | Learner makes connections between corresponding steps in the verbal chain and the pictorial chain and justifies the steps on the basis of knowledge of electricity. | • Problem/task<br>• Standards of learning<br>• Objectives<br>• Assessment |

*Source:* From *Multimedia Learning* by R. E. Mayer, 2001, Cambridge, UK: Cambridge University Press. Copyright 2001. Reprinted with the permission of Cambridge University Press.

| FIGURE 1–4 | Lesson Plan Template for Web-Enhanced Learning Activity |
|---|---|
| Title/topic (Organizing) | State an interesting, attention-getting title. |
| Problem/task (Integrating) | State the problem or task the learner needs to solve or perform. |
| Curriculum area (Organizing) | State the curriculum subject area to which the learning activity relates. |
| Grade level (Organizing) | State the grade level or range for which the learning task is appropriate. |
| Standards of learning (Integrating) | State subject-specific standards and grade-specific technology standards to be addressed by the project. |
| Objectives (Integrating) | State the learning goals, objectives, or purpose of the project relative to the curriculum and technology standards. |
| Background information (Selecting) | Provide orienting or organizing information about the project, including prerequisite learning, facts, concepts, or rules needed to complete the project. |
| Scenario (Organizing) | Develop a context for the project based on a real-world problem or task that will focus attention on the subject matter and generate learner interest in the project. |
| Procedures (Organizing) | Describe the step-by-step procedures the learner should follow to complete the project. Describe any alternative approaches or adaptations that learners may use. Allow for deviation. |
| Resources (Selecting) | State what Web resources are available for the learner to appropriately and successfully complete the project's stated goals, objectives, or purpose. Identify other resources that would enhance the learning experience. |
| Teaching/learning strategies (Organizing) | Describe the teaching and learning methods used to complete the project (may be included in the procedures). Consider teaching methods that address different learning needs. If appropriate, consider alternative teaching methods for teaching the same information or skills. |
| Assessment (Integrating) | State what the learner will do to demonstrate understanding and mastery of objectives (should be directly tied to the objectives). State what assessment process (rubrics) will be used to determine whether learners have understood the material and activities of the lesson. |
| Credits/references (Selecting) | If the project was adapted from another project or lesson plan, provide credits. If original sources are used in background information, list references. |

If additional background information is needed, the teacher could provide printed handouts with background information or could direct students to websites with background information. In some of the tutorials and exercises in this textbook, you will be asked to create a student handout appropriate to the grade level or subject you teach. You can use components from the lesson plan to create handout materials for Web-enhanced learning projects.

## WEL Project Samples

Ms. Cunningham discovered new ideas and resources for technology-based or Web-enhanced projects when she was not necessarily trying to work on lesson plans. So she devised a tool for recording the main elements of the idea or resource that she could file away and revisit later when she was ready to use it. She called her tool a *project sample*.

A project sample is like an abridged lesson plan. In the initial phase of planning a project, you may want to draw up a project sample and then develop the project more fully over time, using the lesson plan template. The project sample includes only the title, problem/task

| FIGURE 1–5 | A Project Sample Template for Web-Enhanced Learning |
|---|---|
| Title/topic | State an interesting, attention-getting title. |
| Problem/task and/or | State the problem or task the learner needs to solve or perform. |
| Background information | Provide orienting or organizing information about the project. |
| Procedures and/or | Describe proposed procedures the learner should follow to complete the project. Describe any alternative approaches or adaptations that learners may use. |
| Resources | State what Web resources you have identified for the learner to complete the project. |
| Assessment | State what the learner will do to demonstrate understanding and mastery of objectives. |
| Credits/references | If the project was adapted from another project or lesson plan, provide credits or URL. |

or background information, procedures, and assessment components (see Figure 1–5). However, you can alter or vary the contents of a project sample to suit your project planning and development needs. A project sample is especially useful for collecting ideas for future projects. For example, if you are surfing the Internet and find an interesting lesson plan that you would like to adapt and use sometime in your classroom, it takes just a minute or two to record the essential information in the project sample template and store it away for future reference.

In chapters 3-6 project samples located on the Companion Website accompany the lessons. You can use these samples (or create similar ones) to develop complete Web-enhanced projects that are appropriate for the subject and/or grade level you teach.

# ■ PRACTICAL CONSIDERATIONS

Several practical considerations should govern the creation of learning tasks and activities using Internet information and communication resources.

## Internet Safety

Although students can have many positive experiences when the Internet is used as an educational tool, they can also be exposed to inappropriate material and can become the targets of crime and exploitation.

### Risks to Students Using the Internet

It is important for teachers and parents to understand the hazards that children and teenagers can encounter on the Internet.

- *Exposure to inappropriate material*—Much content on the Internet is not appropriate for children—for example, pornographic or sexually explicit photographs and material; hate group or racist websites; promotional material about drugs, alcohol, or tobacco; information about cults or fringe groups; or recipes for making bombs and explosives. And adults must remember that children can be victimized through conversations on the Internet, as well as through the transfer of harmful information and material.

- *Sexual harassment and exploitation*—Children and teenagers can encounter e-mail, chat, or bulletin board messages that are harassing, demeaning, or belligerent. In addition, some individuals attempt to sexually exploit children through online services;

some attempt to seduce children through the use of attention, affection, or kindness, whereas others attempt to engage in sexually explicit conversation. Sexual predators can target and stalk children online while maintaining their anonymity because on-line interactions permit deception about identity, age, and intentions.

■ *Physical molestation*—Children can provide online information or arrange encounters that can risk their own safety or that of family members. In some cases pedophiles have used e-mail, chat rooms and bulletin boards, to gain children's confidence and then have arranged face-to-face meetings, sending bus tickets or money to cover the cost of travel or traveling themselves to meet the children. On-line predators may initiate off-line contact quickly or spend a long time preparing children for face-to-face encounters. Sexual predators use gifts, such as CDs and electronic games, to attract children off line.

■ *Legal and financial risks*—Children and teenagers can knowingly or unknowingly participate in Internet transactions that have a negative legal or financial consequence. Children can incur a billable expense, provide a parent's credit card number, or participate in an activity that violates another person's rights.

■ *Criminal activity*—Children and teenagers can also knowingly or unknowingly become involved in criminal activity on the Internet—for example, sending computer viruses, hacking, gambling, illegally purchasing or distributing narcotics and weapons, defrauding, or illegally copying software or other copyrighted material.

### Internet Safety Tips for Teachers and Parents

The existence of hazards is not a reason to avoid using the Internet in the classroom. The best strategy is to teach students about both the benefits and the dangers of cyberspace so that they safeguard themselves from potentially dangerous situations. At the same time teachers must exercise caution:

■ *Take responsibility for what students are doing on the Internet*—The best way to ensure that students have positive online experiences is to know what they are doing on the Internet. You should spend time with students while they are online and have them show you what they are doing.

■ *Use filtering and blocking software*—Most K–12 schools are required to install software that filters out or blocks access to undesirable content or contacts on the Internet. A number of filtering or blocking programs are available for home use as well. Such programs can be configured to filter out sites that contain nudity, sexual content, or hateful or violent material or sites that advocate the use of drugs, tobacco, or alcohol. Some filtering programs can prevent children from revealing information about themselves, such as names, addresses, or telephone numbers. In addition, most Web browsers contain filtering features that restrict access to sites that have been rated appropriate for children. You can find a directory of filtering and blocking programs at http://kids.getnetwise.org/tools/ but such programs should not be relied upon as a complete solution.

■ *Never give out identifying information*—Students' home addresses, school names, and telephone numbers should never be provided in a public message, such as chat or bulletin boards or classroom Web pages. Nor should photographs of individual children be posted on classroom websites. Instead, photos of their projects and work products can be posted. With younger children it is a good idea to create a classroom e-mail address, which you can monitor as students participate in online discussions. In addition, children and teenagers should never be allowed to arrange a face-to-face meeting with another computer user without teacher or parent intervention and permission. Adults should also be cautious about revealing personal information, such as social security numbers, credit card or bank information, mailing addresses, or e-mail addresses.

■ *Set reasonable rules and guidelines for computer and Internet use by students*— Discuss the rules for Internet use, and post them in the classroom or the computer lab as a reminder. Monitor students' compliance with these rules, and be aware of the amount of time children and teens spend on the computer. Excessive use of on-line services can be a clue to a potential problem.

Online services should not be used as electronic babysitters. Because the Internet is a virtual, or artificial, reality, teachers should instruct their students in two fundamental principles of Internet use:

1. *Just because information is published online, it is not necessarily true.* Because there are no editorial guidelines or restrictions for posting information on the Internet, students will probably encounter misinformation published by disreputable sources. Chapter 5 provides strategies to help students evaluate website content for authenticity and validity.

2. *People online may not be who they seem to be.* The virtual reality of the Internet facilitates deception, making it easy for people to pretend to be someone else and to misrepresent their intentions. Instruct students not to click on any links that are contained in an unsolicited e-mail or an e-mail from someone they do not know. Such links can lead to inappropriate websites. In addition, instruct students never to respond to messages or bulletin board items that are suggestive, obscene, belligerent, or threatening or that make them feel uncomfortable. You should encourage students to report any questionable message and should then forward a copy to the technology coordinator or network administrator of your school or school district.

## Copyright and Fair Use

The copyright protections that are normally associated with print also apply to the use of text, images, video, and audio on the World Wide Web. Fair use of copyrighted materials, however, permits their use for educational purposes such as criticism, commenting, news reporting, teaching, scholarship, and research. The Consortium of College and University Media Centers (CCUMC), convened a group of publishers, authors, and educators in the mid-1990s to draft guidelines for applying the fair use exemption of the Copyright Act of 1976. These guidelines can assist teachers and students in creating multimedia projects that include portions of copyrighted works but do not require the permission of copyright owners. In addition, the →**TEACH Act** of 2001 expanded the scope of educators' rights to perform and display copyrighted works.

Go
to the Companion
Website and browse *Chapter 1
Lesson Links: The TEACH Act
of 2001* to learn more about
this topic.

The fair use guidelines identified in Table 1–3 are not a legal document and thus are not legally binding. These guidelines represent only a consensus view of what constitutes fair use of a work that is included in a multimedia educational project. Nonetheless, the checklist provides teachers with a quick reference for classroom learning activities. It should be noted that downloaded resources must have been legitimately acquired by the source website and may not be reposted on another website without permission. However, links to resources can be posted.

School or classroom acceptable-use policies can clarify the fair use of copyrighted materials for teachers and students. Such policies should include the following components:

- A disclaimer of school liability if a student or staff member violates copyrighted material
- Restrictions on making copies of school-owned copyrighted commercial software, music, images, or other materials
- Restrictions on downloading copies of copyrighted commercial software, music, images, or other materials
- A procedure for monitoring materials posted to the school's website
- Guidelines for obtaining permission to use copyrighted materials
- Guidelines for what materials can be copied and what the limitations are for making copies of copyrighted materials

| TABLE 1–3 | Checklist of Fair Use Guidelines for Educational Multimedia Projects |
|---|---|
| **Information resource** | **Fair use** |
| Graphic images in collected works | 15 images or 10% of all images in a collection, whichever is less |
| Motion media (i.e., film or videotape productions) | Up to 10% of the total or 3 minutes, whichever is less |
| Multimedia project | No more than two copies |
| Music, lyrics, or music video | Up to 10% of the work but no more than 30 seconds from an individual musical work |
| Numerical data sets (i.e., databases or spreadsheets) | Up to 10% of the total or 2,500 fields or cell entries, whichever is less |
| Photographs or illustrations | A complete image but no more than 5 from one artist or photographer |
| Poetry | Up to 250 words or an entire poem of less than 250 words, but no more than three poems or excerpts from one poet or 5 poems or excerpts from different poets |
| Text material | Up to 10% of the total or 1,000 words, whichever is less |

*Source:* Retrieved July 1, 2005, from http://www.ccumc.org/copyright/ccguides.html.

Teachers face enormous challenges in complying with copyright and fair use laws when they use the Internet for teaching and learning in the classroom. However, teachers can find many ways to model honesty and can ably use the Internet and World Wide Web to support active learning in the classroom.

## Plagiarism

Using the Internet for learning creates additional opportunities for plagiarism. **Plagiarism** refers to using someone else's words or ideas and passing them off as one's own. It is dishonest, unethical, and perhaps illegal. Copying words or ideas from someone else without giving credit, failing to put a quotation in quotation marks, giving incorrect information about the source of a quotation, and copying a majority of the words or ideas from a source are all acts of plagiarism. Changing the words of an original source is not sufficient to prevent plagiarism.

Teachers should help students develop effective literacy skills to avoid plagiarizing their source materials. Teachers can use several strategies: Make assignments clear and be specific about outcomes. Provide a list of resources and require students to formulate solutions based on them. Use rubrics for assessment that require specific components and process steps in student products. Teach students effective methods of citing sources, both electronic and print.

One of the best tools teachers have for preventing plagiarism of Internet information resources is to practice integrity and trustworthiness themselves. Just as teachers expect students to refrain from cheating on tests, teachers should abide by fair-use and copyright laws, knowing when and what may be copied for educational use and citing information resources when copyrighted information is fairly used. When teachers model integrity in their own educational practices, they demonstrate to students that how one learns is just as important as what one learns.

## Evaluation of Website Content

Because almost anyone can publish information on almost any topic, there is relatively little quality control over documents published on the Internet. Additionally, Web search engines are designed to identify and locate Web documents but not determine the appropriateness of those Web documents for individual needs (Hill & Hannafin, 1997). Consequently, it is important that teachers equip students with practical methods for exploring the Internet and acquiring a proper perspective for the information they encounter there. Students and teachers need to examine websites critically to determine their authority, authenticity, and applicability to purpose. A comprehensive discussion of evaluating website content is presented in a later chapter.

## Universal Design

**Universal design** is a concept that describes usability by the broadest range of people. When applied to the development and design of Web pages, universal design is called →__Web accessibility.__ The premise of universal design, as it is applied to the learning environment, is that a curriculum should include alternatives to make it accessible to and appropriate for individuals with different backgrounds, learning needs, abilities, and disabilities in widely varied learning contexts.

Go to the Companion Website and browse *Chapter 1 Lesson Links: Web Accessibility* to learn more about this topic.

Universal design for learning recognizes the unique nature of each learner and the need to accommodate differences by creating learning experiences that are appropriate for individual learners and that maximize their ability to progress through the curriculum. Lance and Wehmeyer (2001) developed a checklist that describes features of instructional materials for various principles of universal design (see Table 1–4). For example, instructional materials should present information in chunks that can be completed in a reasonable time frame to accommodate low physical and cognitive effort by the learner.

Web-enhanced learning activities should be designed to accommodate the needs of all learners by providing easy resource selection and delivery, alternative pathways to information, connections to experts and mentors, access to a variety of materials, multiple ways to publish work, and placement of widely varying content in structured curricular frameworks. The Internet makes it possible to design projects that are both flexible and versatile.

| TABLE 1–4 | Universal Design in Instructional Materials |
|---|---|
| **Universal design principle** | **Features of instructional materials** |
| Equitable use | Materials can be used by students who speak various languages, address a variety of levels in cognitive taxonomies, provide alternatives that appear equivalent and, thus, do not stigmatize students. |
| Flexible use | Materials provide multiple means of representation, presentation, and student expression. |
| Simple and intuitive use | Materials are easy to use and avoid unnecessary complexity, directions clear and concise and examples provided. |
| Perceptible information | Materials communicate needed information to user independent of ambient conditions or user sensory abilities, essential information highlighted, and redundancy included. |
| Tolerance for error | Students have ample time to respond, are provided feedback, can undo previous responses, can monitor progress, and are provided adequate practice time. |
| Low physical and cognitive effort | Materials present information in chunks that can be completed in a reasonable time frame. |

*Source:* From *Universal Design Checklist* by G. D. Lance and M. L. Wehmeyer, 2001, Lawrence, KS: University of Kansas, Beach Center of Disabilities. Copyright 2001 by University of Kansas. Reprinted with permission.

### Building Your Toolkit:
## Using the WEL Lesson Plan Template

You may want to use lesson plans that you find from educational resources on the Web. The WEL lesson plan is a flexible tool that can be adapted for content obtained from other sources. (You can download a word processing file with a lesson plan template from the Companion Website or create your own template using word processing or spreadsheet software.) The Educator's Reference Desk website you reviewed in the 1.1 Building Your Toolkit Enrichment Activity (on the Companion Website) is a good source for lesson plans. That website also includes a Write-a-Lesson-Plan Guide to help you develop good lesson plans.

| STEP | PROCEDURE |
|------|-----------|
| 1. | Download the WEL lesson plan template document, **WELLessonPlan.doc,** from the Companion Website and the WEL project prototype document, **WELProjectSample.doc,** also from the Companion Website, and save them on your computer; or you can prepare lesson plan and prototype documents with a word processing or spreadsheet program based on the examples presented in Figures 1–4 and 1–5. |
| 2. | Open your Web browser and then the Educator's Reference Desk website in your Web browser at **http://www.eduref.org/**. |
| 3. | Click on the **Lesson Plans** tab and then the **Write a Lesson Plan Guide.** You can view it in your browser or print it out to read it. |
| 4. | At the end of the tutorial are a number of sample lesson plans. Select a lesson plan from the list that would be appropriate for the grade level and/or subject you teach and view it in your browser or print it out. |
| 5. | Use the information on the lesson plan you selected, and adapt it for a project you would like to present in your classroom. Use the WEL project sample template (or the complete WEL lesson plan template) to adapt the lesson plan. |

> **Go to the Companion Website** and browse *1.2 Building Your Toolkit Enrichment Activity: Resources for Educational Standards.* Use the resources in the enrichment activity to identify national educational standards for creating Web-enhanced learning activities.

## REFLECTIONS

Today's classrooms must prepare students to think critically; analyze and synthesize information to solve technical, social, economic, political, and scientific problems; and work productively in groups. The use of Internet technologies in the classroom provides teaching and learning tools that permit application of a powerful set of instructional methodologies and encourages teachers to design complex learning tasks and activities.

In the following chapters of this textbook you will learn to locate and use Internet and Web resources and plan and develop Web-enhanced learning activities. This text will present a number of Web-based tools and resources that will help you improve your teaching skills and practices in using technology. As you learn to create relevant, curriculum-based learning activities using the Internet, you should let the educational practices in Figure 1–6 assist you.

## EXERCISES TO REVIEW AND EXPAND YOUR SKILLS

### Set 1: Reflecting on Practice

■ *Closing the case*—The case study scenario presented at the beginning of this chapter presented Diane Cunningham, a teacher developing technology-enhanced, problem-based learning units. Develop an ending for the case study that includes solutions for

| **FIGURE 1–6** | **Educational Practices for Highly Effective Project Planning Using Web-Enhanced Learning** |
|---|---|

1. **Borrow and build.**   Use a value-added approach. Take advantage of the limitless information resources of the Internet. Start with someone else's good idea or lesson plan and make it better.

2. **Create a hook.**   Base the learning activity on real-world problems or issues that are relevant to students.

3. **Know what resources are out there.**   Conduct your own research so that you are familiar with the topic and have some idea of the availability of online tools and resources.

4. **Cite sources.**   Model responsible use of information acquisition. When you use other people's information, reference their materials. Besides setting a good example, you may motivate students to search original sources for additional information.

5. **Rehearse lesson procedures.**   Practice the steps or events of learning that you are asking students to perform during the learning activity.

6. **Evaluate Web resources.**   Or better yet, teach students how to evaluate Web resources for themselves.

7. **Learn with your students.**   You don't have to be an expert on every topic that your students research, but you do need to be an expert on how to learn. Model learning by learning with your students.

8. **Differentiate learning.**   Web-enhanced learning activities should be flexible and adaptable to the differing learning needs and abilities of students in your classroom.

the issues that it raised: Ms. Cunningham was selected to be one of the teachers in a pilot project for creating technology-rich classrooms, but she was not sure how she would integrate technology into her regular teaching routine and was concerned that the technology would sidetrack her from the curriculum objectives. Based on the information presented in this chapter, what could the district technology coordinator have told Diane to alleviate her concerns about her capability to use technology to support curriculum objectives? How will teaching and learning in her classroom change if she starts using Web-enhanced learning to integrate technology into the classroom curriculum?

■ *Web course management tools*—You (or your team) are appointed as a committee to recommend a course management tool for adoption by your school or college. Compare the features of Blackboard and WebCT (or other tools) and generate a recommendation. In making your recommendation, consider the anticipated role and importance of developing materials for the World Wide Web in your school or college.

   • Does publishing course materials on the Web enhance teaching and learning? Why or why not?

   • Will the use of the Web for publishing materials eventually replace printed textbooks? Why or why not?

   • Should instructors take the time to create Web courses even when they plan to meet face-to-face with students in the classroom? Explain.

   • What features of Web course management tools best support teaching and learning?

■ *TEACH act*—Surf the Web and find out more about the TEACH Act. Create a list of dos and don'ts of materials that you could copy or duplicate for use in your classroom. Conduct a classroom debate on this question: Do copyright laws hinder or promote the free flow of ideas and intellectual content?

■ *Web accessibility*—View the home page of your school or college or another popular website. Consider this question: How do people with disabilities surf the Web? Create a list of the typical functions or features of the Web page that might prevent students who are blind or deaf or who have motion or mobility impairments from obtaining a complete understanding of the information on the Web page (e.g., "Click here"). For each limiting function, suggest one or more solutions that would make it possible for a person with one of these disabilities to gain a complete understanding of the information on the Web page.

## Set 2: Expanding Your Skills

*Learning Objectives for Higher Order Thinking Skills.* Benjamin Bloom (1956) described higher order thinking in his taxonomy of educational objectives. Bloom introduced the idea of a hierarchy of different forms of thinking, from simple to complex or from lower to higher orders. Now, higher order thinking is used synonymously with problem solving and critical thinking. Indeed, the ability to think critically is essential if individuals are to live, work, and function effectively in our current and changing society. Students must make choices, evaluations, and judgments every day regarding information to obtain, use, and believe or plans to make and actions to take.

In 2000 Lorin Anderson, a former student of Benjamin Bloom, and a team of cognitive psychologists revised Bloom's original taxonomy to maintain its relevance in regard to current approaches to learning, they combined both the cognitive process and knowledge dimensions. As a result of their investigation, a number of significant structural improvements were made that can help teachers write or revise learning objectives for active, student-centered classrooms.

In the following list, the term to the left of the arrow shows Bloom's original taxonomy, and the term to the right shows Anderson's revised taxonomy:

| | |
|---|---|
| Knowledge | → Remembering |
| Comprehension | → Understanding |
| Application | → Applying |
| Analysis | → Analyzing |
| Synthesis | → Creating |
| Evaluation | → Evaluating |

The category names were changed from noun to verb forms because thinking is considered to be an active process and verbs describe actions. For example, knowledge is an outcome or product of thinking, whereas the action of thinking is depicted in remembering.

This revision of Bloom's taxonomy supports a student-centered approach to teaching and learning. Learning objectives for the teacher-centered approach of the original taxonomy used verbs such as *recognize, list, describe, identify, retrieve,* or *name* to ensure that students could recall or remember information. Verbs such as *interpret, exemplify, summarize, infer,* or *paraphrase* were used to ensure that students could explain or understand concepts or ideas. Learning objectives for a student-centered approach ensure that students can use or transfer new knowledge to another familiar situation, justify a decision or course of action, or generate new ideas or products—using verbs such as *implement, apply, compare, organize, critique, judge, hypothesize, design, construct, plan,* or *produce.*

Bob Hoffman is the general editor of *The Encyclopedia of Educational Technology,* an online publication of San Diego State University, Department of Educational Technology. In an article about the revised Bloom's taxonomy at http://coe.sdsu.edu/eet/Articles/bloomrev/, information and resources are provided to help teachers write learning objectives ensuring that all levels of the cognitive process are used and that students learn different types of knowledge. Browse the online article and use the technique demonstrated in it to write three learning objectives for a student-centered classroom of the grade level and/or subject you teach.

## Set 3: Using Productivity and Web-Authoring Tools

■ *Develop Your Own Lesson Plan Template*—Browse the websites presented in this chapter for lesson plans, and use a word processing or spreadsheet program to create your own lesson template that is appropriate for the grade level and/or subject you teach.

| FIGURE 1–7 | A Modified Project Sample Template |
|---|---|
| Title/topic | State an interesting, attention-getting title. |
| Standards of learning | State subject-specific standards and grade-specific technology standards to be addressed by the project. |
| Problem/task | State the problem or task the learner needs to solve or perform. and/or |
| Background information | Provide orienting or organizing information about the project. |
| Procedures | Describe proposed procedures the learner should follow to complete the project. Describe any alternative approaches or adaptations that learners may use. and/or |
| Resources | State what Web resources you have identified for the learner to complete the project. |
| Assessment | State what the learner will do to demonstrate understanding and mastery of objectives. |
| Credits/references | If the project was adapted from another project or lesson plan, provide credits or URL. |

■ *Lesson Plan PowerPoint Presentations*—Use a multimedia presentation program such as PowerPoint to create a WEL project sample for a lesson plan you identified in this chapter. Place each component of the project sample on a different slide(s), and insert hyperlinks for the Web resources so that you can link to the website directly from the slide.

■ *Lesson Plan Digital Index*—For times when you encounter an online learning resource or activity but do not have time to record it as a project sample, use a spreadsheet program to create a digital index to keep track of useful resources. In the spreadsheet document set up a column for resource title, resource URL, and a short description. You could also add another column for the type or category of the resource (e.g., lesson plan, content page). Include some of the educational resources you have located in this chapter in your digital index.

### Set 4: Creating Your Own Web-Enhanced Project

Throughout this textbook you will be asked to develop WEL project samples or complete WEL lesson plans that are useful and appropriate for the grade level and/or subject you now teach or plan to teach. Use the websites for educational resources and standards discussed in the Building Your Toolkit tutorials and the enrichment activities for this chapter to identify topics for Web-enhanced learning activities that you want to develop more fully as you progress through the text. Locate online lesson plans that address these topics, and then locate corresponding educational standards for the topics. Plan a curriculum-based Web-enhanced learning project using the WEL project sample template, and include an element that addresses educational standards. Figure 1–7 provides a modified template for this activity.

## REFERENCES

Anderson, L., & Krathwohl, D. (2001). *A taxonomy for learning, teaching and assessing: A revision of Bloom's taxonomy of educational objectives*. New York: Longman.

Bloom, B. S., & Krathwohl, D. R. (1956). *Taxonomy of educational objectives: The classification of educational goals: Handbook I. Cognitive Domain*. New York: Longman, Green.

Bruce, B. C., & Levin, J. A. (1997). Educational technology: Media for inquiry, communication, construction, and expression. *Journal of Educational Computing Research, 17*(1), 79–102.

Brush, T. A., & Saye, J. (2000). Implementation and evaluation of a student-centered learning unit: A case study. *Educational Technology Research and Development, 48*(3), 79–100.

Christie, M. (2002, April). *The role of culture and context in achievement beliefs: An exploration.* Paper presented at the annual meeting of the American Educational Research Association, New Orleans, LA.

Collis, B. (1997). Pedagogical re-engineering: A new approach to course enrichment and re-design with the WWW. *Educational Technology Review, 8,* 11-15.

Davis, E. A., & Krajcik, J. S. (2005). Designing educative curriculum materials to promote teacher learning. *Educational Researcher, 34*(3), 3-14.

Derry, S. J. (1990, April). *Flexible cognitive tools for problem solving instruction.* Paper presented at the annual meeting of the American Educational Research Association, Boston.

Grabowski, B. L., Koszalka, T. A., & McCarthy, M. (2000). *The Web-Enhanced Learning Environment Strategies Handbook and Reflection Tool.* Pennsylvania State University, College of Education. Retrieved January 30, 2003, from http://www.ed.psu.edu/nasa/welessite/weles.pdf

Hannafin, M. J., Hill, J. R., & Land, S. M. (1997). Student-centered learning and interactive multimedia: Status, issues, and implication. *Contemporary Education, 68,* 94-99.

Harris, J. (1998a). Curriculum-based telecollaboration: Using activity structures to design student progress. *Learning & Leading with Technology, 26*(1), 6-15.

Harris, J. (1998b). *Virtual architecture: Designing and directing curriculum-based telecomputing.* Eugene, OR: International Society for Technology in Education.

Hill, J. R., & Hannafin, M. J. (1997). Cognitive strategies and learning from the World Wide Web. *Educational Technology Research & Development, 45*(4), 37-64.

Hoogveld, A. W. M., Paas, F., Jochems, W. M. G., & van Merrienboer, J. J. G. (2001). The effects of a Web-based training in an instructional systems design approach on teachers' instructional design behavior. *Computers in Human Behavior, 17,* 363-371.

Jonassen, D. (2000). *Computers as mindtools for schools.* Upper Saddle River, NJ: Prentice Hall.

Jukes, I., Dosaj, A., Macdonald, B. (2000). *NetSavvy: Building information literacy in the classroom.* Thousand Oaks, CA: Corwin Press.

Lance, G. D., & Wehmeyer, M. L. (2001). *Universal design checklist.* Lawrence, KS: University of Kansas, Beach Center of Disablties.

Mayer, R. E. (2001). *Multimedia learning.* Cambridge, UK: Cambridge University Press.

McCain, T., & Jukes, I. (2001). *Windows on the future: Education in the age of technology.* Thousand Oaks, CA: Corwin Press.

Oliver, R. (2000). When teaching meets learning: Design principles and strategies for Web-based learning environments that support knowledge construction. In R. Sims, M. O'Reilly, & S. Sawkins (Eds.), *Learning to choose: Choosing to learn. Proceedings of the 17th Annual ASCILITE Conference* (pp. 551-560). Lismore, NSW: Southern Cross University Press.

Oliver, R., Omari, A., Herrington, J., & Herrington, A. (2000). Database-driven activities to support Web-based learning. In R. Sims, M. O'Reilly, & S. Sawkins (Eds.), *Learning to choose: Choosing to learn. Proceedings of the 17th Annual ASCILITE Conference* (pp. 551-560). Lismore, NSW: Southern Cross University Press.

Pedersen, S., & Liu, M. (2003). Teachers' beliefs about issues in the implementation of a student-centered learning environment. *Educational Technology Research and Development, 51*(2), 57-76.

Reeves, T. C., & Reeves, P. M. (1997). The effective dimensions of interactive learning on the WWW. In B. H. Khan (Ed.), *Web-based instruction* (pp. 59-66). Englewood Cliffs, NJ: Educational Technology.

Riel, M., & Fulton, K. (2001). The role of technology in supporting learning communities. *Phi Delta Kappan, 82*(7), 518-523.

Rosenberg, M. J. (2001). *E-learning: Strategies for delivering knowledge in the digital age.* New York: McGraw-Hill.

Shulman, L. S. (1986). Those who understand: Knowledge growth in teaching. *Educational Researcher, 15*(2), 4-14.

Tennyson, R. D. (2001). Defining core competencies of an instructional technologist. *Computers in Human Behavior, 17,* 355-361.

Trilling, B., & Hood, P. (1999). Learning, technology, and education reform in the knowledge age or "We're wired, webbed, and windowed, now what?" *Educational Technology, 39*(3), 5-18.

Vermunt, J. D., & Verloop, N. (1999). Congruence and friction between learning and teaching. *Learning and Instruction, 9,* 257-280.

Weimer, M. (2002). *Learner-centered teaching: Five key changes to practice.* San Francisco: Jossey-Bass.

# CHAPTER 2

# Teaching and Learning Theories for Web-Enhanced Learning

Jennifer Edwards is a junior in college. She was recently admitted to the teacher education program and is completing the curriculum requirements for elementary education certification. The college of education in which she is enrolled recently modified the structure of the teacher preparation program to include the use of technology-enhanced learning as an instructional methodology. The methods courses were integrated into a 1-year strand, during which teacher candidates spend part of their time in class and part of their time in K–12 classrooms.

As a part of this integrated methods program, student teachers are expected to teach two technology-enhanced lessons using project-based learning methodologies. They spend time in their college class preparing these instructional activities. Although Jennifer has used computers and the Internet in her educational experience, she does not consider herself a technology expert and so she was concerned about her ability to use technology in the classroom.

At first she had a difficult time designing instructional activities that integrated technology into a problem-based lesson. She had learned about a variety of teaching and learning theories and strategies in her teacher education courses, but she did not know how technology could be used to support these methodologies.

Fortunately, Jennifer's supervising instructor provided her with a procedure for developing learning activities enhanced by computer and Internet technologies and resources. The first step was to select and develop a topic that supported learning outcomes consistent with curriculum goals. Next she identified the kinds of thinking and learning students should do to accomplish these outcomes. Then she created rubrics to authentically assess these outcomes through the creation of products of learning. Finally, she located and evaluated websites that supported the learning outcomes and described the procedures for using the Web resources to find a solution.

Although Jennifer found that it required more planning time to create technology-enhanced lessons, she noticed that when she used the technology-enhanced, problem-based learning units in her student teaching, the students become interested and engaged in completing their assignments. Best of all, Jennifer realized that she did not have to be a technology expert to use computers and the Internet in her teaching.

# NEW TERMS

anchored instruction

authentic assessment

case-based learning

coaching

collaborative learning

constructivism

discovery learning

generative learning

information processing theory

inquiry learning

mentoring

problem-based learning

project-based learning

scaffolding

Web essay

| National Educational Technology Standards for Teachers | National Educational Technology Standards for Students |
|---|---|
| The following NETS•T are addressed by the lesson content and learning activities in this chapter:<br><br>**II. Planning and Designing**<br><br>  **A.** Design technology-enhanced learning opportunities to support diverse needs<br>  **B.** Apply current research on teaching and learning with technology<br>  **C.** Identify, locate, and evaluate technology resources<br>  **D.** Plan for the management of technology resources<br>  **E.** Manage student learning in a technology-enhanced environment<br><br>**III. Teaching, Learning, and the Curriculum**<br><br>  **A.** Facilitate technology-enhanced experiences to address standards<br>  **B.** Use technology to support learner-centered strategies<br>  **C.** Apply technology to develop students' higher order skills<br>  **D.** Manage student learning activities | **1. Basic Operations and Concepts**<br>  • Demonstrate sound understanding of technology<br>  • Be proficient in the use of technology<br><br>**2. Social, Ethical, and Human Issues**<br>  • Understand ethical, cultural, and societal issues related to technology<br>  • Practice responsible use of technology<br>  • Develop positive attitudes toward technology<br><br>**3. Technology Productivity Tools**<br>  • Use technology to enhance learning, increase productivity, and promote creativity<br>  • Use tools to collaborate, prepare publications, and produce creative works |

# OVERVIEW

As was mentioned earlier, today's classrooms need to prepare students to become citizens of the information age. Students must think critically; analyze and synthesize information to solve technical, social, economic, political, and scientific problems; and work productively in groups. For schools and classrooms to address these skills, instructional approaches must focus on rich, multidisciplinary, and sometimes collaborative learning tasks with complex sets of learning objectives (van Merrienboer, 2002).

Integrating technology into the curriculum of the classroom is becoming an inseparable part of good teaching (Pierson, 2001); however, it relies on sound pedagogy. The use of technology as a tool for teaching and learning in the classroom should create learning tasks that extend information retrieval to problem solving, promote the deep processing of ideas, increase student engagement with the subject matter, promote teacher and student motivation for learning, and increase student-to-student and student-to-teacher interaction (Earle, 2002).

Using technology to support teaching and learning makes it possible to use powerful methodologies such as cases, projects, and problems that are meaningful, holistic, and representative of authentic or real-world tasks. Their use requires teachers to design and develop learning tasks and activities that enhance the classroom curriculum.

Several learning theories and teaching strategies can create the conditions for active learning in the classroom. These include anchored instruction, case-based learning, cooperative learning, inquiry learning, problem-based learning, and project-based learning. The common thread running through these approaches is that learning tasks and activities are organized around a central question that creates the need for acquiring and processing certain information.

Teachers can use a project-based approach to create learning activities in which students use the information resources on the Internet to construct knowledge. With such an approach students work on projects that are meaningful activities situated in contexts that simulate real-world problems and conclude with final products that present solutions to the problems.

## Lesson 2.1    Theories and Strategies for Active Learning

### FOCUS QUESTIONS

- What is information processing theory, and how does it explain learning?
- What are several instructional theories and learning models on which Web-enhanced learning is based?
- What is generative learning, and how does it support Web-enhanced learning activities?
- What are several teaching and learning strategies that can be used in the classroom to support generative learning?

## ■ LEARNING THEORIES

Most modern pedagogy is influenced by cognitive learning theories, which place more emphasis on factors that are internal to the learner than on factors within the environment, which are emphasized by behavioral theories (Smith & Ragan, 1999). Information processing theories have been one of the most influential contributions of cognitive learning theory to instructional design practice (Smith & Ragan, 1999) and to learning and developmental psychology (Bransford, Brown, & Cocking, 2000).

**Information processing theory** is based on a set of hypothesized structures in the brain that work much like a computer. For learning to occur, a series of transformations of information takes place in or through these structures. According to information processing theory, the human brain receives information (input), performs operations on it to change its form and content (processing), stores and locates it and generates responses to it (output). Processing involves gathering and representing information, or *encoding;* storing information, or *retention;* and getting at the information when needed, or *retrieval.* The diagram in Figure 2–1 provides a simplified representation of information processing theory.

Mayer (2001) suggests a model for multimedia learning with dual channels for processing that is closely related to Paivio's (1986) dual-coding theory. The assumption of Mayer's model is that there are separate channels for processing auditorily and visually represented information. Mayer's multimedia learning model is particularly appropriate and applicable for the design and development of student-centered multimedia learning environments, such as those represented by Web-enhanced learning activities.

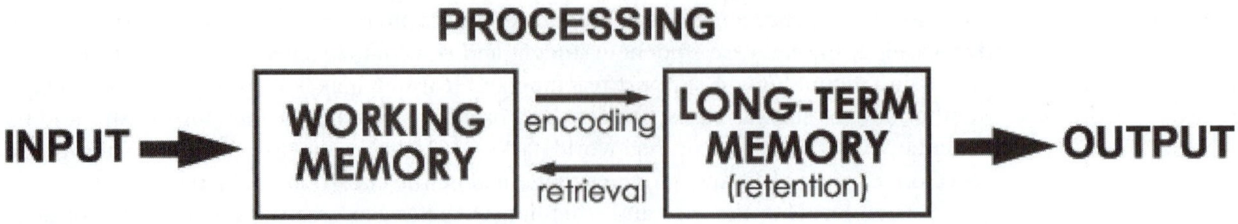

## PROCESSING

**FIGURE 2–1:** **Information Processing Theory**

Active learning can be viewed as a process of building mental models that represent the key parts of the presented material and their relations (Mayer, 2001). Although improvements in retention enable learners to remember information better, learners whose understanding is improved are able to use the information to solve new problems, called *transfer*. Learning activities that are technology-based or technology-enhanced can facilitate understanding to produce deeper and richer learning because they can assist learners in building mental models (Mayer, 2001).

Web-enhanced learning, as it is presented in this textbook, is based on several learning models and teaching strategies that facilitate encoding and retrieval of information to improve retention and increase understanding. The use of Internet technologies can also increase the effectiveness of inputs into working memory by providing interesting and relevant resources that engage students and motivate them to learn.

A contemporary view of learning is that students come to school with a range of prior knowledge, skills, beliefs, and experiences and that they construct new knowledge and understandings based on what they already know and believe (Bransford, Brown, & Cocking, 2000). This view of learning is called **constructivism.** A constructivist philosophy of learning assumes that all knowledge is constructed from previous knowledge. Thus, a pedagogy based on constructivist theory would recognize "the knowledge and beliefs that students bring to a learning task, use this knowledge as a starting point for new instruction, and monitor students' changing conceptions as instruction proceeds" (Bransford et al., 2000, p. 11). Although several interpretations or elaborations of constructivism exist, for the purposes of this textbook, a constructivist approach helps learners actively make sense of the world by constructing new meanings and understandings.

## ■ TEACHING AND LEARNING METHODOLOGIES

Several learning models or methods facilitate student's construction of knowledge, including anchored instruction, case-based learning, cooperative learning, inquiry learning, problem-based learning, and project-based learning. These approaches all revolve around a central question or theme, which creates the need for acquiring and processing information that can be used to construct useful knowledge. The question can take the form of a problem, case, issue, situation, or project. And although the question or problem may be somewhat unstructured, students have a common learning goal, usually based on some component of the curriculum.

### Anchored Instruction

Anchored instruction refers to instructional strategies that create authentic learning experiences. Anchored instruction was developed by the Cognition and Technology Group at Vanderbilt (CTGV) under the leadership of John Bransford, to whom the theory or method is generally attributed. **Anchored instruction** places students in the context of a problem-based story. They take on authentic roles while investigating the problem—identifying gaps in their knowledge, researching the information needed to solve the problem, and developing solutions. Learning activities are designed around the "anchor" of the contextualized case study or problem situation. Curriculum materials permit learners to actively manipulate, question, and become involved in the situation (Bransford, Sherwood, Hasselbring, Kinzer, & Williams, 1990) as the teacher coaches them through the learning process.

With anchored instruction the task must be realistic. Students take ownership based on the relevancy of the story or scenario and its relatedness to everyday problems and experiences. As students identify with the problem, they become actively involved in generating a solution. Thus, anchored instruction results in the deep development of knowledge structures, highly transferable to other situations (Bransford et al., 1990).

Web-enhanced learning can use the principles of anchored instruction, taking advantage of the multimedia features of the Web—audio, video, and graphics—to promote realism. And because all or most of the required data or information should be embedded within the story line, the hypertext linking capabilities of Web pages can support the chunking of information and the branching to related resources. For example, a collection of websites could be organized to provide virtual field trips.

## Case-Based Learning

**Case-based learning** uses cases or complex problems that are typically based in fact and are designed to stimulate classroom discussion and collaborative analysis. In case-based learning students receive a realistic case that supports curriculum goals and then formulate strategies to analyze the data and generate possible solutions. Students imagine themselves in the situation described by the case, make decisions, and explain their rationale for their choices. Cases allow students to acquire substantive knowledge and develop analytic, collaborative, and communication skills.

Because case-based learning is a flexible methodology, it can easily be incorporated into Web-enhanced learning. Cases can provide a structured presentation with a common ending or an open-ended presentation with students exploring the different outcomes resulting from their choices. Although cases can be as simple as printed stories, the multimedia features of the Web can add graphics, audio, and video as well as links to additional resources. Internet communication tools can be used to allow teachers and students to discuss, debate, and debrief cases with one another and with experts online. A more detailed discussion of case-based learning methodologies for Web-enhanced learning activities is provided in chapter 9.

## Collaborative Learning

**Collaborative learning,** or cooperative learning, involves two or more peers engaged in an activity that requires them to maintain some agreement and reach a shared solution. Collaborative learning assumes that a shared goal, mutual respect, tolerance, trust, and clear lines of responsibility are established and that the team works on common materials that can take many forms. The teacher facilitates decisions, but students are actively involved in constructing a solution; communication occurs in both formal and informal environments. Collaborative or cooperative learning extends learning beyond the immediate collaboration by adding to the collective knowledge of the classroom.

Web-enhanced learning often uses collaborative/cooperative learning methodologies. For example, Web pages can be used to present a scenario to an entire class with each student on a cooperative team then assigned a role to research a smaller portion of a larger issue. Team members share and compile their data, developing a solution to the situation and constructing a resource to teach others about their topic and add to the collective knowledge of the class.

Internet communication tools can facilitate collaboration among students, allowing them to communicate asynchronously with e-mail and discussion boards or synchronously with chat rooms. These communication tools usually permit file exchanges as well, which support the collaborative development of work products and solutions.

## Inquiry Learning

**Inquiry,** or **discovery, learning** uses questioning strategies to engage students in discovering rules and relationships and generating new knowledge and understandings. With this approach students are required to discover the rules behind concepts. The role of the teacher is shifted from presenting subject matter to activating conversation to encourage students to discover answers or solutions. The teacher coaches students by questioning, provides context to the topic, draws upon students' prior and prerequisite knowledge, gives feedback, and provides help.

Although inquiry learning is often associated with a science curriculum, it is one of the best ways to implement Web-enhanced learning in almost any subject area. With inquiry-based learning students formulate investigative questions, obtain factual information, and then build knowledge that reflects their answer to the original question; with Web-enhanced learning the factual information is obtained from Web resources. Because inquiry learning involves numerous process and thinking skills, it provides a rich and meaningful experience for students, either as individual learners or in cooperative teams. Inquiry also permits different permutations of the learning task to accommodate all types of learners.

Using Web-enhanced learning with an inquiry approach works something like this: Students are presented with an essential question that they research to develop a list of related questions, choices, or strategies in response to the main question. Students develop a search strategy for locating information by closely examining the related questions for keywords and using Web search engines to locate information resources. Students then evaluate the Web resources they have collected and determine whether the information is related to their essential question, useful for answering their related questions, and reliable. If so, they use it to build knowledge relative to the original question. And finally, they develop exhibits to represent that knowledge and understanding.

The student exhibit can have many forms—for example, **Web essays,** which are documents published on the Web that contain information in multiple formats, including text, sounds, pictures, graphics, and movies. Or students can use Web page editing software or productivity tools to create exhibits such as printed reports or multimedia presentations. A more detailed discussion of using inquiry-based learning for Web-enhanced learning activities is provided in chapter 9.

## Problem-Based Learning

**Problem-based learning** begins with the introduction of a real-world problem. Students are encouraged to confront the problem, construct their individual understanding of it, and finally find an answer for it while teachers provide guidance and resource material (Dillon & Zhu, 1997). Problem-based learning is similar to anchored instruction and case-based learning but may be more open-ended and less structured.

As denoted by its name, problem-based learning relies on problems to drive the curriculum. The problems, which may be ambiguous and unstructured, do not test skills but assist in the development of the skills themselves. The problems are not meant to result in a single, static solution; instead, solutions evolve as new information is gathered in an iterative process. As in anchored instruction, students solve the problems, while teachers function as coaches and facilitators who give guidance only on how to approach problems. Moursund (1999) notes that problem-based learning is a type of project-based learning (see the discussion in the following section).

Web-enhanced learning is highly compatible with a problem-based learning approach. Students can conduct research using the search tools and resources of the Web. The teacher would not typically develop materials to teach specific content but would require students to access databases, slides, documents, or other relevant information resources. These reference materials would be shared in the form of recommended hypertext links to Web-based resources.

### Project-Based Learning

**Project-based learning** organizes learning around projects, which are complex tasks based on authentic, challenging problems or questions that involve students in critical thinking and culminate in realistic products (Thomas, 2000). Project-based learning resembles problem-based learning in the use of authentic content, authentic assessment, teacher facilitation, cooperative learning, and reflection. Project-based learning is distinctive, however, in using problems that are better structured or better defined.

Indeed, all the methods described here are some form of project-based learning, but project-based learning itself is more concerned with the products of learning and emphasizes the mastery of learning, whereas several of the other methods, such as problem-based learning, focus on learning process as much as product (Howard, 2002). A more detailed discussion of using project-based learning for Web-enhanced learning activities is the subject of the next lesson in this chapter.

## ■ TEACHING AND LEARNING STRATEGIES

The use of technology in the classroom permits many of the key instructional variables to be placed in the hands of the learners (Smith & Ragan, 1999). Web-enhanced learning assumes that the learner is not a passive receiver of information and uses inquiry or exploration methodologies to allow the student to generate knowledge. Therefore, teachers should employ instructional strategies that help students construct meaningful understandings of the information they find.

### Generative Learning

**Generative learning** is a process of generating ideas by reorganizing facts and information into more flexible knowledge structures that reveal relationships among ideas or by identifying gaps in knowledge or conflicts between ideas. Comprehension occurs by formulating connections between perceived information, prior knowledge, and other memory components (Wittrock, 1990). Generative learning requires the student to actively participate with the content; it encourages deep thinking and development of new knowledge through recall, reflection, inquiry, and elaboration of previous knowledge. Instructional interventions that promote reflection and interaction with content are key strategies for generative learning.

With Web-enhanced learning generative learning strategies (Wittrock, 1974; 1990) should be used to encourage learners to encounter content in such a way that they can construct their own meaning. Such strategies allow students to experiment with information to create a personal understanding of the subject to be learned; students generate knowledge by forming mental connections among concepts. The teaching strategies that follow can support generative learning in the classroom.

### Authentic Assessment

Learning tasks that use powerful methodologies such as cases, projects, and problems require a different approach to assessment. In student-centered classrooms open-ended assessment techniques that involve students in examining their own learning and understanding are more useful than objective tests (Shepard, 2000). **Authentic assessment** allows evaluation of student exhibits or work products that represent the culmination of a set of learning tasks.

Traditional assessment involves paper-and-pencil testing, but Web-enhanced learning should employ other techniques, such as rating items on scales, observing student performances, critiquing student work products, or conducting student interviews. Assessment can also include student portfolios consisting of exhibits or artifacts that demonstrate mastery of skills. With authentic assessment credit is given on the basis of process—for example, how well a student works on a team—as well as product.

Authentic assessment supports generative learning because student exhibits generate organizational relationships through such elements as titles, headings, questions, objectives, summaries, graphs, tables, and main ideas. Student exhibits can also integrate relationships between what students see, hear, or read and what they have in memory from prior experience and learning through such creations as metaphors, analogies, examples, pictures, applications, interpretations, paraphrases, and inferences.

Other student exhibits can include videotaped or digital portfolios that document interests and accomplishments; journals with weekly entries about project tasks and activities; multimedia presentations demonstrating a solution to a problem; written or printed reports, charts, graphs, or graphical illustrations; and original works on a multidisciplinary theme.

## Coaching and Mentoring

Coaching and mentoring are training and development strategies used by professionals to help colleagues improve their professional practice; both are based on a collegial relationship. **Coaching** is a partnership in which colleagues observe one another in the practice of their profession and hold focused discussions prior to and following observations. **Mentoring** uses the same techniques but involves an expert professional who is assigned to help a novice professional learn new knowledge and skills to improve professionally.

Coaching and mentoring are powerful teaching strategies that are especially appropriate for student-centered classrooms in which students are generating knowledge. Coaching and mentoring help students become more conscious learners through self-assessment and reflection and encourage them to examine their own internal processing mechanisms. Coaching and mentoring techniques include responsive listening, open-ended questioning, descriptive and constructive feedback, and clarification through nonjudgmental responses and reactions. Coaching and mentoring can occur on several levels, including teacher to student, student to student, and mentor to student.

An example of the coaching and mentoring model in educational practice is Generation Y (**http://www.genyes.org**). In the Gen Y model students are paired with partner-teachers at their school. Each student-teacher team decides what lesson plan, curriculum unit, or other school need will be addressed by a collaborative, technology-enriched curriculum project, which the partner-teacher and the Gen Y student produce together. The result of this partnership is authentic, project-based learning for students and professional development in technology for teachers. Students learn not only the technology skills necessary to complete the project, but also the soft skills such as planning, collaborating, and managing.

## Scaffolding

**Scaffolding** provides learners with direction and motivation for solving problems or completing learning activities. Scaffolding generally refers to interactions between teachers and students to support learning. For example, teachers may provide feedback, explanations, directions, examples or nonexamples, or demonstrations that help learners access relevant information for solving problems and reduce the number of steps necessary to solve those problems.

Wood, Bruner, and Ross (1976) introduced the metaphor of scaffolding to describe the way an expert tutor supports a young child's progress in completing a relatively difficult task. Bruner (1978) described scaffolding as a temporary intellectual support a teacher uses to help students ascend to a higher level of understanding. With scaffolding, students are provided with assistance in accomplishing a learning task; but as their competence increases, the assistance is gradually decreased, or faded. The primary purpose of scaffolding is to enable students to regulate and direct their own learning of a specific task or of learning in general.

Scaffolding provides sufficient structure to keep students productive and motivated. The challenge for teachers is to provide the right amount of structure in a learning environment (Dabbagh, 2003). Low scaffolding is needed when students possess prior knowledge and are highly motivated for a learning task, whereas high scaffolding is needed when students possess little or no prior knowledge and are not motivated (Smith & Ragan, 1999).

Jamie McKenzie (2000) identifies several characteristics of scaffolding strategies: They should provide clear directions, clarify purpose, keep students on task, offer assessment to clarify expectations, point students to worthy sources, deliver efficiency, create momentum, and reduce uncertainty, surprise, and disappointment.

In learning environments that promote interactive and collaborative learning, teacher and student roles become increasing reciprocal (Dabbagh, 2003). In other words, as teachers assume more supportive or facilitative roles in learning, scaffolding is shared by the teacher, peers, and Internet resources, all of which can provide supportive structures or scaffolds to help students perform and learn in new ways. The following chapters of this textbook provide many examples and explanations of using Internet technologies and resources as scaffolds for teaching and learning.

---

## *Building Your Toolkit:*
## Theory Into Practice Online Database

Theory Into Practice (TIP) is a database that makes learning and instructional theory more accessible to educators. The database contains brief summaries of 50 major theories of learning and instruction, which can also be accessed by learning domain or concept. Each description includes an overview, the scope or application, an example, principles, and references. Connections between specific theories or to underlying concepts are identified by highlighted text within the articles.

### STEP    PROCEDURE

1.       Open your Web browser and then the website Theory Into Practice at **http://tip.psychologyorg/.** A Web page similar to the screen shot in Figure 2–2 should be displayed.

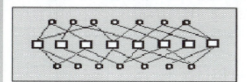

# Explorations in Learning & Instruction:
# The Theory Into Practice Database

Welcome to the Theory Into Practice (TIP) database!

TIP is a tool intended to make learning and instructional theory more accessible to educators. The database contains brief summaries of 50 major theories of learning and instruction. These theories can also be accessed by learning domains and concepts.

- About TIP
- The theories
- Learning domains
- Learning concepts
- About the Author
- Other related web sites

For more information about many of the theories and theorists included here, see the "People & History" section of http://www.psychology.org

**FIGURE 2–2:   The Theory Into Practice Web Page**

*(Continued)*

## Building Your Toolkit:
### Theory Into Practice Online Database (Continued)

| STEP | PROCEDURE |
|------|-----------|
| **2.** | Look up and review several theories by selecting **The theories** link. Some theories that have relevance for Web-enhanced Learning are anchored instruction, andragogy, constructivist theory, GOMS, GPS, lateral thinking, minimalism, situated learning, social development theory, and symbol systems. List aspects of these theories that have application for teaching practices that integrate technology. |
| **3.** | Look up and review several domains by selecting the **Learning domains** link on the TIP home page. Some of the domains that have relevance for Web-enhanced learning are computers, decision making, problem solving, procedures, and reasoning. List aspects of these domains that have application for teaching practices that integrate technology. |
| **4.** | Based on these theories and domains, write a short description of your beliefs about learning and the ways technology can be used to support these beliefs. |

**Go to the Companion Website and browse 2.1 Building Your Toolkit Enrichment Activity: Educational-Research-to-Practice Resources. Use the Internet resources in the enrichment activity to locate educational technology research that applies to classroom teaching practices.**

## Lesson 2.2  A Project-Based Approach to Web-Enhanced Learning

### FOCUS QUESTIONS

- What is project-based learning, and how does it support a Web-enhanced learning approach?
- How can project-based learning be used in the classroom?
- What are the educational features and benefits of project-based learning?

### ■ AN OVERVIEW OF PROJECT-BASED LEARNING

A project-based learning approach is characterized by long-term investigation, a solution to a main question or problem, and the development of project artifacts that demonstrate an understanding of the question or problem (Blumenfeld, Soloway, Marx, Krajcik, Guzdial, & Palinscar, 1991). Thus, project-based learning is resource intensive and requires adequate tools in the classroom. Web-enhanced learning using a project-based approach can be deployed in a classroom with one or more computers that have access to the Internet. The Web provides virtually unlimited resources and numerous tools, many of which you will learn about in this text, to support project-based learning.

With project-based learning students analyze, interpret, and synthesize information resources and then use development tools to construct or represent information in a new format, such as a word processing document, spreadsheet, database, Web page, or multimedia program. For example, Jennifer Edwards, the student teacher introduced at the beginning of this chapter, developed a technology-enhanced, project-based lesson on historiography and the use of primary sources. Her lesson plan assigned teams of students to collect primary source materials from their local community and then analyze the relationships among national, state, and local histories based on these primary sources. Student groups were to digitize and create documents that were based on their analyzed primary sources and could be published on Web pages. They were to publish their projects online as a digital collection or archive. Future classes could then add their projects to this digital library to expand the collective knowledge of local history and its relationship to national and state historical events.

Project-based learning allows teachers to guide students through in-depth studies of real-world topics. The use of projects in classrooms was first advanced by Kilpatrick (1918) and has since been defined in a variety of ways. A project is an in-depth investigation of a real-world topic conducted by a class, small groups, or individual students of any age. This textbook uses *project-based learning* to refer to students working on projects that are meaningful activities situated in curricular contexts that simulate real-world problems or activities and conclude with a final product that addresses the problem or activity.

# ■ THE ADVANTAGES AND CHALLENGES OF PROJECT-BASED LEARNING

As was mentioned earlier, project-based learning focuses more on the learning product than the learning process (Howard, 2002); it emphasizes mastery of lesson content. Projects can motivate students to learn by allowing them to be actively involved in their own learning, which can result in high-quality work (Berliner, 1992). Although projects are structured, they still provide a flexible framework for teaching and learning.

Moursund (1999) described project-based learning as learner-centered, problem or task oriented, and authentically assessed. He lists 10 positive outcomes of project-based learning in the classroom:

1. *Developing expertise.* Students often gain a high level of expertise on a specific topic.
2. *Improving research skills.* Projects require students to use and develop research skills.
3. *Improving higher order thinking skills.* Students must use critical thinking skills to accomplish the project.
4. *Participating in a project.* Students learn to work with other students to successfully complete a project.
5. *Learning to use information technology.* Students employ information technology to complete a project.
6. *Conducting self-assessment and peer assessment.* With projects students are accountable for their own work and performance.
7. *Developing a portfolio.* Projects require students to produce a product that may become a part of the student's portfolio.
8. *Engaging in a project.* Projects are highly motivational for students, causing them to become engaged in the learning tasks required to successfully complete the project.
9. *Being a part of a community of scholars.* Projects allow students to contribute to the collective knowledge of the classroom and beyond.
10. *Working on important ideas.* Projects allow students to work on relevant, real-world activities or problems. (pp. 7–9)

Figure 2–3 lists the basic characteristics of project-based learning: Essentially, it involves meaningful and relevant learning activities, real-world contexts, collaboration among learners, and student exhibits that demonstrate learning. Knowledge and skills are learned as students acquire and apply information within the context of the learning activity. Because projects are designed to be realistic, interesting, and relevant, students are prompted to discuss and collaborate with other students and with persons who model expert behaviors. Thus, students learn to think as experts and are enabled to transfer their learning to other contexts. Projects can be open ended with no prescribed approach or solution, requiring students to generate their own questions, plans, solutions, and products. The products or exhibits that students create contribute to the collective knowledge and understanding of the classroom community.

| FIGURE 2–3 | Common Features of Project-Based Learning |
| --- | --- |

1. Learning activities are meaningful and relevant and involve students in complex situations that are challenging and highly motivating.
2. Learning is situated in contexts that simulate real-world problems or questions.
3. Curricular outcomes are identified up front, but learning outcomes are not completely predictable.
4. Learning often relies on collaboration and communication among students for decision making and problem solving.
5. Teachers provide guidance as needed but encourage students to engage in metacognitive thinking.
6. Students draw from multiple information sources and disciplines to solve problems and design solutions.
7. Students learn teamwork and skills for managing and allocating resources such as time and materials.
8. Students create complex, intellectual products that demonstrate their learning.

Implementing project-based learning in the classroom may seem like an overwhelming or impossible task to many new and existing teachers. For example, Grant (2002) notes that the in-depth investigations conducted in project-based learning require more class time, leaving less time for other content in the curriculum. In addition, with project-based learning students need externalized support (i.e., scaffolding) to organize, articulate, and reflect on ideas throughout that in-depth investigation (Land, 2000). And project-based learning may require teachers to instruct students in group dynamics, negotiation, and conflict management because students are usually inexperienced in working in teams.

Not surprisingly, teachers may encounter some difficulty in developing Web-enhanced, project-based lessons at first, especially if they have been teaching for a number of years and have developed instructional approaches that are quite different from the project approach. However, project-based methodologies permit teachers to begin slowly, supplementing the curriculum with just a few projects at first. As teachers get more comfortable with the approach, they can gradually increase the frequency as well as the degree of complexity and technology integration in the design and implementation of the projects.

## Building Your Toolkit:
## Online Tutorial for Project-Based Learning

Project-based learning organizes teaching and learning around projects. In a review of the research on project-based learning, Thomas (2000) observed that both students and teachers prefer project-based learning over traditional classroom methods and that project-based learning is equivalent to or slightly better than other models of instruction in producing gains in general academic achievement. More significant is the evidence that project-based learning is an effective method of learning complex processes and procedures, such as planning, communicating, problem solving, and decision making. The George Lucas Educational Foundation provides an online tutorial for implementing project-based learning.

| STEP | PROCEDURE |
| --- | --- |
| 1. | Open your Web browser and then the Web page of the George Lucas Educational Foundation's instructional module on project-based learning at **http://www.glef.org/modules/PBL.** A Web page similar to the screen shot in Figure 2–4 should be displayed. |

*(Continued)*

***Building Your Toolkit:***
**Online Tutorial For Project-Based Learning (Continued)**

# INSTRUCTIONAL Module
**THE GEORGE LUCAS**
**EDUCATIONAL**
**FOUNDATION**
## Project-Based Learning
**www.glef.org**

**Home**

**Why Is PBL
Important?**

**What
Is PBL?**

**How Does
PBL Work?**

**Teaching
About PBL**

The Project-Based Learning (PBL) module is designed for either a two- to three-hour class or session or a one- to two-day workshop, and is divided into two parts.

**Join GLEF's InClass Community today!**

- Share ideas
- Lend support
- Discuss procedures and practices

Part One, **Guided Process**, is designed to give participants a brief introduction to project-based learning. It answers the questions **"Why is Project-Based Learning Important?"**; **"What is Project-Based Learning?"**; and **"How Does Project-Based Learning Work?"** The Guided Process includes the **Teaching About PBL** section and a PowerPoint® presentation, including presenter notes. This presentation can be shown directly from the Web site or can be downloaded for use as a stand-alone slide show. The video segment, "Newsome Park" demonstrates project-based learning in action at Newsome Park Elementary School in Newport News, Virginia. The Teaching About PBL section contains two additional examples (Journey North and Mountlake Terrace High School) of project-based learning.

**FIGURE 2–4:   Web Page of Instructional Module on Project-Based Learning**

*Source:* From George Lucas Educational Foundation Instructional Module on Project-Based Learning at http://www.glef.org/modules/PBL. Used with permission.

| STEP | PROCEDURE |
|---|---|
| 2. | Complete the online instructional module by clicking on each of the following module segments and completing Steps 3, 4, and 5: <br><br> • **Why Is Project-Based Learning Important?** <br> • **What Is Project-Based Learning?** <br> • **How Does Project-Based Learning Work?** |
| 3. | Read the first segment of the instructional module **(Why Is Project-Based Learning Important?),** and list five reasons that project-based learning is important. |
| 4. | Read the second segment of the instructional module **(What Is Project-Based Learning?),** and view the video segment. List four characteristics of project-based learning. |
| 5. | Read the third segment of the instructional module **(How Does Project-Based Learning Work?),** and list and describe the steps for project-based learning. |
| 6. | Select the link **Teaching About PBL,** and download or run online the PowerPoint presentation on project-based learning. Be sure to read through the speaker notes for each slide. You may want to keep a copy of the presentation to use as a seminar to teach students or other teachers about project-based learning. Complete each of the following activities by reading the article and viewing the accompanying video segment: |

*(Continued)*

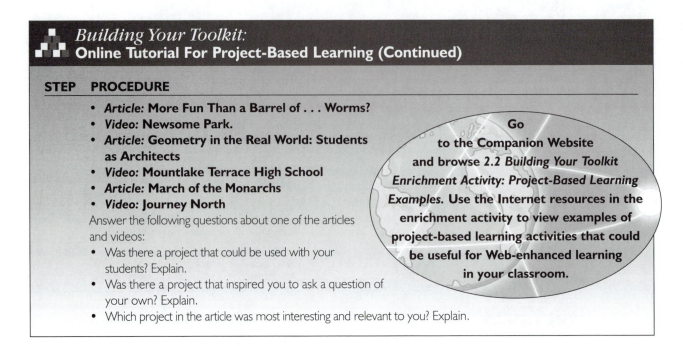

**STEP   PROCEDURE**

- *Article:* **More Fun Than a Barrel of . . . Worms?**
- *Video:* **Newsome Park.**
- *Article:* **Geometry in the Real World: Students as Architects**
- *Video:* **Mountlake Terrace High School**
- *Article:* **March of the Monarchs**
- *Video:* **Journey North**

Answer the following questions about one of the articles and videos:

- Was there a project that could be used with your students? Explain.
- Was there a project that inspired you to ask a question of your own? Explain.
- Which project in the article was most interesting and relevant to you? Explain.

Go to the Companion Website and browse *2.2 Building Your Toolkit Enrichment Activity: Project-Based Learning Examples*. Use the Internet resources in the enrichment activity to view examples of project-based learning activities that could be useful for Web-enhanced learning in your classroom.

# REFLECTIONS

Web-enhanced learning is based on a number of learning theories and strategies that facilitate the active participation of students in learning (see Figure 2–5). These methodologies are effective because they use communication technologies and information resources on the Internet to create student-centered, resource-rich, project-based learning environments.

This chapter provides a theoretical basis for designing, developing, and delivering classroom instruction in an active, student-centered learning environment that is supported by Internet technologies and is called Web-enhanced learning. This chapter also discusses and demonstrates the use of project-based learning as an appropriate approach to Web-enhanced learning in the classroom.

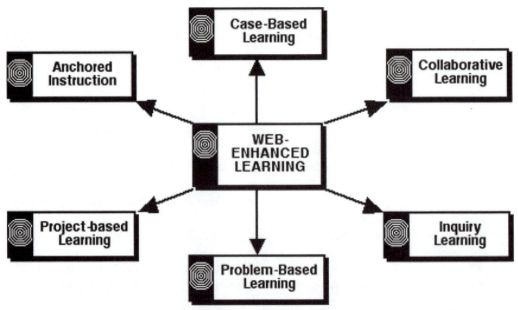

**FIGURE 2–5:   Methodologies on Which Web-Enhanced Learning is Based.** (Diagram created using *Inspiration*® by Inspiration Software,® Inc.)

# EXERCISES TO REVIEW AND EXPAND YOUR SKILLS

## Set 1: Reflecting on Practice

- *Closing the Case.* Jennifer Edwards must teach two technology-enhanced units using problem-based learning methodologies as a part of her teacher preparation program and student teaching experience. Although Jennifer was proficient in her personal use of computer technology, she found it difficult to integrate technology into her student teaching practice. Based on the information presented in this chapter, what instructional theories or strategies would you mention to Jennifer to help her integrate technology in her teaching practices? What would you tell her about project-based learning to help her integrate technology into her teaching practices?

- *Self-Analysis of Beliefs about Teaching and Learning.* Chapter 1 stated that the instructional tasks a teacher assigns reveal the teacher's theories and beliefs about teaching and learning. Reflect on the kinds of instructional tasks you have assigned or have been taught to assign, and list a representative sample of these tasks. What do they indicate about the theoretical approaches to teaching and learning to which you subscribe? Thinking about the instructional theories presented in this chapter, write a statement of your beliefs about teaching and learning. How does technology support your beliefs?

## Set 2: Expanding Your Skills

*Theories of Learning.* Use the Theory Into Practice database (http://tip.psychology.org/) to select a learning theory or model, and prepare a multimedia presentation to describe that theory or model and identify features that could support technology integration in the classroom. Your presentation should include the following components: description of the theory or model, leading theorists or proponents of the theory, the theory's view of the learning process, locus of learning according to the theory, the theory's contribution to education and pedagogy, the educator's role according to the theory, and features of the theory that support technology integration.

## Set 3: Using Productivity and Web-Authoring Tools

- *Theories-of-Learning Document.* Use a word processing or spreadsheet program to create and complete a table of the information in Set 2.

- *Instructional Theory PowerPoint Presentation.* Use the multimedia presentation you completed in Set 2 and insert hyperlinks to an associated Web resource.

- *Presentation of Best Practices in Technology Integration.* Use a multimedia presentation program such as PowerPoint to create a presentation on research-based educational practices in technology integration in the classroom. You can use information from the CARET website at http://caret.iste.org/ for the talking points of your presentation. Insert hyperlinks for Web resources used in the presentation.

- *Problem-Based-Learning Workshop.* Use a multimedia presentation program such as PowerPoint to create a workshop you could present to other teachers on project-based learning. Use the Web resources presented in this chapter to develop your presentation.

## Set 4: Creating Your Own Web-Enhanced Project

Plan a curriculum-based Web-enhanced learning project based on the teaching and learning theories and strategies described in this chapter. You can use the project sample you developed in Set 4 of chapter 1 or a new topic. Use the WEL project sample template, and include an element that addresses teaching and learning strategies (see Figure 2–6).

| FIGURE 2–6 | A Project Sample Template That Includes Strategies |
|---|---|
| Title/topic | State an interesting, attention-getting title. |
| Standards of learning | State subject-specific standards and grade-specific technology standards to be addressed by the project. |
| Problem/task | State the problem or task the learner needs to solve or perform. and/or |
| Background information | Provide orienting or organizing information about the project. |
| Procedures | Describe proposed procedures the learner should follow to complete the project. Describe any alternative approaches or adaptations that learners may use. and/or |
| Resources | State what Web resources you have identified for the learner to complete the project. |
| Teaching/learning strategies | Describe the teaching and learning methods used to complete the project (may be included in the procedures). Consider teaching methods that address different learning needs. If appropriate, consider alternative teaching methods for teaching the same information or skills. |
| Assessment | State what the learner will do to demonstrate understanding and mastery of objectives. |
| Credits/references | If the project was adapted from another project or lesson plan, provide credits or URL. |

# REFERENCES

Berliner, D. C. (1992). Redesigning classroom activities for the future. *Educational Technology, 32*(5), 7–13.

Blumenfeld, P. C., Soloway, E., Marx, R. W., Krajcik, J. S., Guzdial, M., & Palinscar, A. (1991). Motivating project-based learning: Sustaining the doing, support the learning. *Educational Psychologist, 26,* 369–398.

Bransford, J. D., Brown, A. L. & Cocking, R. R. (Eds.). (2000). *How people learn: Brain, mind, experience, and school.* Washington, DC: National Academy Press.

Bransford, J. D., Sherwood, R. D., Hasselbring, T. S., Kinzer, C. K., & Williams, S. M. (1990). Anchored instruction: Why we need it and how technology can help. In D. Nix & R. Spiro (Eds.), *Cognition, education, and multimedia: Exploring ideas in high technology* (pp. 115–141). Hillsdale, NJ: Lawrence Erlbaum.

Bruner, J. (1978). The role of dialogue in language acquisition. In A. Sinclair, R. Jarvella, and W. J. J. Levelt (Eds.), *The child's conception of language* (pp. 241–256). New York: Springer.

Dabbagh, N. (2003). Scaffolding: An important teacher competency in online learning. *Tech Trends, 47*(2), 39–44.

Dillon, A., & Zhu, E. (1997). Designing Web-based instruction: A human-computer interaction perspective. In B. H. Khan (Ed.), *Web-based instruction.* Englewood Cliffs, NJ: Educational Technology.

Earle, R. S. (2002). The integration of instructional technology into public education: Promises and challenges. *Educational Technology Magazine, 42*(1), 5–13.

Grant, M. M. (2002). Getting a grip on project-based learning: Theory, cases, and recommendations. *Meridian: A Middle School Computer Technologies Journal, 5*(1). Retrieved June 27, 2005, from http://www.ncsv.edu/meridian/win 2002/514.

Howard, J. (2002). Technology-enhanced project-based learning in teacher education. *Journal of Technology and Teacher Education, 10*(3), 343–364.

Kilpatrick, W. H. (1918). The project method. *Teachers College Record, 19,* 319–335.

Land, S. M. (2000). Cognitive requirements for learning with open-ended learning environments. *Educational Technology Research and Development, 48*(3), 61–78.

Mayer, R. E. (2001). *Multimedia learning.* Cambridge, UK: Cambridge University Press.

McKenzie, J. (2000). *Beyond technology: Questioning, research and the information literate school.* Bellingham, WA: FNO Press.

Moursund, D. (1999). *Project-based learning using information technology.* Eugene, OR: International Society for Technology in Education.

Paivio, A. (1986). *Mental representations: A dual coding approach*. Oxford, England: Oxford University Press.

Pierson, M. E. (2001). Technology integration practice as a function of pedagogical expertise. *Journal of Research on Computing in Education, 33*(4), 413-430.

Shepard, L. A. (2000). The role of assessment in a learning culture. *Educational Researcher, 29*(7), 4-14.

Smith, P. L., & Ragan, T. J. (1999). *Instructional design.* Upper Saddle River, NJ: Prentice Hall.

Thomas, J. W. (2000). *A review of research on project-based learning.* San Rafael, CA: Autodesk Foundation.

van Merrienboer, J. J. G. (2002). Computer-based tools for instructional design: An introduction to the special issue. *Educational Technology Research and Development, 50*(4), 5-9.

Wittrock, M. C. (1974). Learning as a generative process. *Educational Psychologist, 11*, 87-95.

Wittrock, M. C. (1990). Generating processes of comprehension. *Educational Psychologist, 24*(4), 345-376.

Wood, D. J., Bruner J. S., & Ross, G. (1976). The role of tutoring in problem solving. *Journal of Child Psychology and Psychiatry, 17*(2), 89-100.

# CHAPTER 3

# Internet Technologies for Teaching and Learning
## *An Overview*

When Carla Hockenbury first became a computer teacher at William Davies Middle School, she taught computer skills as a related arts class. As the school began to integrate computer technology into the curriculum, teachers scheduled their classes in Ms. Hockenbury's computer lab to use computer technology and the Internet to enhance the activities taking place in the classroom. Now, when teachers bring their classes to the computer lab, the subject teacher works with the class on the content of a project, and Ms. Hockenbury assists the teachers and students in using technology to complete the learning tasks.

Besides facilitating the use of the computer lab, Ms. Hockenbury helps teachers and students through Web pages she creates to support curriculum-related projects with Internet resources. She also has students set up e-mail accounts so they can help each other by "buddying up" in completing cooperative assignments or can request information about a learning task from experts.

Research for learning activities is an important use of the Internet in Ms. Hockenbury's computer lab. She created a learning activity called Web Detective to assist students in evaluating the reliability of material they find online. Scavenger hunts and virtual tours are other online research activities she commonly uses with students. For example, she has created a scavenger hunt that addresses plagiarism and copyright issues, and she has all seventh graders visit the online version of the Smithsonian American Art Museum and select a piece of artwork they would like to write about. After students complete the research on their projects, they publish Web pages that present their findings and conclusions. Some recent examples include an online career museum and book reviews for books on the accelerated reading list.

In addition, Ms. Hockenbury helps teachers use the Internet to find new ideas, lesson plans, and learning activities. She publishes a site-of-the-week for teachers on the weekly computer lab schedule. She thinks that the Internet is a great resource for teachers who are integrating technology into their classrooms.

## NEW TERMS

asynchronous communication          chat room
bulletin board service              discussion list
chat                                e-mail

emoticons
FTP
Gopher
HTML
HTTP
instant messaging
Internet
Internet2
Internet videoconferencing
Internet whiteboard
intranet
listserv
Majordomo
message board
Netiquette
newsgroup

packets
portal
pull technology
push technology
synchronous communication
TCP/IP
Telnet
thread
URL
Usenet
Web browser
Webcasting
Web log
Webmail
Web server
World Wide Web

## National Educational Technology Standards for Teachers

The following NETS•T are addressed by the lesson content and learning activities in this chapter:

**I. Technology Operations and Concepts**

  **A.** Demonstrate understanding of technology concepts and skills

  **B.** Demonstrate continual growth in technology knowledge and skills

**VI. Social, Ethical, Legal, and Human Issues**

  **A.** Model and teach legal and ethical practice related to technology use

  **B.** Enable and empower diverse learners

  **C.** Identify and use technology resources that affirm diversity

  **D.** Promote safe and healthy use of technology resources

  **E.** Facilitate equitable access to technology resources

## National Educational Technology Standards for Students

The following NETS•S are addressed by the lesson content and learning activities in this chapter:

**1. Basic Operations and Concepts**

- Demonstrate sound understanding of technology
- Be proficient in the use of technology

**2. Social, Ethical, and Human Issues**

- Understand ethical, cultural, and societal issues related to technology
- Practice responsible use of technology
- Develop positive attitudes toward technology

**3. Technology Productivity Tools**

- Use technology to enhance learning, increase productivity, and promote creativity
- Use tools to collaborate, prepare publications, and produce creative works

**4. Technology Communications Tools**

- Use telecommunications to collaborate, publish, and interact with others
- Use varied media and formats to communicate information and ideas

# OVERVIEW

The Internet is a loosely structured network of computers that cross geographical, political, educational, and cultural boundaries. The Internet has two main features that can support a wide range of learning activities in the classroom: information resources and communication technologies. This chapter and chapter 4 provide a discussion of the communication technologies, whereas chapters 5 and 6 focus on the use of the information resources. Chapters 7, 8, 9, and 10 demonstrate ways in which these features can be combined and deployed to address a number of learning goals.

It is important to be familiar with the various Internet communication technologies to be able to use them in the classroom. To help you better understand these technologies, this chapter presents descriptions of a number of them, some of which are useful for classroom instruction. Teachers should be familiar with how each technology can be used so that they can choose the Internet technologies and resources that are most likely to be embraced by their students and that permit the level of control and manageability appropriate for their classes and grade levels.

The Internet supports both synchronous and asynchronous communication channels. Synchronous communication requires all communicating parties to be present when communication occurs, whereas asynchronous communication does not. Because of the unstructured nature of asynchronous and synchronous communication, it is important to establish clear rules and expectations for Internet communication sessions. *Netiquette* refers to network etiquette—the dos and don'ts of online communication.

## Lesson 3.1  Internet Technologies

### FOCUS QUESTIONS

- What is the Internet and how did it get started?
- What technologies does the Internet support?
- What information and communication functions do Internet technologies perform?
- How can Internet technologies support teaching and learning in the classroom?

## ■ A BRIEF HISTORY OF THE INTERNET

The **Internet** is a global network of networks through which computers communicate. It is an infrastructure consisting of computers, cables, wires, and other telecommunications devices plus the protocols to allow these computers to easily communicate with each other. The Internet has had a profound effect on almost every aspect of our lives, changing the way we do business, communicate, and even educate ourselves.

Several → Internet histories have been written that describe the origins of the Internet and the motivations of the researchers and funding agencies that participated in its original development. The Internet was developed in the 1970s as a U.S. Department of Defense network called the ARPAnet (Hafner & Lyon, 1996). The defense department's Advanced Research Projects Agency (ARPA or DARPA) had initiated a research program to investigate communication protocols that would allow different types and models of computers in various geographical locations to communicate with each other across multiple networks.

**Go to the Companion Website and browse *Chapter 3 Lesson Links: Internet Histories* to learn more about this topic.**

The Internet today uses the ARPAnet structure and is a collection of computer networks linked through different media, connecting many campus networks, commercial networks, and government networks across the world. By the end of 1989 the original Department of Defense ARPAnet had been retired and turned over to the National Science Foundation to form what is now called the Internet (Hafner & Lyon, 1996). Thereafter, the Internet linked universities around North America and then connected to research facilities in Europe. Use of the Internet exploded during the 1990s, when it was expanded to allow private companies and individuals to connect to it. Eventually, management of the

Internet was transferred from U.S. government agencies to independent, international organizations.

Today the Internet is a loosely structured network of computers that cross geographical, political, educational, and cultural boundaries. There is no centralized governing body exercising management or control over its operations, allowing it to emerge incrementally through the designs and inventions of Internet users. However, technical bodies contribute specifications, standards, and protocols to support the interoperability of the Internet among computers and networks. The seemingly infinite amount of information available on the Internet makes it a natural educational resource.

## ■ INTERNET USE IN THE CLASSROOM

Ms. Hockenbury, the computer teacher you met at the beginning of this chapter, has made Internet use a part of her classroom curriculum. Based on that experience, she has prepared a list of the 10 best ways to use Internet technologies and information resources in the classroom (see Figure 3–1). You will encounter many of these uses throughout this textbook.

In addition, the National Academy of Sciences has indicated in its publication *How People Learn: Brain, Mind, Experience, and School* that an important use of technology is its capacity to create learning opportunities situated in real-world problems (Bransford, Brown, & Cocking, 2000). The powerful technologies used to mediate the limitless information resources available on the Internet make it possible for teachers to bring real-world problems into their classrooms for students to explore and solve.

Even though the Internet has many educational uses in the classroom, it is not the ultimate solution to all the educational problems a teacher faces. By itself the Internet is only a loosely organized collection of information and technologies. However, in the hands of skillful, tech-savvy teachers guiding students through the complex processes that go into learning, the vast information and communication resources of the Internet can be exploited to create useful knowledge. When teachers employ appropriate strategies and methods to integrate those technologies into the classroom curriculum, the Internet can be a powerful tool to motivate students and engage them in learning.

| **FIGURE 3–1** | **Ms. Hockenbury's 10 Best Uses of the Internet in the Classroom** |
|---|---|

1. **Ask an expert**—Telementoring using Internet communication technologies.
2. **Collaborative projects**—Students in multiple locations around the world working on a common task or project.
3. **Electronic portfolios**—Using multimedia to collect and organize documents that are published on the Internet.
4. **Keypals**—Electronic penpals using e-mail.
5. **Lesson plans**—Tested and proven lesson plans created by other teachers and published on the Internet.
6. **Online learning**—Interactive tutorials or workshops available through the Internet.
7. **Publishing**—Classrooms sharing work with peers by publishing their work on Web pages.
8. **Research**—Searching, locating, and evaluating information resources published on the World Wide Web.
9. **Virtual tours**—Multimedia guided tours allowing students to see the world from their computers.
10. **WebQuests**—An inquiry activity that uses information from the World Wide Web to solve a problem or perform a task collaboratively.

*Source:* Retrieved December 1, 2003, from http://www.hamiltonschools.org/davies/10best/. Reprinted with permission.

# ■ AN OVERVIEW OF INTERNET TECHNOLOGIES

Although we use the term *Internet* to refer to a single entity or structure, the Internet is actually the infrastructure that provides access to or exchanges of information using several telecommunication services, or technologies, across numerous networks. In contrast to the Internet, an **intranet** is a private network that resides within an organization and is not accessible to the public. It uses networking hardware and software for communicating and storing or sharing files within the intranet. Usually a networked computer can access both an intranet and the Internet.

Internet technologies provide access to information that would have been impossible to access just a few years ago. Using the World Wide Web, students have access to virtual libraries, electronic databases, and powerful search engines. They can manipulate and generate information in artificial or exploratory learning environments. The Internet also permits interaction and communication among peers and with experts outside the local classroom, both synchronously and asynchronously. Internet technologies support interaction and collaboration that allow students to share ideas, ask questions, and discuss classroom projects.

The two salient features of the Internet—information resources and communication technologies—can support a wide range of learning activities. Harris (1998) calls these features teleresearch and telecollaboration processes. The information features of the Internet provide access to and manipulation of the vast resources available on the Internet by locating, organizing, and structuring information in ways that help students build new knowledge and understandings. The communication features of the Internet support multiple formats and contexts for interaction and exchange of information with other persons or interactive programs in ways that, again, help students build new knowledge and understandings. Both of these features of the Internet offer a number of tools and resources that can support varied instructional methodologies to address a variety of learning goals.

As the Internet has evolved, some technologies have been replaced by newer ones or have evolved with the Internet. For example, the use of the World Wide Web has, for the most part, made Gopher obsolete. Yet e-mail, one of the original Internet technologies, has grown in use and popularity as the Internet has grown. The following discussion provides summaries of most of the Internet technologies you may encounter in the classroom but is not intended to be comprehensive. Some technologies may not be appropriate for use in classroom instruction.

The establishment of the World Wide Web is the focal point for classifying Internet technologies as old, recycled, or new (see Table 3-1). Technologies that were created prior to the World Wide Web and are not widely used now are considered to be old technologies. Those that were designed primarily to support the delivery of information or communication through the World Wide Web are new technologies. And those that predated the Internet but have been modified or updated to deliver services through the World Wide Web or are still widely used on the Internet are considered to have been recycled.

## Old Internet Technologies

Old Internet technologies were used on the Internet prior to the beginning of the World Wide Web and now are not widely used.

### *Gopher*

**Gopher** brought hierarchically organized text files from servers all over the world to a user's computer. Gopher was developed at the University of Minnesota (where sports teams are called the Golden Gophers) and was prominently used from about 1992 through 1996, when it was effectively replaced by the World Wide Web. For the most part, Gopher servers are no longer active on the Internet because almost all of the original Gopher content has been made accessible on the World Wide Web.

| TABLE 3–1 | Classification of Internet Technologies | | | |
|---|---|:---:|:---:|:---:|
| **Internet technology** | | **Old** | **Recycled** | **New** |
| Bulletin board service | | | ✓ | |
| Chat | | | | ✓ |
| Discussion lists | | | ✓ | |
| E-mail | | | ✓ | |
| File transfer protocol (FTP) | | | ✓ | |
| Gopher | | ✓ | | |
| Hypertext markup language (HTML) | | | | ✓ |
| Hypertext transfer protocol (HTTP) | | | | ✓ |
| Instant messaging | | | | ✓ |
| Message boards | | | | ✓ |
| Telnet | | ✓ | | |
| Transmission control protocol/Internet protocol (TCP/IP) | | | ✓ | |
| Uniform resource locator (URL) | | | | ✓ |
| UseNet | | | ✓ | |
| Videoconferencing | | | | ✓ |
| Web log (blog) | | | | ✓ |
| World Wide Web (WWW or Web) | | | | ✓ |

### *Telnet*

**Telnet** is a protocol that permits basic communication between two host computers. It was developed in the early days of the Internet as an accommodation to overcome simple differences among computers, such as what kind of character set to use. Telnet allowed a person to log on to a host computer through the Internet as a regular user with whatever privileges were granted to the specific application and data on that computer.

## Recycled Internet Technologies

Recycled Internet technologies were used on the Internet prior to the beginning of the World Wide Web but were modified to work as a Web service or are still widely used.

### *Bulletin Board Services*

**Bulletin board services** (BBSs) are electronic message centers that host specific interest groups. A BBS may provide archives of files, personal electronic mail, and any other services or activities of interest to the bulletin board's system operator. Bulletin boards are a particularly good place to find free or inexpensive software products. Messages on BBSs are typically categorized by topics, and any user can submit or read any message.

BBSs were originally a single computer hooked up through a modem to a phone line with special software running that allowed anyone with a modem who called the phone line to connect to the computer, read and leave (i.e., send) messages, and download files. The BBS is unique as an electronic telecommunications service whose origins were not with military or defense organizations but with computer hobbyists and scientists.

The beginning of computer bulletin boards is attributed to Ward Christensen and Randy Suess, who opened the first public BBS in Chicago in the late 1970s. Their Computerized Bulletin Board System went online to the public in 1979 and operated like a virtual thumbtack bulletin board, where participants could read and post messages. As others responded to the messages, an ongoing virtual discussion was created. Christensen and

Suess published an article describing the technology they used, and virtual bulletin boards begin popping up all around the country. America Online (AOL) and CompuServe are examples of commercial BBSs; Microsoft Network (MSN) was originally a commercial BBS.

BBSs supplied their own content and sometimes interconnected with other BBSs, but in the early 1990s BBSs began connecting to the Internet, expanding the range of content available to BBS members, who had previously operated within the confines of one BBS or several interconnected BBSs. By the mid-1990s membership in BBSs began to decline as the graphics-oriented World Wide Web became more widely available, and eventually BBSs either became Web portals or were absorbed into the World Wide Web and were reconstituted as individual websites operated by government, educational, and research institutions.

### Electronic Mail

**E-mail** was one of the original Internet technologies, yet it remains probably the most popular technology used on the Internet. E-mail allows messages comprised of text and other media to be sent between computers. It was invented during the 1960s, when computer scientists devised ways of exchanging short messages within a large time-sharing computer system. By 1970 electronic message traffic was moving smoothly on the Department of Defense network, and by the early 1980s network mail was called *e-mail* and the @ sign became an indispensable component of e-mail addresses. The rise in e-mail traffic was the largest early force contributing to the growth and development of the Internet (Hafner & Lyon, 1996).

E-mail applications usually require both a client program that runs on an individual computer and a server connected to the Internet. Many e-mail servers allow e-mail messages to be retrieved and sent using an application called **Webmail,** which allows e-mail accounts to be accessed through a Web browser program. To use e-mail, you must have an e-mail account on a mail server. Most schools and universities operate mail servers on a local network that is connected to the Internet. You can also obtain e-mail accounts with an Internet service provider (ISP), such as Yahoo! or MSN Hotmail. Students may have accounts at home as well as at school.

An e-mail account is identified by an e-mail address, which has two parts, separated by an @ symbol. To the left of the @ symbol is the account or user name; the part on the right identifies the domain of the mail server where your account resides. The account or user name can be chosen or assigned, but it must be unique within the domain in which it is used. Figure 3–2 illustrates the structure of the e-mail account scm777@hotmail.com. All who use MSN Hotmail will have the same domain—hotmail.com—as the second part of their e-mail addresses; all who use Yahoo! mail will have yahoo.com as the second part of their e-mail addresses; and all who use America Online e-mail will have aol.com as the second part of their e-mail addresses.

There are several ways to set up an e-mail account, but the basics of using e-mail are essentially the same for all applications. Even though different e-mail programs may have

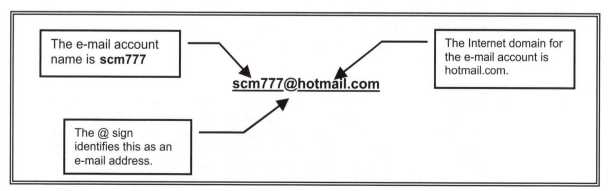

**FIGURE 3–2:    The Structure of an E-Mail Address**

different looks, they all operate fundamentally the same way. An e-mail account will usually operate from one of the following sources:

- *An e-mail account through an ISP*—ISPs usually provide e-mail accounts as part of the fee for a connection to the Internet. This type of account is usually accessed through a phone line or cable connection.

- *An e-mail account through a school or university (or business) network*—These accounts often use a full-featured e-mail program, such as Microsoft Outlook, Outlook Express, or Eudora. These client e-mail applications often come preloaded on a computer or may be downloaded for free or for a small license fee. These programs have many features and are configured by the individual user or a network administrator to operate with an Internet connection through a local area network.

- *An e-mail account through a Web-based e-mail service*—Several **portal** sites that provide a structured gateway to the Internet with supporting tools and resources, such as Yahoo! (http://www.mail.yahoo.com) or MSN (http://www.hotmail.com), provide free e-mail in exchange for exposure to advertisements. These e-mail services are easy to use and are usually accessible through any computer connected to the Internet.

Two popular uses of e-mail are e-mail announcement lists and e-mail discussion lists. Announcement lists are used to send messages to a small or large group or a collection of e-mail accounts. Such lists are usually created around particular products or organizations. When you purchase a product, use a service, or join an organization, you may be subscribed to an announcement list. Discussion lists are used to generate information, comments, or feedback from others subscribing to the lists. Discussion lists are usually organized around a particular topic, and you usually subscribe to the list voluntarily because of your interest in the topic.

Announcement lists use a top-down approach: E-mail announcements flow from the manager of the list to the subscribers. Discussion lists use a bottom-up approach: E-mail discussions flow from subscribers to the list manager and then out to other subscribers. With a discussion list you send an e-mail to a specific e-mail address, and the message goes to possibly hundreds or thousands of people who have subscribed to the list.

### File Transfer Protocol

File transfer protocol **(FTP)** is a standard Internet protocol that permits the exchange of files between computers on the Internet. Like Telnet, FTP was developed in the early days of the Internet (it was released as a standard protocol in 1972) to make it possible to share files between computers. FTP is now commonly used to transfer Web page files from the Web page author's computer to a Web server. FTP is also commonly used to download programs and other files from a Web server to a user or client computer. FTP permits deleting, renaming, moving, and copying of files on a server. It can be used as a stand-alone program or application, or it can be built into other programs, such as a program for authoring Web pages that requires the author to move files back and forth between the user computer and the Web server. A Web browser can also perform FTP requests to download programs selected from a Web page. You need to log on to an FTP server, but publicly available files are easily accessed using an anonymous FTP.

### Listservs or Discussion Lists

**Discussion lists** (or **listservs,** discussion forums, electronic mailing lists, or just mailing lists) are automated mail lists—basically, e-mail distributed to a large group. A listserv, or mailing list manager, is a program that receives messages and automatically sends them out to the e-mail addresses of a group of users who have subscribed to the list. Thus, list subscribers can communicate with other list subscribers without having to send individual e-mails to everyone on the list. Each subscriber can post a message to the e-mail address of the mailing list, which serves as an alias for all list subscribers' addresses.

Messages to and from mailing lists are sent and received in the same way that other e-mail messages are. Some of the most popular mailing list management programs are LIST-SERV, ListProc, and Majordomo. Even though LISTSERV is a proprietary and copyrighted name owned by L-Soft International, Inc., the term *listserv* has become the generic name to describe discussion lists. This textbook will use the terms *discussion list, listserv,* and *mailing list* interchangeably to refer to the same asynchronous communication tool so that you will become comfortable with all the terms.

Discussion lists allow many people in diverse locations to exchange information and/or have a discussion through a single e-mail address. Discussion lists focus on a common topic, such as online education in the classroom. To use a discussion list, you subscribe by sending an e-mail message to the specific list address. Once you subscribe, you will usually receive a confirmation message that tells you the guidelines of the list and the way to unsubscribe. You should always save the confirmation message so you will have information about how to send messages to the list or how to unsubscribe from the list.

Discussion lists can be structured in several ways:

- *Moderated*—A discussion list can have a moderator who reviews and approves each message posted to the list.
- *Unmoderated*—Without a moderator messages are automatically posted to all subscribers on the list without approval.
- *Open*—A discussion list can allow anyone to subscribe.
- *Closed*—A discussion list can be limited to certain subscribers, who must get approval before joining.
- *One-way or broadcast*—A discussion list can allow subscribers to receive messages from the list but not post new ones.
- *Two-way*—A discussion list can allow subscribers to post as well as receive messages.

There are several primary ways to host and manage a discussion list. First, the discussion list can be hosted on your own server, using mailing list software such as Majordomo or LISTSERV. Your school or school district network may provide the capability of setting up and hosting a classroom discussion list. If not, you can pay an Internet service provider to host a discussion list for you, although the best choice for a classroom is to use a free mailing list hosting service. However, free services usually include advertisements attached to the bottom of posted messages, which may not be appropriate for some classrooms. For a small fee most free services allow you to run an advertisement-free list. For example, Yahoo Groups charges a small monthly fee per list for messages without advertisements.

### Newsgroups

**Newsgroups** began as a means of communication between mainframe computers at large universities. Newsgroups use a network service called **Usenet,** which was originally implemented between 1979 and 1980 by Steve Bellovin, Jim Ellis, Tom Truscott, and Steve Daniel at Duke University and has evolved into a large distributed news network (Hafner & Lyon, 1996). Usenet permits any member to participate in a public dialogue with everyone else in the newsgroup. As it grew to become international in scope, it became probably the largest decentralized information resource in existence until the advent of the World Wide Web.

UseNet is not a formal network but is comprised of networked computers that exchange articles tagged with predetermined subject headers for groups with specific areas of interest (i.e., newsgroups). Any computer that can attach itself to the Internet can become part of UseNet. News articles are handled as electronic mail messages by most computers and are processed as news information by applications called news readers, which send and receive the messages, although most Web browsers are capable of processing Usenet articles.

Usenet newsgroups are distributed among thousands of computers called news servers, which are operated by Internet service providers, universities, companies, and other

| FIGURE 3–3 | Newsgroup Discussion Categories |
|---|---|

- **alt.** Any conceivable topic
- **news.** Info about Usenet news
- **biz.** Business products, services, reviews
- **rec.** Games, hobbies, sports
- **comp.** Hardware, software, consumer info
- **sci.** Applied science, social science
- **humanities.** Fine art, literature, philosophy
- **soc.** Social issues, culture
- **misc.** Employment, health, and much more
- **talk.** Current issues and debates

organizations. Each server receives copies of all messages in a newsgroup and stores them in a database. News servers automatically exchange, or propagate, these messages among themselves, to keep each other's databases up to date.

Newsgroups can be unmoderated, with anyone able to post submissions, or moderated, with submissions automatically directed to a moderator, who edits or filters and then posts the article. Postings to unmoderated groups are automatically propagated to the newsgroup, whereas postings to moderated groups are not propagated until approved by the moderator.

Newsgroups are hierarchically classified (see Figure 3–3). Newsgroup discussion categories, such as alt, are organized into topics, such as alt.animals, which are again divided into even more specific topics, such as alt.animals.dogs. Ultimately, the classification leads to a newsgroup containing messages from people who are interested in one particular topic, such as alt.animals.dogs.beagles. The different parts of a newsgroup's name are always separated by a period.

Each newsgroup contains threads that are more or less a continuous chain of messages on a single topic. Messages, or articles or postings, are linked to one another by a common subject in much the same way that you link to an originating e-mail message when you reply to it.

Because alt newsgroups, especially, may contain content and discussions that are inappropriate for classroom use, Internet filters in schools may limit or prevent access to newsgroups.

Newsgroups are different from discussion lists in several ways. Postings to a newsgroup are made to a central location rather than to e-mail accounts, and Usenet articles remain on a server, whereas discussion list messages come to an e-mail account. Further, discussion lists need only an e-mail program to view the discussion; newsgroups need a news reader or Web browser.

### Transmission Control Protocol/Internet Protocol

**TCP/IP** (transmission control protocol/Internet protocol) is the basic communication language, or protocol, of the Internet. It can also be used in a local area network. The collection of networks eventually called the Internet was named for the first word of Internet protocol (Hafner & Lyon, 1996).

The Internet can best be described as one large worldwide network connecting many smaller networks. It is a packet-switching network. **Packets** are like little envelopes of information packaged and routed according to network availability. Each packet has a destination address and is transported from one place to another until it is delivered to the correct address. A packet may go through a series of networks before it reaches its final destination; the protocols that make the packet transformation possible are called transmission control protocol and Internet protocol, or TCP/IP.

TCP/IP is a two-layer program. TCP manages the assembling of a message or file into smaller packets that are transmitted over the Internet and are then reassembled into the original message. The other layer, IP, handles the address part of each packet so that it gets to the right destination. A Gateway computer checks the address to see where to forward the message.

TCP/IP uses a client/server model of communication, in which a computer user (i.e., a client) requests and is provided a service, such as receiving a Web page, by another computer (i.e., a server) in the network. TCP/IP communication is primarily point to point, meaning each communication is from one point, or host computer, in the network to another point, or host computer.

## New Internet Technologies

New Internet technologies support the use of the World Wide Web.

### Chat

**Chat** is real-time communication between two or more people using computers, usually through the Internet. Any online, real-time conversation is chat or a form of chat. Most networks, online services, and conferencing programs offer a chat feature. A **chat room** is a virtual space where a chat session takes place. Technically, a chat room is a communications channel, but the term *room* supports the chat metaphor.

Because chat is intended for two-way communication, it supports a high level of interactivity among users. The client application installed on the user computer transmits every character typed in real time or a complete message that is sent when the user presses the ENTER key. The standard for establishing chat among large groups of people is known as Internet relay chat (IRC). IRC uses chat rooms for people to meet and discuss topical issues related to the overall theme set by the room. IRC could be considered the real-time equivalent of newsgroups.

In a chat session the participants may be physically located anywhere in the world but are able to communicate almost instantly by typing text, which immediately appears on the screens of all participants in the chat session. A newer browser, such as Netscape Communicator 4.x or Internet Explorer 4.x, is often all that is needed to participate in Web-based chats.

Chat can be used effectively to support Web-enhanced learning in the classroom. Some of the benefits include the following:

- Chat sessions are a good way to access experts in a field of study. For example, a science class might invite a renowned scientist to join the class's chat session at a specific time, allowing the expert to remain at home or in the office.

- Teachers can provide online office hours as a chat session, allowing more than one person to benefit from the discussion. When others participate, varied points of view are expressed to all participants.

- Most chat tools keep a record or a log of conversations. Students can then use the transcript of the conversation to recall important parts of the discussion. And students who are unable to participate in the chat can review the transcript of the discussion. Transcripts can also be used by the teacher to evaluate student participation.

- Chat sessions can be relatively spontaneous. For example, if a controversial topic is in the news, an instructor can schedule a chat session that day to discuss it.

### Hypertext Transfer Protocol

Hypertext transfer protocol **(HTTP)** is the underlying protocol used by the World Wide Web. HTTP defines how messages are formatted and transmitted and what actions Web servers and Web browsers should take in response to various commands. For example, when you enter a URL in your browser, you send an HTTP command to the Web server directing it to fetch and transmit the requested Web page. In contrast to FTP, HTTP transfers the contents of a Web page into a Web browser only for viewing, whereas FTP transfers the contents of entire files from one device to another and stores them on the receiving computer. FTP is a two-way system in which files can be transferred back and forth between server and client computers. HTTP is a one-way system in which files are transferred from the Web server into the Web browser of the client computer. When HTTP appears in a URL, it means that the user is connecting to a Web server and files are transferred but not downloaded and stored.

### Hypertext Markup Language

Hypertext markup language (**HTML**) is the language in which Web pages are written. HTML uses a simple system for denoting instructions, called tags, to convey the content and structure of a hypertext document, or Web page. Hypertext is a term coined by Ted Nelson in 1965 to describe text that includes links or shortcuts to other documents, allowing the reader to easily jump from one text to related texts, and consequently from one idea to another, in a nonlinear fashion. In addition to hypertext, Web pages now commonly include other media, and it may be more accurate to use the term *hypermedia* instead of *hypertext*. HTML files, or Web pages, use HTTP to transfer Web pages from a Web server through the World Wide Web to a client computer, where they are parsed and displayed using a **Web browser** program.

### Instant Messaging

**Instant messaging** is a form of chat that provides a more personal or private interaction between chatters but requires specialized software to be downloaded to a user's computer. There are several different instant messaging systems available, including ICQ (I Seek You), AOL Instant Messenger, Yahoo! Messenger, and MSN Messenger. With instant messaging you create buddy or contact lists of other users with whom you wish to correspond, all of whom must be using the same instant messaging program. When one of the people on your list logs on to the system, you are notified by some means, such as a sound, a pop-up box on the screen, a flashing menu bar, or some other attention-getting device. You can then chat interactively or transfer files. If you happen not to be online, a message may still be sent but is not delivered until you log in. In this case, instant messaging reverts to an asynchronous communication similar to e-mail.

Because of the lack of an instant messaging standard, instant messaging may not be a good choice for Web-enhanced learning in the classroom. It is difficult for a teacher to provide instant messaging support to students without installing multiple programs. If you do use instant messaging in your classroom, you must decide which program to use and then provide students with instruction. Each student should establish buddy lists and should add the teacher to the list so that the teacher will be notified and can simply respond instead of having to actively enroll each student. Students can take responsibility for creating their own contact lists with each other.

Instant messaging has a number of advantages over online chat rooms. Instant messaging programs are popular, and many students will have some form of instant messaging installed on their computers. In addition, instant messages are delivered even if the contact is not currently online. However, the best use of instant messaging is for online office hours. Students with questions usually like to receive help immediately, and instant messaging lets them know whether the teacher is currently available.

### Internet2

**Internet2** is a consortium of over 200 universities working in partnership with industry and government to develop and deploy advanced applications for learning and research. The Internet2 project is not a single, separate network but joins its members together through many advanced campus, regional, and national networks.

Internet2 is itself a collection of communication and information-sharing technologies. For example, a major function of Internet2 is adding sufficient network infrastructure to support real-time multimedia and high-bandwidth interconnections and thus to enable applications such as telemedicine, digital libraries, and virtual laboratories that are not possible with the technology underlying today's Internet.

Internet2 is not intended to be a future replacement for the Internet but is intended to investigate and develop new ways to use the Internet and the Internet2 infrastructure for educational and research purposes. Its organizers plan to share their developments with other networks, including the Internet.

### Message Boards

**Message boards,** bulletin boards or forums, or threaded discussions usually refer to a Web-based asynchronous communication tool that allows you to post a message for people to read at their own convenience. Message boards work similarly to newsgroups but function differently from discussion lists. With discussion or mailing lists, messages are received in subscribers' e-mail inboxes because messages are pushed from the Web server to the client computer. Message boards require messages to be pushed from the client computer to a Web server, participants go to a bulletin board on a Web server to read the messages. A message or bulletin board is the equivalent of a newsgroup on the Web.

With an Internet-based message board, you go to a specific location on the Web and post a message consisting of a subject title and a message body. When other people have read the message, they can post a message in reply or post a different message with a different subject heading. Multiple posts referring to one particular subject title are called a **thread** of discussion. The series of messages, or posts, can evolve into complex, multilayered conversations that are similar in many respects to face-to-face conversations.

### Uniform Resource Locator

A uniform resource locator **(URL)** is the address or location on the World Wide Web of a document or file that resides on a Web server connected to the Internet. The URL is the most fundamental innovation of the Web, it is the specification used by any program, computer, or server connected to the Internet to locate a resource on the Web. The URL allows a Web document or resource that is published on a Web server to be found by any Web browser.

Because URLs generally use HTTP to transfer documents or files to the Web browser of a requesting computer, URLs usually begin with http://. An understanding of the structure of URLs is useful for determining the accuracy and reliability of information on a website. For example, a Web address of **http://www.mysite.com/myfolder/mydoc.html** uses http to transfer a Web document named **mydoc.html** from the folder, **my folder,** in a → <u>domain</u> named **www.mysite.com** on a public Web server (see Figure 3–4) to a Web browser on a computer connected to the Internet.

Go to the Companion Website and browse *Chapter 3 Lesson Links: Domain Name* to learn more about this topic.

### Videoconferencing Technologies

**Webcasting** is a term taken from *World Wide Web* and *broadcast.* Sometimes called *Netcasting,* Webcasting refers to the real-time transmission of encoded video under the control of a server to multiple recipients who all receive the same content at the same time. Webcasting is used to deliver live or delayed versions of sound or video broadcasts. It also refers to the delayed or preview versions of movies, music videos, or regular radio and television broadcasts, which promote the live broadcasts.

Webcasting uses so-called **push technology,** in which a Web server seemingly pushes information to the user, in contrast to **pull technology,** in which the user seeks and downloads information, as with a Web browser. In reality, the pushing of information is triggered by a user or a network administrator who preselects the service, it arrives only as the result of client requests. Webcasting is a feature of the Microsoft Internet Explorer browser and

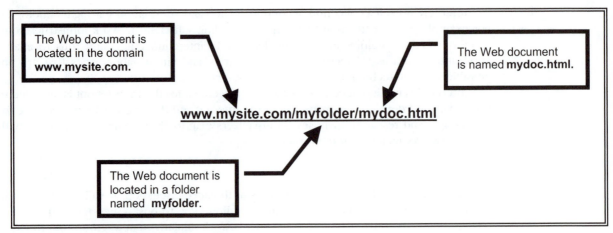

The Web document is located in the domain **www.mysite.com**.

The Web document is named **mydoc.html**.

www.mysite.com/myfolder/mydoc.html

The Web document is located in a folder named **myfolder**.

**FIGURE 3–4:    The Structure of a URL**

Netscape's Netcaster, part of its Communicator suite. Webcasting is also available through separate applications, such as Pointcast and Backweb, which run on current versions of browsers.

**An Internet whiteboard** is an Internet application that allows users to draw objects that can then be transmitted to other users who are simultaneously using the same application. This electronic concept is similar to that of a real-world whiteboard: One participant draws objects that others can see, and the other participants can then add to or delete these drawings. An electronic whiteboard allows communicating parties to share textual and graphic information in real time. Internet whiteboards are used in the context of some other communication channel, such as an Internet videoconference or a presentation.

**Internet videoconferencing** is becoming a widely used technology. Its applications and services are usually based on technologies that allow real-time video and audio to be sent and received through computer networks. The advantage of these technologies over older videoconferencing is that they allow videoconferencing to occur over the Internet rather than only through phone lines. Two popular software programs that allow videoconferences are CUSee-Me from Cornell University and NetMeeting from Microsoft. In both cases you need a video camera and a digitizing card to transmit video signals. A microphone, speakers (or headset), and an audio card are required for audio transmission.

### Web Log

A **Web log,** or blog, is an online journal in the form of a Web page that is comprised of links and postings in reverse chronological order. The activity of updating a blog is called *blogging,* and the person who maintains a blog is a *blogger.* The totality of Web logs on the World Wide Web is often called the *blogosphere.*

Web logs are not actually an Internet technology but use Web publishing technologies and tools to disseminate information on the Web. The format of Web logs varies from simple bullet lists of hyperlinks to article summaries with user-provided comments and ratings. Individual Web log entries are usually date- and time-stamped, with the newest post at the top of the page. Some Web logs are maintained by single authors, whereas others have multiple authors. Most are interactive and allow visitors to leave public comments, creating a community of readers centered around the Web log.

Two features common to Web logs are blogrolls and commenting, or feedback. A blogroll is a list of other Web logs that are linked to a Web log entry or article. Blogrolls are one way a blogger creates a context for a blog by listing other blogs that are similar. Blogrolls can be used as a measure of blog authority, ranking blogs according to the number of references found in other blogs—much like Google rankings of search results.

A feedback or comment system allows users to post their own comments on a Web log entry or an article. Some blogs do not allow comments or have a closed commenting system, which requires approval from those running the blog. However, for many bloggers comments are a critical feature. Regular comments on a blog are referred to as the blog's *community.*

Many Web logs are syndicated on the Web by distributing their headlines along with hyperlinks and summaries through a technology called Really Simple Syndication (RSS). An RSS feed simply repackages the content of an entry in a Web log as a list of data items, such as the date of the posting, a summary of the article, and a link to it. A program known as an *RSS aggregator,* or feed reader, can then check RSS-enabled Web log pages for a user and display any updated articles it finds. This process is more convenient than repeated visits to favorite Web logs because it ensures that the reader sees only material that has not been previously viewed.

### World Wide Web

The **World Wide Web** (WWW, or just Web) is the second most popular Internet application, second only to e-mail. The Web is an application built on top of the Internet and used to access information resources through the Internet, using specific protocols to identify and locate that information. The Web allows documents to be viewed in a semiformatted manner, regardless of what brand of computer is viewing them. Although the World Wide Web is one Internet technology, or application, like e-mail, Web browsers such as Internet Explorer or Netscape Navigator are used so extensively to access the Internet that we often think of the Internet in terms of the World Wide Web. Certainly in everyday use the Internet and the World Wide Web can be considered one and the same.

The World Wide Web was invented in 1989 by Tim Berners-Lee while working at CERN (Conseil Européen pour la Recherche Nucléaire), the European Particle Physics Laboratory. Berners-Lee, now director of the →World Wide Web Consortium (W3C), wrote the first Web browser and Web server programs in 1990 (Berners-Lee, 1999). The World Wide Web is a body of software, protocols, and conventions that provide for the viewing and publication of text and multimedia documents stored on computers known as **Web servers.**

Go to the Companion Website and browse *Chapter 3 Lesson Links: World Wide Web Consortium* to learn more about this topic.

---

### Building Your Toolkit:
### Using a Web Browser

To create learning activities that are supported by Internet technologies, you need to be proficient in surfing the Net so that you can model this skill for your students. You surf the Net (actually the World Wide Web) using a computer program called a **Web browser,** which allows you to view Web pages and other Web documents, usually stored on Web servers. Microsoft Internet Explorer and Netscape Browser are the most widely used Web browsers.

Current statistics indicate that most Web surfers are using Microsoft Internet Explorer running on a computer that uses the Microsoft Windows operating system. Therefore, many of the screen shots in this book will also follow that convention. The tutorials, however, will be applicable to any browser, any browser version, and any computer operating system (e.g., Microsoft Windows, Macintosh, and Linux) on which the Web browser is running.

You probably already know how to use a Web browser and already have your preferred Web browser. The following exercise is intended to review the basic skills needed to use a Web browser and to sharpen and expand those skills. Start by opening the Web browser program on your computer. Opening the browser also opens the website that has been set as the home or default website. Thus, home is the website to which the browser links when you first start the program (or when you click on the Home icon or button on your browser). The following steps demonstrate the use of the main features of a Web browser on a computer using the Windows operating system. These steps may differ slightly for different browser versions or for browsers on a Macintosh computer. Figure 3–5 illustrates all the buttons that are used in Steps 2–13 in the following exercise using the Internet Explorer browser.

*(Continued)*

# Building Your Toolkit:
## Using a Web Browser (Continued)

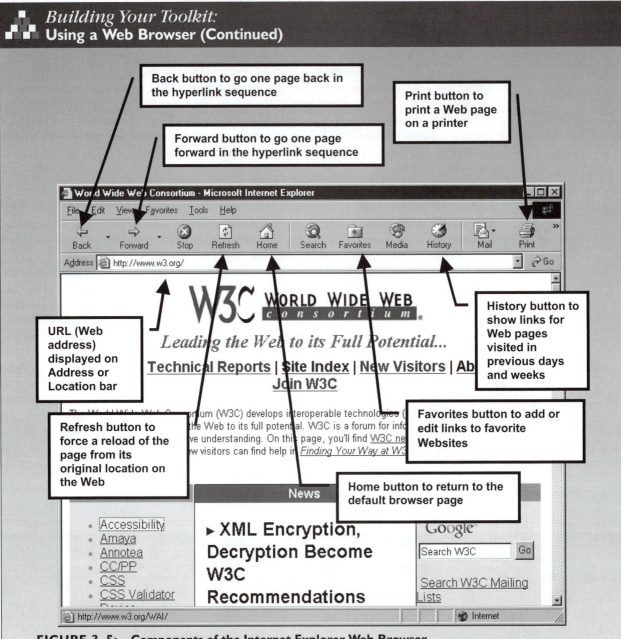

**Back button to go one page back in the hyperlink sequence**

**Print button to print a Web page on a printer**

**Forward button to go one page forward in the hyperlink sequence**

**History button to show links for Web pages visited in previous days and weeks**

**URL (Web address) displayed on Address or Location bar**

**Favorites button to add or edit links to favorite Websites**

**Refresh button to force a reload of the page from its original location on the Web**

**Home button to return to the default browser page**

**FIGURE 3–5:   Components of the Internet Explorer Web Browser**

| STEP | INTERNET EXPLORER | NETSCAPE BROWSER |
|---|---|---|
| **1.** | To view home Web address, select **Tools > Internet Options,** and then select the **General** tab. Click **OK** to close the Internet Options dialog box. | To view home Web address, select **Edit > Preferences** and then select the **Navigator** category. Click **OK** to close the Preferences dialog box. |
| **2.** | In the **Address** bar of the browser window, type in the following URL: **www.w3c.org**. Press **ENTER**. | In the **Location** bar of the browser window, type in the following URL: **www.w3c.org**. Press **ENTER**. |

*NOTE:* Because most versions of Web browsers now add http:// to the Web address, you do not need to include it when entering Web addresses in the Address or Location bar of your browser window.

**3.**   Click the **Back** icon or button. The Back button reverts the browser display to one page back in the sequence of Web pages to which you have hyperlinked (or just linked) during the current browser session.

*(Continued)*

| STEP | INTERNET EXPLORER | NETSCAPE BROWSER |
|---|---|---|
| 4. | Click the **Forward** icon or button. The Forward button advances the browser display one page ahead in the sequence of pages you have hyperlinked (or just linked) to during the current browser session. | |
| 5. | Click the **Home** icon or button. The Home button returns you to the page set as the default home page for the browser program on your computer. | |
| 6. | Enter the following URL into the Address bar: **www.discovery.com**. Press **ENTER**. | Enter the following URL into the Location bar: **www.discovery.com**. Press **ENTER**. |
| | *NOTE*: When you start typing the information in the Address or Location bar—or in a field on a Web page or in a box for a user name or password—the AutoComplete lists possible matches as you type, if you've typed a similar entry before. If a suggestion in the list matches what you want to enter in that field, click the suggestion. If no suggestion matches what you are typing, continue typing. | |
| 7. | Surf the Discovery website by clicking hyperlinks on the Web page and by using the navigation bars and buttons (displayed as either text or graphics) on the sides, top, or bottom of the Web page. Consider how you might use some of the information found on the website as content for a lesson or instructional activity. | |
| 8. | When you view a Web page with content that is interesting or appropriate for a subject you teach, bookmark it for future reference by selecting **Favorites** from the **menu bar** and then selecting **Add to Favorites** from the pop-up menu. Enter different information in the **Name** box if the default information does not provide a distinctive title for the Web page name. Click **OK**. | When you view a Web page with content that is interesting or appropriate for a subject you teach, bookmark it for future reference by clicking the **Bookmarks** button and selecting **Add a Bookmark** from the pop-up menu. (You can use **Edit Bookmark** to change the name of the page. Click **OK**.) |
| 9. | Print the content of the Web page you are viewing by selecting **File > Print** or clicking the **Print** icon. (Check with your instructor before actually printing.) | |
| 10. | To view a list of the sites you have previously visited, click the **History** button. The History bar appears on the left side of the window, listing links for websites and pages visited in previous days and weeks. In the History bar, click a week or day, then click a website folder to display individual pages, and then click the page icon to display the Web page. You can hide the History bar by clicking the **History** button again. A drop-down list of recently viewed pages is also available by clicking the down arrow at the right end of the Address bar. | To view a list of the sites you have previously visited, select **Communicator > Tools** and then select **History**. A window with a list of links for websites and pages visited in previous days and weeks is displayed. Close the History window after viewing it. |
| 11. | To delete Web address history from the browser, click **Tools > Internet Options** and select the **General** tab. Under **History** click **Clear History**. All Web address history (including history used for the AutoComplete feature) is deleted from the computer. Click **OK** to close the Internet Options dialog box. | To delete Web address history from the browser, select **Edit > Preferences** and select the **Navigator** category. Under **History** click **Clear History**. All Web address history (including history used for the AutoComplete feature) is deleted from the computer. Click **OK** to close the Preferences dialog box. |
| 12. | Your Web browser stores Web pages and related files (such as graphics) in a temporary folder. These files are stored on your computer to increase the speed with which a Web page is displayed for pages you frequently visit or have already visited by opening Web pages first from your hard disk instead of from a remote Web server. | |
| | This folder is named the Temporary Internet Files folder. If you think a newer version of a Web page is available after you have already viewed it, click the **Refresh** icon or button to force the browser to reload the Web page from its original location on the Web server. | This folder is named Cache. If you think a newer version of a Web page is available after you have already viewed it, click the **Reload** icon or button to force the browser to reload the Web page from its original location on the Web server. |

*(Continued)*

*Building Your Toolkit:*
**Using a Web Browser (Continued)**

| STEP | INTERNET EXPLORER | NETSCAPE BROWSER |
|------|-------------------|------------------|
| 13. | Increasing the size of the Temporary Internet Files or Cache folder can increase how fast previously visited pages are displayed while also decreasing the space available for other files on your computer. Emptying the folder decreases the amount of space it uses on your hard disk. You may find it necessary occasionally to clear the Temporary Internet Files or Cache folder when files become corrupted and do not display correctly or when a newer version of the Web page is available. | |

To delete the file contents of the Temporary Internet Folder from the browser, select **Tools > Internet Options,** then select the **General** tab, and click the **Delete Files** button.

To delete the file contents of the Cache folder from the browser, select **Edit > Preferences** and expand the **Advanced** category, then select **Cache**, and click the **Clear Disk Cache** button.

> **Go** to the Companion Website and browse *3.1 Building Your Toolkit Enrichment Activity: Creating a Web Archive for Off-Line Browsing.* **Follow the procedure in the enrichment activity for storing Web pages on your computer in a Web archive for off-line browsing.**

> **Go** to the Companion Website and browse *3.1 Project Sample: Understanding the Internet.* **Use the project sample as the foundation for a learning activity to introduce the Internet into the classroom. Adapt the project sample to the subject area and/or grade level that you teach.**

## Lesson 3.2    Online Communication

### FOCUS QUESTIONS

- What is the difference between synchronous and asynchronous communication on the Internet?
- What are examples of synchronous and asynchronous communication technologies?
- What rules, social conventions, and techniques are used for online communication?

### ■ SYNCHRONOUS AND ASYNCHRONOUS MODES

The Internet supports both synchronous and asynchronous communication channels. **Asynchronous communication** is communication that occurs without regard to time or location; it is not necessary for all communicating parties to be present when communication occurs. With asynchronous communication a message is sent but is not necessarily received (accessed and read) immediately. **Synchronous communication** is communication that occurs in real time and is highly interactive; all communicating parties are simultaneously present. With synchronous communication a message is sent and immediately received.

Information exchanges using the Internet, whether synchronous or asynchronous, can support both individual and group learning. Communication over the Internet can take place by individuals communicating with other individuals, individuals communicating with groups, or groups communicating with other groups (Harris, 1998). For educational purposes this textbook classifies Internet communication technologies in two categories: interpersonal communication and group communication. Interpersonal communication occurs one to one between individuals holding a private or public conversation. A student having an e-mail conversation with a teacher or a chat with a peer is an example of interpersonal communication. Group communication is used to communicate the same information to multiple individuals and occurs when an individual communicates with a group. Group communication is always a public conversation. A teacher distributing assignment information to a class, using a distribution list or message board, is an example of group communication.

When using synchronous or asynchronous communication to support information exchanges, it is important to establish classroom guidelines for online communication and specific learning objectives for each information exchange assignment. Additionally, students should learn online communication techniques and use appropriate communication practices when engaging in information exchanges.

## ■ NETIQUETTE

Because of the unstructured nature of asynchronous and synchronous communication, it is important to establish clear rules and expectations for Internet communication sessions. You should establish ground rules ahead of time that focus discussions on learning goals and make it easier to evaluate student participation. For example, prior to an information exchange, you might provide a list of topics for discussion so that students can be prepared to conduct a meaningful conversation. Complex questions should also be distributed prior to the session, but online brainstorming activities may not need advance preparation.

Rules and expectations for information exchanges should be made clear in general guidelines for online communication. **Netiquette** means network etiquette and refers to the dos and don'ts of online communication. It covers both common courtesy and the informal rules of surfing the Net (see Figure 3-6).

| FIGURE 3–6 | The Core Rules of Netiquette |
| --- | --- |

**Rule 1: Remember the human.** Be polite and courteous. Do not be offensive. There's a real person behind the computer that is accessing your online communication. Furthermore, whenever you communicate through the Internet, your words are written, and chances are good that they are stored somewhere where you have no control over them.

**Rule 2: Adhere to the same standards of behavior online that you follow in real life.** Be ethical and do your best to act within the laws of society and cyberspace.

**Rule 3: Know where you are in cyberspace.** When you enter a domain of cyberspace that is new to you, spend some time listening to the chat or reading the archives. Get a sense of how the people who are already there act before you participate.

**Rule 4: Respect other people's time and bandwidth.** It's your responsibility to ensure that the time spent reading your e-mail or posting to a discussion list is not wasted.

**Rule 5: Make yourself look good online.** In cyberspace you will be judged by the quality of your writing, so spelling and grammar do count.

**Rule 6: Share expert knowledge.** Do not be afraid to share what you know. It is especially polite to share the results of your questions with others.

**Rule 7: Help keep flame wars under control.** *Flaming* is what people do when they express a strongly held opinion without holding back any emotion. Netiquette forbids the perpetuation of flame wars, that is, a series of angry letters, most of which come from two or three people and are directed toward each other, dominating the tone and destroying the camaraderie of a discussion group.

**Rule 8: Respect other people's privacy.** Do not snoop into other people's e-mail.

**Rule 9: Don't abuse your power.** Knowing more than others, or having more power than they do online, does not give you the right to take advantage of them.

**Rule 10: Be forgiving of other people's mistakes.** If you do decide to inform someone of a mistake, point it out politely and preferably by private e-mail rather than in public. Give people the benefit of the doubt; assume they don't know any better.

*Adapted from Netiquette* by V. Shea, 1994, San Francisco: Albion Books. Available online at http://www.albion.com/netiquette/book/.

| FIGURE 3–7 | Emoticons for Online Conversations |
| --- | --- |

| | EYES : = | | NOSE – * ^ (or blank) | | MOUTH > ) 0 ( < |
| --- | --- | --- | --- | --- | --- |
| :–> | ambivalent or indifferent | :-9 | delicious, yummy | : O | shocked |
| :–( | angry or frowning | :-6 | exhausted | : ) or :–) or =) | smile |
| >–] | asleep | | | :–0 | surprised |
| (: : ( ) : : : ) | bandage | ^ 5 | high five | ^ | thumbs up |
| \–0 | bored | | | :–& | tongue tied |
| :–c | bummed out | :–# | lips are sealed | :–\ | Undecided |
| : ( ) | can't stop talking | :~/ | mixed up | :–0 | wow |
| : *) | clowning | :–@ | screaming | >–O | Yawning |

The composition of online messages often ignores conventional rules of capitalization, punctuation, and other grammatical rules. Although online communication facilitates a sense of freedom, it does not accommodate nonverbal communication or changes in inflection, thus making it much easier for the recipient of a message to misunderstand its meaning or to draw the wrong conclusion based solely on its written content, style, and formatting.

Using written communication styles and techniques that are appropriate, positive, and easy to understand is important for Web-enhanced learning activities. Messages should not contain ambiguous or inaccurate content but should clearly communicate and clarify the positions of the sender. The appropriate use of **emoticons** can be a good way to express emotion in written, text-based, asynchronous communications. Emoticons use text symbols to represent a face that is turned 90 degrees counterclockwise (see Figure 3-7).

## Building Your Toolkit:
## Subscribing to a Professional Discussion List

K–12 teachers can sometimes become isolated in their classrooms because of scheduling requirements and teaching duties. Professional discussion groups provide an opportunity for ongoing discussions among teachers without interrupting the class schedule. Teachers.net (http://www.teachers.net/) is a sponsored website containing a variety of resources, including chat rooms, lessons plans, live meetings, discussion groups, and an online newsletter. Teachers.net calls its discussion lists mailrings and offers several, including grade-level and subject groups. There is no cost to join, you subscribe to a group(s) by completing a Web form. Anyone who subscribes receives instructions for posting to and receiving e-mail from teacher colleagues around the world.

### STEP    PROCEDURE

1.   Open your Web browser and then the Teachers.net discussion group page at **www.teachers.net/mailrings**. A Web page with a form similar to that in Figure 3–8 should be displayed.

2.   Complete the form to join a discussion group appropriate to the grade level and/or subject area you teach.

- Select one or more discussion groups by clicking the check box beside the name of the discussion group you want to join.
- If you want to join a discussion group with teachers in your state, click on the down arrow of the pull-down list for **Your State Mailrings,** and select your state from the list. If you do not want to join a state mailring, uncheck the check box beside **Select State**.
- If you do not want to receive the online newsletter or information about events, uncheck the **Teachers.Net Gazette** and **EVENTS@Teachers.Net** check boxes.
- Enter your e-mail address in the **E-Mail** field.
- Click the **Subscribe** button to join the discussion group(s) you have selected.

*(Continued)*

*Building Your Toolkit:*
## Subscribing to a Professional Discussion List (Continued)

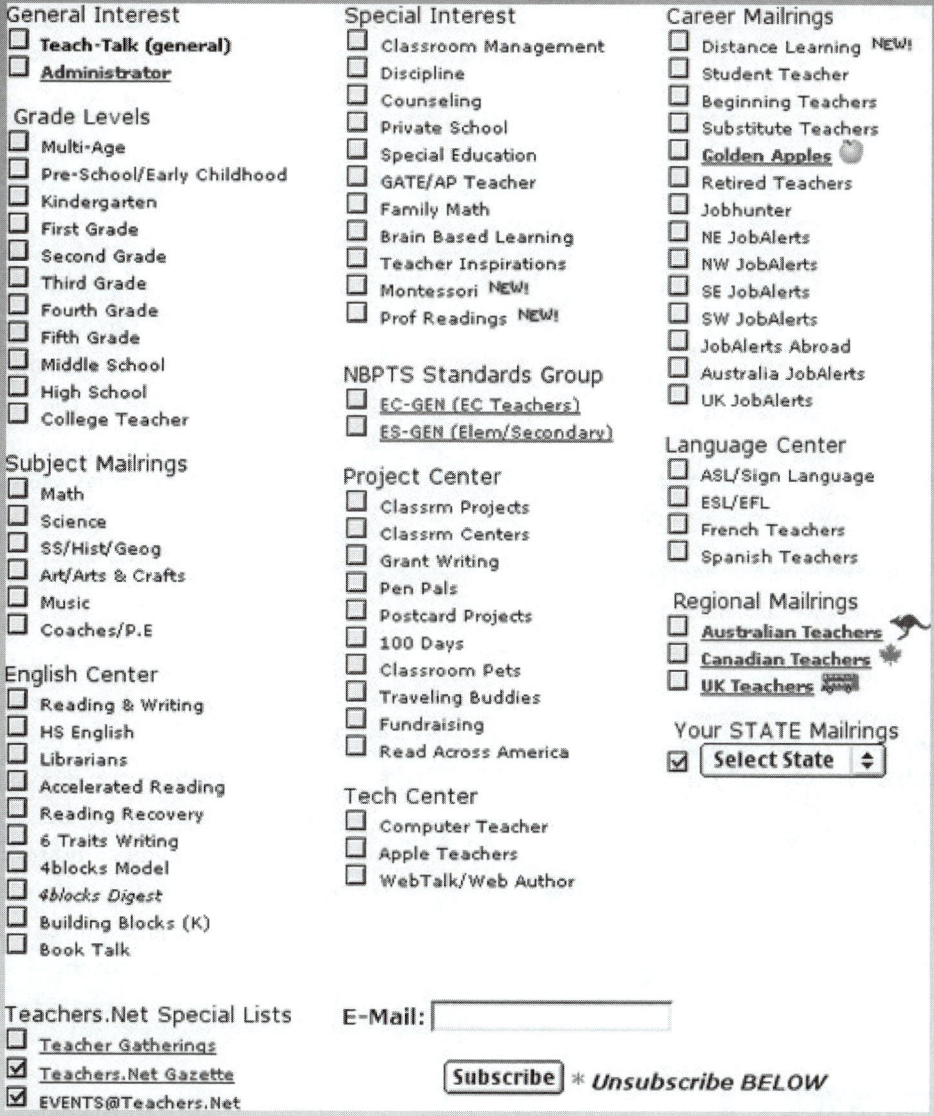

**General Interest**
- ☐ **Teach-Talk (general)**
- ☐ Administrator

**Grade Levels**
- ☐ Multi-Age
- ☐ Pre-School/Early Childhood
- ☐ Kindergarten
- ☐ First Grade
- ☐ Second Grade
- ☐ Third Grade
- ☐ Fourth Grade
- ☐ Fifth Grade
- ☐ Middle School
- ☐ High School
- ☐ College Teacher

**Subject Mailrings**
- ☐ Math
- ☐ Science
- ☐ SS/Hist/Geog
- ☐ Art/Arts & Crafts
- ☐ Music
- ☐ Coaches/P.E

**English Center**
- ☐ Reading & Writing
- ☐ HS English
- ☐ Librarians
- ☐ Accelerated Reading
- ☐ Reading Recovery
- ☐ 6 Traits Writing
- ☐ 4blocks Model
- ☐ *4blocks Digest*
- ☐ Building Blocks (K)
- ☐ Book Talk

**Teachers.Net Special Lists**
- ☐ Teacher Gatherings
- ☑ Teachers.Net Gazette
- ☑ EVENTS@Teachers.Net

**Special Interest**
- ☐ Classroom Management
- ☐ Discipline
- ☐ Counseling
- ☐ Private School
- ☐ Special Education
- ☐ GATE/AP Teacher
- ☐ Family Math
- ☐ Brain Based Learning
- ☐ Teacher Inspirations
- ☐ Montessori NEW!
- ☐ Prof Readings NEW!

**NBPTS Standards Group**
- ☐ EC-GEN (EC Teachers)
- ☐ ES-GEN (Elem/Secondary)

**Project Center**
- ☐ Classrm Projects
- ☐ Classrm Centers
- ☐ Grant Writing
- ☐ Pen Pals
- ☐ Postcard Projects
- ☐ 100 Days
- ☐ Classroom Pets
- ☐ Traveling Buddies
- ☐ Fundraising
- ☐ Read Across America

**Tech Center**
- ☐ Computer Teacher
- ☐ Apple Teachers
- ☐ WebTalk/Web Author

**Career Mailrings**
- ☐ Distance Learning NEW!
- ☐ Student Teacher
- ☐ Beginning Teachers
- ☐ Substitute Teachers
- ☐ Golden Apples 🍎
- ☐ Retired Teachers
- ☐ Jobhunter
- ☐ NE JobAlerts
- ☐ NW JobAlerts
- ☐ SE JobAlerts
- ☐ SW JobAlerts
- ☐ JobAlerts Abroad
- ☐ Australia JobAlerts
- ☐ UK JobAlerts

**Language Center**
- ☐ ASL/Sign Language
- ☐ ESL/EFL
- ☐ French Teachers
- ☐ Spanish Teachers

**Regional Mailrings**
- ☐ Australian Teachers
- ☐ Canadian Teachers
- ☐ UK Teachers

**Your STATE Mailrings**
- ☑ Select State ↕

**E-Mail:** [＿＿＿＿＿＿＿＿]

[Subscribe] * *Unsubscribe BELOW*

**FIGURE 3–8:   A Subscription Form for Teachers.net Mailrings**
*Source*: Retrieved from http:// teachers.net. @ Copyright 2004 Teachers.net. All rights reserved. Reproduced with permission.

3.  Teachers.net mailrings and many other discussion lists use a common Internet management program called **Majordomo**, which automates the management of Internet mailing lists. Majordomo controls a list of addresses through existing e-mail systems but performs no mail delivery itself. When you click the subscribe button, Majordomo requires you to confirm your subscription by sending a message similar to the following to your e-mail account:

Someone (possibly you) has requested that your e-mail address be added to or deleted from the mailing list "[group]@lists.teachers.net."

If you really want this action to be taken, please send the following commands (exactly as shown) back to "majordomo@lists.teachers.net":

auth [authorization number] subscribe [group] [e-mail address]

If you do not want this action to be taken, simply ignore this message and the request will be disregarded.

*(Continued)*

### Building Your Toolkit:
## Subscribing to a Professional Discussion List (Continued)

| STEP | PROCEDURE |
|---|---|
| **4.** | The best way to confirm your subscription without making any typing errors is to copy and paste the authorization command to a new e-mail message. You would copy the command, reply to the Majordomo confirmation e-mail, paste the authorization command into the body of the e-mail, delete all other text from the e-mail, and send your confirmation. When you have successfully confirmed your subscription to a discussion list, Majordomo sends you a notification and a welcome message. |
| **5.** | Once you receive notification that you have successfully joined the discussion list, you should enter an e-mail address into your address book for the discussion group(s) you have joined. (If you had joined the WebTalk group, you would enter webtalk@lists.teachers.net into your address book.) You can initiate a discussion by sending an original e-mail to your discussion group, or you can reply to messages received from other members of your discussion group. |
| **6.** | Send an e-mail message to the discussion group you have joined concerning a question or issue appropriate to the discussion group, and solicit the views of other members of the group. Respond to someone's comments, being sure to use appropriate netiquette when writing your messages. |
| **7.** | Majordomo provides instructions for unsubscribing from a discussion group, but you can easily unsubscribe by using the Web form at Teachers.net. On the Web form at **www.teachers.net/mailrings**, scroll down to the **Unsubscribe from a Mailring** section of the form, click on the down arrow for the pull-down list, and select the appropriate discussion group(s) from the list. If you wish to unsubscribe, enter your e-mail address (exactly as you subscribed), and click the **Unsubscribe** button. You will receive a confirmation from Majordomo when you have successfully unsubscribed. |

**Go to the Companion Website and browse 3.2 *Building Your Toolkit Enrichment Activity: Joining a Student Discussion Group*. Use the information in the enrichment activity for creating learning activities using online communication among students.**

**Go to the Companion Website and browse 3.2 *Project Sample: Netiquette and Internet Ethics*. Use the project sample as the foundation for a learning activity to introduce guidelines for participation in online communication. Adapt the project sample to the subject area and/or grade level that you teach.**

## REFLECTIONS

Internet technologies and information resources make it possible to organize classrooms into learning communities with students, teachers, and community members all playing vital roles in directing the course of education (Riel, 1998). Using synchronous and asynchronous communications on the Internet, students can interact with many more people and ideas. According to Riel, the structure of future learning environments will be determined by how students, teachers, and the community use these new educational tools (see Table 3–2).

The powerful technologies and information resources available on the Internet can bring learning to life in the classroom. It can even make learning exciting and fun. Internet technologies and resources have the potential to motivate and engage students as active learners because of the capacity for informative communication and collaboration and relevant multimedia resources. There are a number of ways teachers can use the Internet in the classroom:

- Access worldwide information sources such as newspapers and magazines, online encyclopedias, historical documents, government documents, research papers, books, maps, directories, and guides

| TABLE 3–2 | The Evolution of Instructional Tools |
|---|---|
| **Past tools for learning** | **Promising power tools for learning** |
| Textbooks and worksheets | Primary sources and student-created materials |
| Linear text student writing | Hypertext, multimedia productions |
| Models and materials | Virtual creatures and simulations |
| Direct observations | Tools for remote observations |
| Educational films, broadcast reality | Virtual worlds interact with reality |
| Teacher delivers lectures | Many expert voices in classroom |
| Student reports to teacher on learning | Student generates lessons for others |

*Source:* From *Education in the 21st Century: Just-in-Time Learning or Learning Communities* by M. Riel, 1998. Retrieved September 25, 2003, from http://gsep.pepperdine.edu/~mriel/office/papers/jit-learning/index.html. Reprinted with permission.

- Communicate with experts on almost any subject
- Take a virtual field trip to the Smithsonian or other museums, space missions, sports teams, or television and movie studios
- Work on projects with schools located thousands of miles away
- Listen to music while your class learns about composers and musicians
- View video clips created by other students from around the world
- Obtain access to free government and scientific databases worldwide
- Find thousands of free graphics, pictures, and animations
- Use online programs and simulations to demonstrate scientific and mathematical principles and calculations
- Access thousands of educational resources such as lesson plans and WebQuests, most of which are free for use in your classroom

# EXERCISES TO REVIEW AND EXPAND YOUR SKILLS

## Set 1: Reflecting on Practice

- *Closing the Case.* The case study scenario presented a middle-school computer teacher, Carla Hockenbury, who has identified the 10 best ways to use the Internet in the classroom. What role would you want the computer teacher in your school to have in relation to your students and the other teachers in the school? What technology information and assistance should the computer teacher provide to your students and the other teachers in your school? What is your favorite example of a way to use the Internet in the classroom, and why is it your favorite?

- *World Wide Web Consortium.* In small groups discuss the role and importance of the W3C for
  - developing common protocols to ensure the interoperability of the Web and promote its evolution
  - encouraging an open forum for discussion of the technical evolution of the Web

  Should the Internet have more control? Who/what should control the Internet? Summarize those points on which the group reaches consensus, and report to the whole class.

- *Domain Names.* You (or your team) have been assigned the task of recreating a new system or hierarchy for naming locations on the Internet. Develop a new naming system, and use charts or graphs and narrative as necessary to demonstrate how your new naming system works. You might want to use design or outline software such as Inspiration for this activity.

- *Emoticons.* The use of emotion in asynchronous conversations is often discouraged, especially when it leads to heated discussions that result in flaming.
  - What role should emotion play in asynchronous communication?
  - Do emoticons provide an appropriate outlet for displaying emotion or nonverbal behavior in an asynchronous conversation? Why?
  - Do emoticons serve to increase understanding about the intentions of the author? Why?

  Create one or two emoticons for emotions or nonverbal behavior that are not included in Figure 3–7.

- *Newsgroups.* Setting up a newsgroup may not be feasible for most teachers because it is a much more complex procedure than setting up a message board. Because newsgroup articles are propagated throughout Usenet, you must have the consent of Usenet administrators, and different hierarchies of newsgroups have different rules for creating new groups. If the topic is of broad international interest, one of the so-called Big 8 hierarchies (comp, humanities, misc, news, rec, sci, soc, or talk) or alt is logical. If the topic is basically of local or regional interest, you should look for an appropriate national, regional, or local newsgroup hierarchy. On the Google Groups website (http://www.google.com/groups) you can select the link for Help and find an FAQ about setting up a newsgroup. Then just follow the links that describe the official procedures for setting up a newsgroup.
  - What newsgroup hierarchy would be appropriate for setting up a classroom newsgroup?
  - List the procedures for starting a newsgroup under the hierarchy that you have selected.

### Set 2: Expanding Your Skills

***Advanced Web Browsing and Customizing Your Browser.*** You can customize the operation of the Web browser on your computer through several settings: You can set the home page, set default programs, and customize the look and feel of the browser.

- *Setting Your Home Page.* You can change the home page that comes up when you load your Web browser program. For Internet Explorer select **Tools > Internet Options** and then select the **General** tab (see Figure 3–9). For Netscape Browser select **Edit > Preferences.** Then enter the URL for the Web page you want to use as the home page for your browser and click **OK** to close the dialog box. Test what you have done by clicking on the **Home** button on your Web browser.

**FIGURE 3–9: Setting the Internet Explorer Home Page**

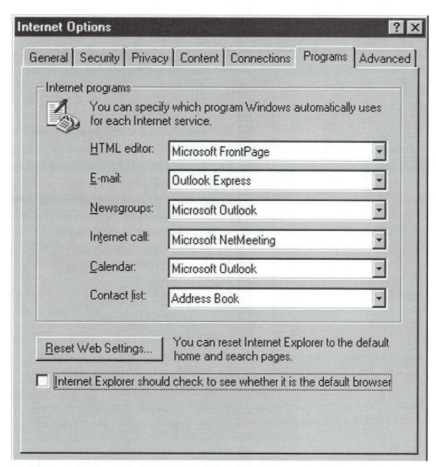

**FIGURE 3–10:   Setting Default Programs in Internet Explorer**

- *Setting Default Programs in Internet Explorer.* You can set which program the browser automatically uses for different Internet services. For Internet Explorer select **Tools > Internet Options**, and then select the **Programs** tab (see Figure 3–10). If you set your e-mail program to Outlook Express, your browser will automatically run Outlook Express if you click on an e-mail address on a website. You can configure other programs, such as your HTML editor, your newsgroup reader, your calendar, and so on. You can also set whether you want Internet Explorer to be the default Web browser. (You may not want it to be if you use another Web browser more often than Internet Explorer.)

- *Customizing the Look and Feel of the Web Browser.* By modifying the advanced options, you can control the look and feel of the Web browser. For Internet Explorer select **Tools > Internet Options**, and then select the **Advanced** tab (see Figure 3–11). For Netscape Browser select **Edit > Preferences**, and then expand **Advanced** in the Category frame on the left side of the dialog box (see Figure 3–12). Features include launching the Web browser directly into a full screen window when you run it, displaying error messages or not, automatically checking for updates or not, and showing friendly URLs. In Internet Explorer if you are unsure of what a feature does, you can click the **?** icon in the top right-hand corner and then click on the option you want more information about. A dialog box will appear with more information. You can always restore the default settings by clicking the Restore Defaults button on the bottom right.

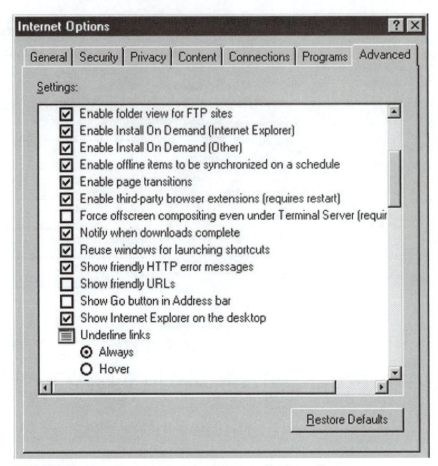

**FIGURE 3–11: Customizing the Internet Explorer Browser**

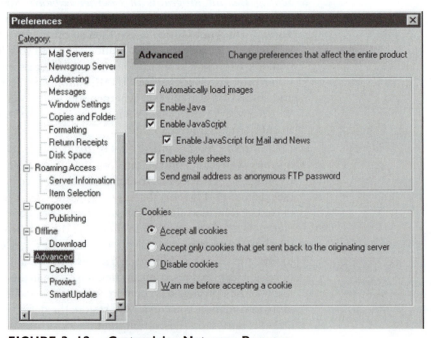

**FIGURE 3–12: Customizing Netscape Browser**

## Set 3: Using Productivity and Web-Authoring Tools

- *Internet Technologies Presentation.* Use a multimedia presentation program such as PowerPoint to create a lesson you can present to your class on Internet technologies. Use the information in this chapter to develop the talking points for your presentation and make the content appropriate for the grade level you teach. Insert clip art in your presentation to correspond to each of the Internet technologies you include.

- *Internet Technologies Handout.* Create a student handout of Internet technologies that is appropriate for the grade level you teach. Insert clip art to correspond to each of the Internet technologies you describe. Use Inspiration or another diagramming tool to create a diagram that identifies and gives an overview of the Internet technologies you describe and any relationships among them. Paste the diagram into the student handout document.

- *Workshop on the Best Uses of the Internet in the Classroom.* Use Ms. Hockenbury's 10 best uses of the Internet in the classroom as the basis for a multimedia presentation you could share with other teachers in a workshop on using the Internet in the classroom. As you advance through this textbook, use the information in the various chapters to determine your own top 10 list of best uses and to develop the talking points for your presentation.

## Set 4: Creating Your Own Web-Enhanced Project

- *Internet Technologies.* Plan a project that uses one or more of the Internet technologies described in this chapter. You can use the project sample you developed in Set 4 at the end of chapter 2 or a new topic. Plan a curriculum-based, Web-enhanced learning project using the WEL project sample template, and include an element that addresses Internet technologies and resources (see Figure 3–13).

- *WEL Lesson Plans.* Expand one of the project samples for this chapter from the Companion Website—Understanding the Internet or Netiquette and Internet Ethics—into a WEL lesson plan that is appropriate for the grade level and/or subject that you teach.

### FIGURE 3–13

| | |
|---|---|
| Title/topic | State an interesting, attention-getting title. |
| Standards of learning | State subject-specific standards and grade-specific technology standards to be addressed by the project. |
| Problem/task | State the problem or task the learner needs to solve or perform.<br>and/or |
| Background information | Provide orienting or organizing information about the project. |
| Procedures | Describe proposed procedures the learner should follow to complete the project. Describe any alternative approaches or adaptations that learners may use. |
| Resources | State what Web resources are available for the learner to appropriately and successfully complete the project's stated goals, objectives, or purpose. Identify other resources that would enhance the learning experience. |
| Teaching/learning strategies | Describe the teaching and learning methods used to complete the project (may be included in the procedures). Consider teaching methods that address different learning needs. If appropriate, consider alternative teaching methods for teaching the same information or skills. |
| Assessment | State what the learner will do to demonstrate understanding and mastery of objectives. |
| Credits/references | If the project was adapted from another project or lesson plan, provide credits or URL. |

# REFERENCES

Berners-Lee, T. (1999). *Weaving the Web: The original design and ultimate destiny of the World Wide Web by its inventor.* New York: HarperCollins.

Bransford, J. D., Brown, A. L. & Cocking, R. R. (Eds.). (2000). *How people learn: Brain, mind, experience, and school.* Washington, DC: National Academy Press.

Hafner, K., & Lyon, M. (1996). *Where wizards stay up late: The origins of the Internet.* New York: Touchstone Simon & Schuster.

Harris, J. (1998). *Virtual architecture: Designing and directing curriculum-based telecomputing.* Eugene, OR: International Society for Technology in Education.

Riel, M. (1998). *Education in the 21st century: Just-in-time learning or learning communities.* University of California at Irvine, Center for Collaborative Research in Education. Retrieved September 25, 2003, from http://gsep.pepperdine.edu/~mriel/office/papers/jit-learning/index.html

Shea, V. (1994). *Netiquette.* San Francisco: Albion Books. Also available at http://www.albion.com/netiquette/book/

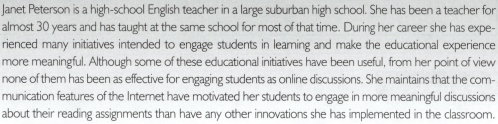

# CHAPTER 4

# Using the Internet for Communication

Janet Peterson is a high-school English teacher in a large suburban high school. She has been a teacher for almost 30 years and has taught at the same school for most of that time. During her career she has experienced many initiatives intended to engage students in learning and make the educational experience more meaningful. Although some of these educational initiatives have been useful, from her point of view none of them has been as effective for engaging students as online discussions. She maintains that the communication features of the Internet have motivated her students to engage in more meaningful discussions about their reading assignments than have any other innovations she has implemented in the classroom.

For the last several years Ms. Peterson has been creating a closed online discussion group for her two literature classes using Yahoo's e-groups. A closed group is a members-only group. The discussion group has allowed her students another option for entering into classroom discussions; they can continue discussions started in class or start discussions that can be continued in class. In addition, Ms. Peterson can pose questions for discussions, provide links to related information, take polls, and post messages to the class. She can also remind students of upcoming events, homework assignments, schedule changes, and even days when there is no school.

Ms. Peterson has found that with the online discussion group some students who might otherwise hesitate to ask a question in class or enter into a classroom debate are more likely to become engaged because they have time to reflect before asking questions or making comments. Ms. Peterson says that for other students the online discussion group is a great way to keep them on track. Although she is nearing the end of her career, Ms. Peterson thinks that Internet technologies make it a great time to be a teacher.

## NEW TERMS

chatiquette
flaming
keypals

spam
virus

| National Educational Technology Standards for Teachers | National Educational Technology Standards for Students |
|---|---|
| The following NETS•T are addressed by the lesson content and learning activities in this chapter: | The following NETS•S are addressed by the lesson content and learning activities in this chapter: |

**National Educational Technology Standards for Teachers**

The following NETS•T are addressed by the lesson content and learning activities in this chapter:

**I.  Technology Operations and Concepts**

**A.** Demonstrate understanding of technology concepts and skills

**B.** Demonstrate continual growth in technology knowledge and skills

**VI. Social, Ethical, Legal, and Human Issues**

**A.** Model and teach legal and ethical practice related to technology use

**B.** Enable and empower diverse learners

**C.** Identify and use technology resources that affirm diversity

**D.** Promote safe and healthy use of technology resources

**E.** Facilitate equitable access to technology resources

**National Educational Technology Standards for Students**

The following NETS•S are addressed by the lesson content and learning activities in this chapter:

**1.  Basic Operations and Concepts**
- Demonstrate sound understanding of technology
- Be proficient in the use of technology

**2.  Social, Ethical, and Human Issues**
- Understand ethical, cultural, and societal issues related to technology
- Practice responsible use of technology
- Develop positive attitudes toward technology

**3.  Technology Productivity Tools**
- Use technology to enhance learning, increase productivity, and promote creativity
- Use tools to collaborate, prepare publications, and produce creative works

**4.  Technology Communications Tools**
- Use telecommunications to collaborate, publish, and interact with others
- Use varied media and formats to communicate information and ideas

## OVERVIEW

Communication and information sharing among computers on the Internet occur through a number of technologies, including e-mail and the World Wide Web. Person-to-person online communication occurs between two or more individuals holding a private or public conversation—for example, a student can have an e-mail conversation or a chat with a teacher or a peer. Online group communication includes more participants and is used to communicate the same information to multiple individuals—for example, a teacher can pose a question to a discussion list, and students can respond at any time. Person-to-person communication tools include e-mail and chat, and group communication tools include discussion groups and message boards.

As was mentioned earlier, e-mail (electronic mail) refers to messages sent via the Internet. Many Internet users got their start using e-mail, which is a fast and easy way to send messages from one person to another or to a group. Messages are typically delivered within seconds or minutes of the time the message is sent.

As discussed in chapter 3, chat is real-time communication between two or more people using computers, usually through the Internet. A chat room is a virtual space where a chat session takes place. During a chat session participants can be physically located anywhere in the world but are able to communicate almost instantly by typing text that immediately appears on the screens of all participants in the chat session.

Listservs or discussion lists are useful for facilitating communication among a group of individuals. A listserv is basically a program on an e-mail server that keeps track of the e-mail discussion lists that are available and the members of each discussion list. When messages come in for a particular list, the listserv program rebroadcasts that message to all of the members of the list.

Message boards or Web-based bulletin boards allow users to post a message that can be read by anyone who accesses the bulletin board. Message board discussions are threaded, meaning that messages about a particular topic are grouped together. Thus, users are able to reply and associate their messages with a specific message already posted.

## Lesson 4.1    Person-to-Person Information Exchanges on the Internet

### FOCUS QUESTIONS

- How can e-mail be used to enhance teaching and learning in the classroom?
- What are keypals, and how can you use keypal projects in the classroom?
- How can chat be used to enhance teaching and learning in the classroom?
- What are the rules and procedures for communicating with others using chat?

## ■ USING ELECTRONIC MAIL

When Ms. Peterson started using the Internet in the classroom, she soon realized that it is important for students to have a personal or classroom e-mail account. In the classroom free e-mail service is a good option; although students may have to endure some advertising, these accounts are accessible, functional, and easy to use. However, you should always check with your network administrator and school district policies to learn how e-mail works at your school and what is the best way to create student e-mail accounts.

Although e-mail and the other online communication tools discussed in this chapter have several distinct advantages, they may not always be the best choice for every classroom at every grade level. School policies may limit or prohibit the use of e-mail by students, and filtering programs may prevent access to Web-based e-mail services. If such services can be used, you should remember that they demand no accountability on the part of students and, therefore, may circumvent your school district's policy on proper use of e-mail. Elementary-school teachers may want to set up a classroom e-mail account so that they can monitor messages that are sent and received by young students.

E-mail is a simple way to begin using asynchronous tools in the classroom. Because e-mail programs are relatively simple to use, it does not take long for students to use them effectively; many students probably already have personal e-mail accounts. At least one computer with a connection to the Internet is needed, and access to a computer network connected to the Internet is better. Many classrooms in schools and universities have computers or computer labs that are connected to the Internet.

E-mail penpals, or keypals, are the most basic form of student e-mail projects (see Harris, 1998). **Keypals** are penpals who communicate with one another through the Internet. In a keypal project students are paired with students in classes at other schools; they use e-mail to communicate on any topic and at a frequency they determine between themselves. To be worthwhile, a keypal's project should include assignments that students work on in teams or groups and for which a product is required as the final goal.

The primary advantage of using e-mail in classroom learning activities is that students become engaged in intellectual conversations that are less contrived than those of textbook- or teacher-centered activities. Using e-mail requires students to use and type words carefully and appropriately to express their thoughts. A lot of time is needed, however, to plan and conduct learning activities using e-mail, which often require finding classes with similar learning goals. There are websites available on the Internet to help you find other classrooms to participate in a keypals project.

E-mail and other online communication tools can effectively complement instructional activities. Synchronous and asynchronous online discussions are a pedagogically sound practice because they provide more opportunities for students to become actively involved with curriculum content (Markel, 2001). Online discussion, however, should be used primarily as an addition to in-class discussion, rather than as a substitution for it (Tiene, 2000).

An e-mail assignment can be used as an introductory device for using asynchronous communication. For example, students can e-mail one another and the teacher, and the messages received can be used to create an address book for the class. Later, students can send mail to students in other classes and to keypals in other parts of the country or the world, or they can contact experts and sources for research projects.

Because the amount of correspondence can be overwhelming when you use e-mail for learning activities, you should establish a structure for asynchronous communications in the classroom and should state your policies to students. For example, you might notify your students that you will reply to e-mails within 24 hours. You might also want to set up an additional e-mail account for assignments and then use the auto-reply feature to automatically let your students know that you have received their e-mails. You can use folders to help organize the messages according to their appropriate project, group, or class; students should use key words such as a project title or a class name in the subject line of their messages to assist in sorting and grouping the messages. You should also require students to use signature files so that their names and important contact information appear at the bottom of every message.

When using student e-mail accounts in the classroom, students should be instructed about → e-mail spam and viruses. **Spam** is unsolicited e-mail sent by an individual or a company with which the recipient has had no previous dealings. **Viruses** are self-replicating pieces of computer code, which can be spread by e-mail and can damage a computer by partially or fully attaching themselves to files or applications. Most e-mail programs, including those offered by Internet portals and service providers, have features that allow users to filter in-coming e-mail messages. These filters, however, are not always effective in blocking spam and questionable e-mail messages. Before using e-mail accounts with young children, teachers should be knowledgeable about available measures to prevent or reduce the impact of spam and virus attacks. School or school district networks that provide e-mail accounts for students may offer some antispam and antivirus measures at the server level.

> Go to the Companion Website and browse *Chapter 4 Lesson Links: E-Mail Spam and Viruses: The Dark Side of E-Mail* to learn more about this topic.

---

### Building Your Toolkit:
## Managing E-Mail Accounts and Sending/Receiving File Attachments

An e-mail address is becoming as common as a phone number; it provides a convenient method of communicating with friends, family, colleagues, and students. E-mail accounts have several advanced features that you should be able to use—adding signature information to e-mail messages, sending and receiving file attachments, forwarding e-mail messages from one person to others, and informing others that you are away from your account for an extended period of time. These features allow you to use your e-mail account more productively and effectively. For this tutorial you will need to have a personal e-mail account. If you do not already have an e-mail account, you can sign up for a free Yahoo! Mail account at **http://mail.yahoo.com/** or an MSN Hotmail account at **http://www.hotmail.com/**. Use the e-mail application of your e-mail account to perform each of the following operations:

| STEP | PROCEDURE |
|------|-----------|
| 1. | Locate the formatting options for your e-mail program. Then set up a signature for your e-mail account that includes your name, e-mail address, mail address, phone number, and other appropriate information, perhaps a title or position and institution name. Apply the signature to all new e-mail messages you send. |
| 2. | Send an e-mail with one or more file attachments. E-mail attachments are files sent along with an e-mail message. An attachment can be any kind of file, including formatted word-processed documents, spreadsheets, databases, graphics, and even software. The e-mail message should explain to the recipient the type of file or file format (e.g., Word document, Excel spreadsheet, text file, picture). |

*(Continued)*

---

*Building Your Toolkit:*
**Managing E-Mail Accounts and Sending/Receiving File Attachments (Continued)**

**STEP    PROCEDURE**

- **Sending an attachment.** With most e-mail programs it is easy to send and receive messages containing attachments. To attach a file to an e-mail message, open a new mail message and use your e-mail program to attach a file (usually by clicking on a paper clip icon). The program will display a Find or Browse dialog box, and you can then select the file you want to attach from your computer. A copy of the file will then accompany the message to your recipient.

- **Opening an attachment.** If you receive a file attachment, you should see a note or an icon with your message, indicating that it includes an attachment. Some types of files may be viewable within the message, depending on the e-mail program you use. Usually, files must be viewed with an application that is capable of opening the file. You can either double-click on the file's icon in the message to launch the program and open the file, or you can save the file on your computer. E-mail programs may designate a default folder on your computer where attachments are automatically saved. It is best to save the file to your computer and then launch the application that can find the file on your computer and open it. If you do not have the right program to open a file, you may need to ask the sender to send the file in a format that a program on your computer can read, or you may need to take the file to a different computer with the right program installed and open the file there.

**3.**    To forward a copy of an e-mail you have received to someone else, select the **forward** option while you are viewing the e-mail. Then type in the address field the e-mail address of the intended recipient, add any additional message, and press **Send.**

**4.**    Again, locate the formatting options for your e-mail program. Then activate the auto-reply or vacation mail function; it is useful when you are away and cannot check your e-mail account. Create an auto-reply message, explaining that you are unable to reply to the e-mail message. You can provide information in the auto-reply message about the day of your return or the name of the person who is handling your responsibilities in your absence.

**Go to the Companion Website** and browse *4.1 Building Your Toolkit Enrichment Activity: Creating Information Exchanges Using E-Mail Keypals.* Use the information in the enrichment activity to develop learning activities using information exchanges supported by e-mail.

**Go to the Companion Website** and browse *4.1 Project Sample: Cultural Exchanges Through Internet Keypals.* Use the project sample as the foundation for a learning activity with interpersonal information exchanges. Adapt the project sample to the subject area and/or grade level that you teach.

## ■ USING CHAT

Tommy Eldridge is a high-school social studies teacher and an assistant football coach who frequently used computers at home and in his classroom. Although he commonly required his students to search Internet resources, he did not allow them to use the Internet for communication. He realized, however, that many of his students had considerable experience communicating via e-mail and in chat rooms.

As Coach Eldridge began adapting his social studies courses to include problem solving, he realized that the subject matter could not be adequately addressed with information searches alone. Students need to communicate with experts and peers to better understand the context of a problem and to obtain other perspectives in developing solutions. Consequently, he invited online quest lecturers to chat with his classes, and his students enjoyed the opportunity to interact directly with political leaders and scholars.

In addition, because his coaching duties limit his availability during the school day and after school, Coach Eldridge incorporated online office hours into his schedule and encouraged his students to e-mail their questions to him. He found that he could be virtually available to any student at any time. Coach Eldridge has now become a dedicated user of Internet communication features, which he affirms can add a rich and appealing dimension to classroom learning activities.

Whereas e-mail permits asynchronous person-to-person communication, chat provides real-time Internet conversations. Chat can be difficult to use in the classroom, however, because it is completely unstructured and often confusing. Furthermore, chat rooms are not always safe educational environments; they are susceptible to uninvited guests contributing misinformation or offensive remarks.

Nonetheless, if a teacher is comfortable using chat and moderating a chat room, this communication tool can be quite effective. One of the best uses of chat is to provide access to experts, which would otherwise not be possible. A class chat session allows teachers and students as a group to interact with a guest speaker in real time, thus providing students with real-world experiences related to their subject matter. Before interacting online, students should thoroughly research the topic to be discussed, checking the FAQ page at the guest speaker's website, if available, and any online biography about the speaker. Students should create questions ahead of time for such sessions; they might use an interview approach to ask about a speaker's profession, rather than a specific topic. After the chat session students should be discouraged from sending unsolicited e-mail to the speaker.

Go to the Companion Website and browse *4.1 Building Your Toolkit Enrichment Activity: Using Online Experts to Support Classroom Learning.* Use the information in the enrichment activity to create learning activities using information exchanges with external experts.

Chat can also be used to conduct debates and student-led discussions. Students can post a position on a topic, to which others can respond with their own arguments, followed by a critique of those arguments. A student can also submit a question to the classroom chat forum about material read or discussed in class. That student, then, is responsible for leading the discussion that ensues from the question. Thus, students can become facilitators of their own chat sessions.

Moreover, as Coach Eldridge discovered, chat is a good way to provide additional support for students through virtual office hours. Having a virtual office hour outside the regular school day allows teachers to provide instructional support for homework assignments at a time when students are most likely to need assistance. However, the effectiveness and fairness of virtual office hours (and other online communications with students) beyond the regular school day is dependent on their having out-of-school access to the Internet.

Chat session transcripts can also provide an excellent resource for a number of activities; logs of a chat session can provide a study tool for students and an evaluative tool for teachers. After each chat session teachers can post the transcript to a Web page or send a copy to students through e-mail or a discussion list. Students can then read and review the conversation that took place during the chat. And transcripts permit students who were not present in a chat session to review what transpired.

| FIGURE 4–1 | Procedures for Chat Sessions |
| --- | --- |

1. A participant with a comment or a question should type ! for a comment or ? for a question.
2. Participants type comments one sentence or clause at a time and then press ENTER so the group does not have to look at white space while typing occurs. Individuals with poor typing skills should type an entire statement before submitting it to the chat session.
3. Participants type three forward slash marks (///) at the end of a comment or a question to indicate that the next participant can begin.
4. To request the floor, participants can type ? or ! at any time; the first person to enter a ? or ! has the floor. All participants are responsible for maintaining the flow of conversation.
5. Requests to change the topic of conversation are signaled by typing *new ?* or *new !* If no one objects by typing ! or ?, the participant proceeds with the new topic.
6. Private chats during the discussion are not acceptable.

Because students can get lost in the unstructured atmosphere of a chat session and can fail to participate, chat sessions should always have a clear focus and a way to keep student discussion on track. The teacher should act as a moderator, encouraging all students to contribute to the chat discussion.

Chat rooms follow their own procedures (see Figure 4-1) and have their own form of etiquette, called → **chatiquette,** which defines the social conventions that structure and organize chat sessions. The purpose of chatiquette is not to diminish conversation but to facilitate clear and unambiguous communication. It is a way to make the nonverbal cues of face-to-face conversations available to all participants. To reduce the number of keystrokes when posting messages online, chatiquette permits abbreviations and acronyms (see Figure 4-2).

**Go** to the Companion Website and browse *Chapter 4 Lesson Links: Chatiquette* to learn more about this topic.

| FIGURE 4–2 | Chat Expressions | | |
|---|---|---|---|
| **AAIK** | as far as I know | **L8R** | later |
| **AFK** | away from keyboard | **LMHO** | laughing my head off |
| **ASAP** | as soon as possible | **LOL** | laugh out loud/laughing online |
| **BBFN** | bye bye for now | **LTNS** | long time no see |
| **BBL** | be back later | **LTS** | laughing to self |
| **BBS** | be back soon | **OBTW** | oh, by the way |
| **BRB** | be right back | **OIC** | oh, I see |
| **BTW** | by the way | **OTOH** | on the other hand |
| **BWL** | bursting with laughter | **OTTOMH** | off the top of my head |
| **C&G** | chuckle and grin | **PM** | private message |
| **CID** | cringing in disgrace | **PMFJI** | pardon me for jumping in |
| **CP** | chat post | **POAHF** | put on a happy face |
| **C YA** | see ya | **POD** | piece of data |
| **C YA L8R** | see you later | **POOF** | left the chat room |
| **EMSG** | e-mail message | **QSL** | reply |
| **EOF** | end of file | **RFD** | request for discussion |
| **FC** | fingers crossed | **ROFL** | rolling on floor laughing |
| **FMG** | filling my glass | **RSN** | real soon now |
| **FWIW** | for what it's worth | **RTSM** | read the stupid manual |
| **FYI** | for your information | **RUOK?** | are you OK? |
| **\*G\*** | giggle | **SETE** | smiling ear to ear |
| **(G)** | grin | **SITD** | still in the dark |
| **GFN** | gone for now | **SO** | significant other |
| **GMTA** | great minds think alike | **SUL** | see you later |
| **GTSY** | glad to see you | **SWL** | screaming with laughter |
| **HAGU** | have a good un | **SYS** | see ya soon |
| **HHIS** | hanging head in shame | **TA** | thanks again |
| **IC** | I see | **TIA** | thanks in advance |
| **IMHO** | in my humble opinion | **TIC** | tongue in cheek |
| **IMO** | in my opinion | **TNX** | thanks |
| **IOW** | in other words | **TPTB** | the powers that be |
| **IRL** | in real life | **TTYL** | talk to you later |
| **JMO** | just my opinion | **WB** | welcome back |
| **JTLYK** | just to let you know | **WRT** | with regard to |
| **KIT** | keep in touch | | |

## Lesson 4.2    Online Group Communication

### FOCUS QUESTIONS

- How can discussion lists be used to enhance teaching and learning in the classroom?
- How do you subscribe to and unsubscribe from a discussion list?
- How can message boards be used to enhance teaching and learning in the classroom?
- How do message boards support online communication?

## ■ USING GROUP COMMUNICATION TOOLS ON THE INTERNET

Like interpersonal communication tools, group communication tools can expand the geographical boundaries of your classroom. The tools presented in this lesson utilize asynchronous communication, so that time zones and geographical locations will not make a difference. Thus, discussion can be initiated and continued indefinitely as it evolves into new topics.

Group communication tools are also useful in the classroom for facilitating group work and collaborative learning. For example, like Ms. Peterson, the high-school English teacher you met at the beginning of this chapter, you can establish online discussion groups or classroom message boards to provide other options for engaging students in discussing curriculum content.

Before using group communication tools, however, you should have a clear understanding of how they work, and you should be proficient in their use. If you model confidence and enthusiasm, your students are much more likely to participate eagerly in the learning activities you have planned.

The instructional strategies you employ using Internet communication technologies are not much different from what you would do in the conventional classroom. For example, you want to use Internet technologies to support a community of learning in the classroom, which can flourish when students understand the proper techniques for exchanging views that contribute to the collective creation of knowledge. When students conduct their own research and discuss it with peers, they increase the probability of correctly solving a problem or successfully completing a project.

## ■ USING DISCUSSION LISTS

E-mail discussion lists are useful for facilitating communication among individuals. The Internet contains thousands of discussion groups that are managed by a list server, commonly referred to as a listserv, a list processor, or a list. As mentioned previously, the basic operation of a listserv is to keep track of available e-mail discussion lists and the members of each list. When messages come in for a particular list, the listserv program rebroadcasts that message to all of the members of the list—as if someone had sent an e-mail message to all of the members of a group by entering all of their e-mail addresses in the To field of the message. The listserv program merely automates the process. Lists are often moderated by a list owner, but some lists are simply a free-for-all discussion without anyone filtering the messages.

Most lists can be provided to the user either in a digest form or on a post-by-post basis. Listservs can distribute electronic journals, or e-journals, and newsletters. Most lists and e-journals can be joined by posting an e-mail to the listserv address. Any member of a discussion list can take part in a conversation or can begin a new topic.

To use a discussion list in her classroom, Ms. Peterson had to decide whether to have her own classroom discussion list or to join an existing Internet discussion list. Several listserv programs are freely distributed on the Internet, and many school or school district networks are capable of supporting classroom listservs. Tools are also freely provided on the Internet for setting up your own discussion group.

| **FIGURE 4–3** | **Netiquette for Online Discussions** |
| --- | --- |

- **Be brief.** Remember that the longer your message is, the fewer the people who will bother to read it.
- **Use descriptive subject lines.** Provide a title for the content of your message.
- **Avoid typing in uppercase letters.** Typing in uppercase is considered shouting on the Internet.
- **Avoid getting flamed or flaming others**. Members of discussion groups who do not follow the rules for the discussion group or who ask stupid questions may receive flame mail. **Flaming** is a heated retort of a personally demeaning or derogatory nature. Try to avoid sending flame mail even when someone else has not followed the list rules.
- **Summarize and snip.** Either summarize the previous person's post and add your comments, or include the parts to which you would like to respond and delete the rest.
- **Be careful with humor and avoid sarcasm.** Because nonverbal cues and facial expressions are an important part of humor and sarcasm, it is easy for dry humor and sarcasm to be offensive in Internet communications.
- **Pay attention to the reply address.** Using the reply function on your e-mail program can send your reply directly to the person who posted the original message, or it can send your response to the entire group.
- **Get to know the culture of the group.** You may want to lurk for a while before offering your comments.
- **Know your list addresses.** Send commands to the administrative address and messages to the list address.
- **It is more blessed to give than to receive.** Take the time to share what you know when others make requests or submit questions to the group.
- **Your posts are a reflection on you.** Read your message through before sending it because you will likely find misspellings, missing words, or breaks in logic.
- **Be careful what you say.** Thousands of people may read your message, and what you say may come back to haunt you.
- **When summarizing, summarize!** When you request information from a discussion group, it is common courtesy to offer to summarize and report your findings so that others can benefit as well. The best way to do this is to take all the responses you received and edit them into a single message.
- **Avoid dittos and me-toos.** If you agree with what is posted, there is no need to add to the volume of mail in people's boxes by saying ditto.
- **Mark your spoilers.** If the topic of your post could be difficult or painful for other list members to read, be sure to indicate this in your subject.
- **Take it private.** If a subject has evolved into a conversation between two or three people, correspond privately rather than sending your messages to the list.
- **Save the welcome message.** The system-generated message you receive when you have successfully subscribed to a list usually also contains other useful information (such as how to unsubscribe).

*Source:* From University of Kansas Academic Computing Services at http://www.ku.edu/acs/documentation/docs/listproc/netiquette.shtml. Reprinted with permission.

Ms. Peterson decided to implement her own classroom discussion list. Thus, she had to monitor list traffic, provide thoughtful questions, recommend useful resources, and work behind the scenes to enforce the list guidelines and help list subscribers stay on topic. As with face-to-face discussions in the classroom, good discussion list managers set a welcoming tone, shape the focus of the discussion, manage technical issues and any debates that ensue, and summarize the discussion.

There are social conventions and common courtesies that guide online discussions. For example, when replying to a listserv message, you need to decide whether your reply should go only to the original sender or to the whole list. If the original poster is asking for a specific piece of information that would not be of interest to other list members, it is probably best to reply directly to the individual. But if the original e-mail and your reply are about topics of general concern to list members, then replying to the list would allow them all to follow the ongoing discussion. In general, the same rules of discourse and discussion that pertain to the classroom should be applied to listserv discussions as well. Figure 4–3 provides some basic guidelines for Internet discussions.

| FIGURE 4–4 | Five Simple Rules for Subscribing to and Unsubscribing from a Discussion List |
|---|---|

1. **Send e-mail messages as plain text.** Allow message recipients to select for themselves what size and font they prefer. Do not set your e-mail system to send formatted text.

2. **Always read and keep a copy of the instructions/guidelines when you or your students subscribe to a discussion list.** You may need these instructions later for help in using the list appropriately and for unsubscribing instructions.

3. **Set up e-mail accounts in your contacts list or address book with the e-mail address for posting messages as well as the e-mail address for the list manager.** The e-mail address for managing a list may be different from the e-mail address for posting messages to the list.

4. **Never send subscribe or unsubscribe commands to the e-mail address you use for posting a message.** Posting such requests to the entire discussion list can be embarrassing to you and frustrating to the members of the discussion list.

5. **Unsubscribe from the exact e-mail address from which you subscribed.** If you have several e-mail addresses or your e-mail address can be written in several ways, make sure you use the same address for subscribing and unsubscribing.

Subscribing and unsubscribing from discussion lists is accomplished by sending e-mail messages to a prescribed address. With some discussion lists you can subscribe (or even unsubscribe) from a link on a Web page that automatically sends an e-mail message. Correct spelling and syntax are critical for subscribing and unsubscribing operations because key phrases are parsed by a computer to automatically add you to or delete you from the list.

When you subscribe to a mailing list, you may receive a confirmation that includes the e-mail address for unsubscribing from the list. You should keep that e-mail and any information about additional addresses related to general questions and requests. It is important that you understand the distinction among addresses. E-mail messages that you want distributed to other members of the list should be sent to the list address, whereas e-mail messages to the listserv program should be sent to the administrative address. Figure 4-4 provides a list of guidelines to help you remember the most important steps in subscribing to and unsubscribing from a discussion list.

## *Building Your Toolkit:*
## Setting Up a Yahoo! Groups Account and Discussion List

You may be able to create discussion lists through your school or school district network. If not, you can create a personal listserv, bulletin board, and/or chat forum using Yahoo! Groups, which is a free service that allows you to create and moderate your own discussion list. Yahoo! Groups is an easy-to-use, privacy-protected, and spam-protected discussion environment. You can use the service from the Yahoo! website or through any e-mail program.

Before setting up your discussion list, you should make certain preparations; you should define the purpose of your list, decide who will participate, and choose your list format. Refining the focus of your list will increase its chances for success. Ask yourself the following questions:

- What is the main purpose of the list (e.g., discussion, information exchange, coordination of learning activities)?
- What is my goal in creating a list (e.g., addressing a topic or issue, building a learning community, facilitating teamwork)?
- Which topics are appropriate for discussion, and which are not?
- How much message volume, or traffic, will there be on the list (usually measured by the number of e-mails per subscriber per day)?
- Do I want the list restricted to specific participants or open to anyone?
- Do I plan to moderate the mailing list?

*(Continued)*

## Building Your Toolkit:
## Setting Up a Yahoo! Groups Account and Discussion List (Continued)

- How much time can I spend managing and moderating the list?
- Are the advertisements at the bottom of messages appropriate for my subscribers?

Once you have answered these questions, you are ready to develop guidelines for your mailing list to inform subscribers about the objectives and operating parameters of the list. Because it is your list, you can designate any agenda and establish any rules as long as you declare these rules at the start. If subscribers repeatedly violate list guidelines, you can unsubscribe them from the list.

Mailing list software usually allows you to send a welcome or confirmation message to each new subscriber. Mailing list managers can also send list guidelines periodically to remind subscribers of the rules. When using discussion lists in your classroom, you may want your students to initiate the subscription process themselves, but in this exercise you will register the e-mail addresses yourself. Thus, before starting the tutorial, you should invite two or more participants to join the group created by this activity and obtain their e-mail addresses.

| STEP | PROCEDURE |
|------|-----------|
| 1. | Open your Web browser and then the Yahoo! Groups website **at http://groups.yahoo.com/**. |
| 2. | To sign up for membership in Yahoo! Groups, you must register. If you already have a Yahoo! e-mail account, click on the **Sign In** link. If you do not have a Yahoo! account, go to New User? and click on **Sign Up**. Complete all necessary information fields. |
| 3. | Once your registration is complete, go to Create Your Own Group, and click on **Start a group now**. |

- Select a Yahoo! Groups category for your group. For example, you might choose to select **Schools & Education > K-12**. Then click on **Place my group here**.
- Enter a name, an e-mail group name, and a short description of the group. Click on **Continue**. If required, enter the verification text, and click on **Continue** again.
- Once the group is set up, a confirmation screen will be displayed.

| 4. | Return to the Yahoo! Groups home page. Go to My Groups and select the link for the group you created. |
| 5. | On the navigation bar on the left side of the window, select **Invite** to ask members to join the group. Enter the e-mail addresses of the participants who agreed to join your group. If you enter a message explaining why you are inviting these people to join your group, it will be included with the e-mail invitation. Click the **Submit Invite** button. |
| 6. | When your invited participants subscribe to your list, welcome them by e-mail, and provide list guidelines. |
| 7. | From the navigation bar select the **Management** link, and review the management categories listed. Manage your own discussion list by performing the following functions: |

- Post a general reminder of list guidelines and Netiquette.
- Post a friendly message to thank subscribers for their contributions.
- Encourage list members to introduce themselves.
- Encourage and summarize discussions.
- Provide content to begin discussions.
- Post some resources that are relevant to the discussion.
- Subscribe and unsubscribe users as necessary.

**Go to the Companion Website and browse *4.2 Building Your Toolkit Enrichment Activity: Searching UseNet and Posting to a Newsgroup.* Use the information in the enrichment activity to create learning activities involving newsgroup discussions among students.**

## ■ USING MESSAGE BOARDS

Before there were e-mail accounts, a World Wide Web, or even an Internet, online communication meant posting text messages on electronic bulletin boards where others could read and reply to them. Now electronic bulletin board services are asynchronous communication tools on the World Wide Web. Message boards are useful for online communication because they are relatively easy to access. The information shared resides in an archive, and discussions are threaded, making it easy to check student participation.

Unlike discussion lists, message board messages do not come to students directly by e-mail; students must go to the message board to be able to read and post messages. An advantage to this approach is that postings are collected in one place, specific to the subject at hand. Furthermore, students do not have to have an e-mail account of their own to view messages. However, posting to a message board usually requires an e-mail account.

Online message boards are a great way to extend class participation beyond the classroom. A message board allows students to discuss course topics online, respond to each other's comments, and share ideas. With a message board you can designate the participants, suggest topics for discussion, and monitor students' participation. When using message boards in the classroom, you should build online discussions into your curriculum; students are more likely to participate in online discussions if credit is given for participation.

Online discussions can increase the participation of students who are shy or uncomfortable speaking in front of the whole class. Because some students like to take time to reflect and write their comments, teachers can accommodate a variety of learning styles or preferences by grading participation based on in-class as well as message board discussions. In addition, because message boards provide an opportunity for students to edit their postings, another obvious benefit is the potential for students to practice and enhance their writing skills.

When using online discussions, teachers should allow students enough time to consider their responses and post them. Teachers should also consider the size of the discussion groups; students and teachers find it difficult to keep up with discussions if there are too many responses to read. An effective strategy is to create several smaller discussion groups for one class.

Teachers may choose to be active in the discussion or limit their participation, based on the instructional goals of the discussion. However, successful discussions using message boards are usually the result of the teacher taking an active role in structuring meaningful discussions that are relevant at the current time and motivate students to think and make contributions. Teachers can offer guidance by posing new questions and providing feedback, perhaps organizing discussion by chapter topics in an associated textbook. Teachers should always validate student postings and provide more information when needed.

Online discussions work best if topics discussed on the message board are introduced in class. Meaningful topics that relate to classroom learning activities will promote discussion and facilitate a deeper level of thinking about a discussion topic. One useful instructional strategy is online debates. Individuals or groups can be assigned different sides of a controversial topic, and a vote can be taken at the end to see who had the most convincing argument.

Policies for online discussions need to be clear and well defined and should include how individual students or groups are graded for their contributions to discussions. Guidelines might also specify a minimum number of responses and the minimum length of messages, to encourage students to think harder about the content of a message rather than just replying with very short, superficial comments.

### Building Your Toolkit:
### Creating a Connected Classroom

Nicenet's Internet Classroom Assistant (ICA2) allows virtually any classroom, even those with modest technology resources, access to powerful Internet tools and technologies. ICA2 is a sophisticated communication tool that offers the following features:

- *Conferencing:* You can create your own private, threaded conferencing on topics you choose for the class or allow students to create their own topics.
- *Scheduling:* You can put the class schedule online. With a 7-day advance notice on your class home page, students will have a heads-up display of upcoming assignments and class events.

*(Continued)*

## Building Your Toolkit:
## Creating a Connected Classroom (Continued)

- **Document sharing:** Both students and teachers have the ability to publish their documents on the site, using simple Web-based forms. No knowledge of HTML is needed. Students are one click away from turning in their assignments online, giving their peers feedback on published papers, and receiving teacher comments.
- **Personal messaging:** Similar to traditional e-mail but fully integrated with document sharing and conferencing, personal messaging is a great way to communicate with students, comment privately on conferencing postings, or give private feedback on published papers.
- **Link sharing:** You can share links to pertinent Internet resources sorted by topics that you create.

Nicenet provides the ICA2 free of charge for public use with no advertising. Nicenet makes no profit from your participation, but you must register with the Nicenet website to take advantage of its e-mail and chat features.

**Go to the Companion Website and browse 4.2 *Building Your Toolkit Enrichment Activity: Using a Classroom Message Board*. Use the information in the enrichment activity to create learning activities using information exchanges among students and the teacher.**

| STEP | PROCEDURE |
|------|-----------|
| 1. | Open your Web browser and then the website Nicenet.org at http://www.nicenet.org. On the navigation bar on the right side of the window, select the link **Teachers: Create a Class** in the **New Users Start Here** box. |
| 2. | Complete the registration information, and click the button **Create a Class.** After you create a class, you will be sent a class key code that students can use to sign up for the class. Click **Finish Registration.** |
| 3. | Log in to see your classroom home page. Try out the various features of ICA2 (see Figure 4–5) by making sample postings for the following features:<br>• **Conferencing**<br>• **Link Sharing**<br>• **Documents**<br>• **Class Schedule**<br>• **Class Members** |
| 4. | After you have browsed the features of ICA2, click the **Log out** link on the navigation bar on the left side of the window. |

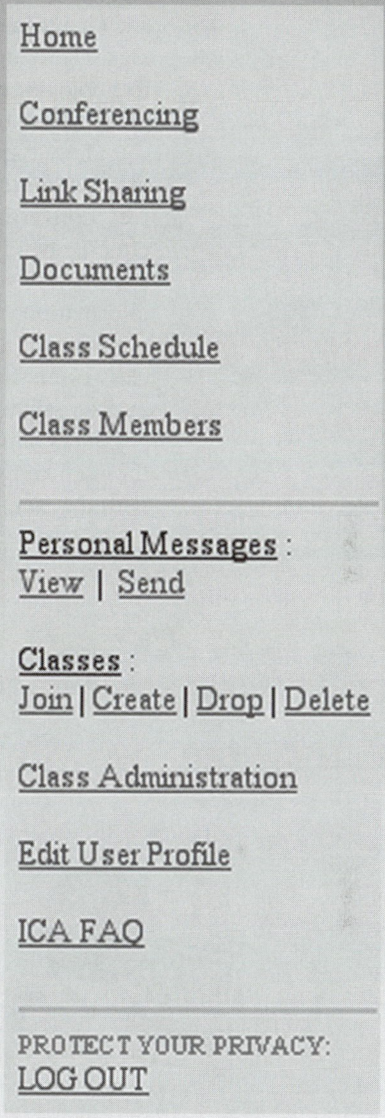

**Go to the Companion Website and browse 4.2 *Project Sample: Ask an Expert About a Topic*. Use the project sample as the foundation for a learning activity that includes interpersonal information exchanges. Adapt the project sample to the subject area and/or grade level that you teach.**

Home

Conferencing

Link Sharing

Documents

Class Schedule

Class Members

Personal Messages :
View | Send

Classes :
Join | Create | Drop | Delete

Class Administration

Edit User Profile

ICA FAQ

PROTECT YOUR PRIVACY:
LOG OUT

**FIGURE 4–5: The Features of Nicenet's Internet Classroom Assistant.**

*Source:* Retrieved August 25, 2004, from http://www.nicenet.org. Reproduced with permission.

## REFLECTIONS

This chapter provides discussion about and tutorials for Internet communication technologies that can be useful in facilitating information exchange in the classroom (see Figure 4–6). E-mail and chat features allow for person-to-person communication, whereas discussion lists and message boards are tools for group discussion. Because many students have experience with these technologies, especially e-mail and chat, teachers can take advantage of that familiarity and integrate these tools into teaching and learning activities to enhance classroom instruction.

Many types of learning activities can be designed and presented with Internet communication technologies. E-mail can be used for projects that engage students in intellectual conversations with the teacher, peers, or other classrooms. Chat can be used effectively for collaborative learning activities, such as online brainstorming sessions, and can provide students with online access to experts. Discussion lists use e-mail accounts for information exchange and are easy to set up and maintain. Many tools and resources are available on the Internet to support topical or thematic discussions within or beyond the classroom. Message boards are also easy to use and access and allow students to participate in discussions outside the classroom.

The communication features of the Internet can extend teaching and learning beyond the well-known information-searching capabilities of the Internet to include interactions with teachers, peers, and experts outside the classroom.

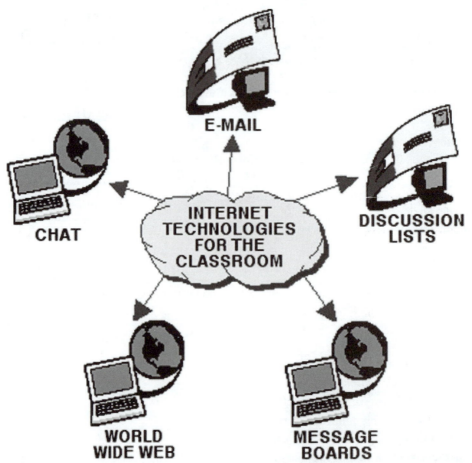

**FIGURE 4–6: Internet Technologies for Information Exchange in the Classroom.**
(Diagram Created in *Inspiration*® by Inspiration Software®, Inc.)

# EXERCISES TO REVIEW AND EXPAND YOUR SKILLS

## Set 1: Reflecting on Practice

- *Closing the Case (1).* Janet Peterson thinks that the online discussion group she created for her two literature classes motivates her students to engage in discussions about the reading assignments more than any other educational innovation she has used. How could a discussion list motivate students to learn in your classroom? What guidelines and procedures would you establish for a class discussion list? What topics would you want students to discuss? When would you use a discussion list, and when would you use a chat room?

- *Closing the Case (2).* Tommy Eldridge is a social studies teacher who would not allow his students to use the Internet for communication. Why would he have restricted that function? How might chat enhance the teaching and learning in your classroom? What guidelines and procedures would you establish?

- *Information Exchanges.* For each of the communication technologies and tools described in this chapter, identify the type of communication channel used, list some advantages and disadvantages in its classroom use, and identify its possible application to particular kinds of learning activities. Some of the issues to consider include the intended audience, ease of creation, ease of use, management concerns, and ease of removal. Use the following table layout to organize your ideas:

| Internet Communication Technology | Synchronous/ Asynchronous | Advantages | Disadvantages | Classroom Application |
|---|---|---|---|---|
| E-mail | | | | |
| Chat | | | | |
| Discussion List | | | | |
| Message Board | | | | |

- *Netiquette.* Review the netiquette lists presented in this and the previous chapter. Determine which guidelines are the most important and appropriate for the Internet technologies you will use and the grade level and/or subject you teach. Formulate your own set of not more than 10 guidelines that you can publish for your students.

## Set 2: Expanding Your Skills

***Subscribe to an Online Journal.*** News lists generally refer to one-way broadcasts, such as electronic newsletters, to people who are interested in a particular subject. For example, many websites allow people to subscribe to e-mail updates from the organization that runs the site. Usually, no communication occurs among the subscribers, although people may sometimes communicate with the editor, much as they would write a letter to the editor of a magazine. You might create an e-mail newsletter of your own to communicate with students and parents. To create a news list, you would need to set up an electronic mailing list that is configured only to send posts from you and not to receive messages from subscribers.

You should also subscribe to an online journal, discussion list, or e-mail service (i.e., announcement list). The following is a partial list of free online resources related to education, technology, and/or teacher education:

- *From Now On: The Educational Technology Journal,* published by Jamie McKenzie at **http://www.fno.org**
- *Educational Technology Review,* published by the Association for the Advancement of Computing in Education at **http://www.aace.org/pubs/etr**
- *InFocus,* an online graduate-student journal published by the Teachers College Record, Columbia University, at **http://www.tcrecord.org** (requires registration)
- *Current Issues in Education,* a peer-reviewed scholarly electronic journal published by the College of Education, Arizona State University, at **http://cie.asu.edu**
- *Edupage,* a free e-mail service that summarizes developments in information technology and is sent three times a week to subscribers by EDUCAUSE at **http://www. educause.edu** select **Resources > Additional Publications > Electronic Newsletters > Edupage**

## Set 3: Using Productivity and Web-Authoring Tools

- *Netiquette Classroom Guidelines.* Use a word processing program to publish the netiquette guidelines you formulated in Set 1. Develop a document that can be used as either a student handout or a classroom poster. Insert clip art in your document that corresponds to and reinforces each of the netiquette guidelines.
- *Workshop on the Best Uses of the Internet in the Classroom.* Use the information presented in this chapter and in the Set 1 exercise on information exchanges to add talking points to your top 10 list of best uses of the Internet, the multimedia presentation started in chapter 3.

## Set 4: Create Your Own Web-Enhanced Project

- *Information Exchange in Space Science.* NASA Quest (http://quest.arc.nasa.gov/) is a rich resource for educators, kids, and space enthusiasts who are interested in meeting and learning about NASA personnel and the national space program. NASA Quest allows the public to share the excitement of NASA's scientific and engineering pursuits, like flying in the shuttle and docking with the international space station, exploring distant planets with amazing spacecraft, and building the aircraft of the future. NASA Quest includes a full suite of synchronous and asynchronous resources:
  - Profiles of NASA experts and stories about their work days
  - Several live interactions with NASA experts per month
  - Audio/video programs over the Internet
  - Lesson plans and student activities
  - Collaborative activities in which kids work with one another
  - Background information and photo sections
  - A place where teachers can meet one another
  - A searchable Q&A area with over 3,000 previously asked questions
  - An e-mail service in which individual questions get answered

Frequent live, interactive events allow participants to come and go according to individual and classroom needs. These projects are open to anyone without cost. Explore the website and select your area of interest, take a look at the calendar of events to find information about upcoming online activities, and search the online lesson plans. Develop a project sample for a project that uses Webcasts and/or chat as instructional strategies for group work and/or information gathering. Use the basic template in Figure 1–5.

- *WEL Lesson Plans.* Expand one of the project samples for this chapter presented on the Companion Website—Cultural Exchanges Through Internet Keypals or Ask an Expert About a Topic—into a WEL lesson plan that is appropriate for the grade level and/or subject that you teach.

# REFERENCES

Harris, J. (1998). *Virtual architecture: Designing and directing curriculum-based telecomputing.* Eugene, OR: International Society for Technology in Education.

Markel, S. L. (2001). Technology and education online discussion forums: It's in the response. *Online Journal of Distance Learning Administration, 4*(2).

Tiene, D. (2000). Online discussions: A survey of advantages and disadvantages compared to face-to-face discussions. *Journal of Educational Multimedia and Hypermedia, 9*(4), 369–382.

# CHAPTER 5

# Locating and Evaluating Information on the Internet

The computer has become one of Sherry Alarcon's most valuable tools in the classroom. Ms. Alarcon, a fifth-grade teacher, says that when teachers integrate technology into good instructional practices, they add a new dimension to their teaching that can motivate and engage students. According to Ms. Alarcon, most students today, even those in low socioeconomic areas, come from homes that are media rich with electronic games, television, radio, CDs, and DVDs. She maintains that her students learn better when they are in a classroom in which lots of technology resources are available for students to experience.

Ms. Alarcon has integrated computer technology and Internet use into almost every aspect of her teaching. For example, while studying geography, her students use the Internet to explore geography resources in the United States, getting material from websites such as the U.S. Geological Survey (**http://www.usgs.gov**) and the National Geographic Society (**http://www.nationalgeographic. com/**) to plan a class field trip. After searching the Internet, the school library, and the classroom book collection, student teams choose a place or a location and map out the trip, describing the sights that can be seen on the field trip. Next, students use a spreadsheet program to estimate the cost of the field trip and create graphs or charts to project how much money needs to be made from various fund-raising activities. Then, each student team creates and presents a multimedia slideshow or video to promote its field trip idea, using maps and pictures downloaded from related websites. All class members then discuss which field trip they would most like to take and vote on the various proposals.

Ms. Alarcon says that information is growing so fast that the main problem faced by her students is how to look at it and make judgments and decisions about it. She says her students need to know whether information is good and how to use it appropriately. At the beginning of each school year Ms. Alarcon presents an orientation to the Internet, explaining that information on the Internet is not always valid. She then explains how to find reliable information on the Internet and how to evaluate its authenticity.

## NEW TERMS

differentiated classroom
digital library
electronic journal

evaluation criteria
hybrid search engines
Google

information literacy
invisible Web
metasearch engines
search engines

searchable databases
search directories
task-relevant knowledge
virtual library

## National Educational Technology Standards for Teachers

The following NETS•T are addressed by the lesson content and learning activities in this chapter:

**I.  Technology Operations and Concepts**

  **A.** Demonstrate understanding of technology concepts and skills

  **B.** Demonstrate continual growth in technology knowledge and skills

**V.  Productivity and Professional Practice**

  **A.** Use technology for ongoing professional development

  **B.** Continually evaluate and reflect on professional practice

  **C.** Apply technology to increase productivity

  **D.** Use technology to communicate and collaborate

**VI. Social, Ethical, Legal, and Human Issues**

  **A.** Model and teach legal and ethical practice related to technology use

  **B.** Enable and empower diverse learners

  **C.** Identify and use technology resources that affirm diversity

  **D.** Promote safe and healthy use of technology resources

  **E.** Facilitate equitable access to technology resources

## National Educational Technology Standards for Students

The following NETS•S are addressed by the lesson content and learning activities in this chapter:

**1.  Basic Operations and Concepts**

  • Demonstrate sound understanding of technology

  • Be proficient in the use of technology

**2.  Social, Ethical, and Human Issues**

  • Understand ethical, cultural, and societal issues related to technology

  • Practice responsible use of technology

  • Develop positive attitudes toward technology

**3.  Technology Productivity Tools**

  • Use technology to enhance learning, increase productivity, and promote creativity

  • Use tools to collaborate, prepare publications, and produce creative works

**5.  Technology Research Tools**

  • Use technology to locate, evaluate, and collect information

  • Use technology tools to process data and report results

  • Evaluate and select new information resources and technology

## OVERVIEW

Many constructive learning activities involve students collecting, compiling, comparing, and reporting different types of information. Web-enhanced learning activities often involve information searches and the acquisition and processing of information. Both searching for and validating information obtained from the Internet are important learning activities when using Internet information resources.

The wealth of information available on the Web greatly broadens the scope of information that is available to students in classrooms. There are virtual libraries and digital collections, websites for professional and standards-oriented organizations, government resources, periodicals, newspapers, magazines and journals, books, encyclopedias, and educational content sites—all on the Web. When students are taught to use search technologies and effective search strategies to solve problems and complete projects, they are better able to transfer search techniques to other problem-solving contexts. Developing an information search strategy for the classroom is the first step in addressing complex problems and issues requiring critical thinking.

Because there are no universal quality controls for publishing documents on the Internet, anyone with the know-how and access rights to a Web server can publish pages on the Web. Thus, the information published on Web pages may not have undergone the scrutiny of peers, experts, or professionals and thus may be inaccurate. When an Internet search is conducted, it is important for teachers and students to distinguish resources that are relevant and appropriate from those that are not.

## Lesson 5.1    Identifying Internet Sources of Educational Information

### FOCUS QUESTIONS

- What kinds of information resources are available on the Internet?
- How can Internet information resources be used for educational purposes?
- What is the invisible Web?

## ■ LOCATING EDUCATIONAL INFORMATION ON THE INTERNET

The information students need and use to complete project-based learning activities can come from a number of sources, including personal experiences, books, articles, expert opinions, encyclopedias, and the World Wide Web. One of the greatest features of the Internet is that it offers students relatively inexpensive access to a wealth of information across a vast range of fields, which can increase students efficiency in searching for information. Indeed, information searches are the most basic function of Web use. However, the increased amount of information that can be accessed requires students to become adroit at locating appropriate sources. A variety of Internet search technologies, content-related websites, and Web databases are available to help them.

### Virtual Libraries and Digital Image Collections

A **virtual library** is designed to extend or simulate in a virtual space many of the services and capabilities of brick-and-mortar libraries. Usually managed by libraries and librarians, these virtual libraries identify electronic resources referred and reviewed by professionals, particularly librarians. Virtual libraries filter out many of the irrelevant, personal, and corporate pages that commercial search engines produce. Although copyright and subscription issues may limit the capability of virtual libraries to provide references to scholarly articles and books, newspaper articles, and professional magazine pieces, many of these resources can be acquired by academic or fee-based library or subscription services. Some examples of virtual libraries include the following:

- The Librarian's Index to the Internet (http://lii.org/) is a searchable, annotated subject directory with thousands of Internet resources selected and evaluated by librarians for their usefulness to users of public libraries. This index provides a well-organized point of access for reliable and trustworthy Internet resources.
- Infomine (http://infomine.ucr.edu/) is a virtual library of Internet resources relevant to faculty, students, and research staff at the university level. It contains useful Internet resources such as databases, electronic journals, electronic books, bulletin boards, mailing lists, online library card catalogs, articles, directories of researchers, and many other types of information. Infomine was built by librarians from several colleges and universities.
- The Internet Public Library (http://www.ipl.org) is a project of the University of Michigan School of Information and is designed to provide students and professionals

in the library and information science profession with a place to learn about the practice of librarianship in the digital age. Hundreds of students have been involved in designing, building, creating, and maintaining this website and its various services, and volunteer librarians throughout the world have been involved remotely in answering reference questions.

These virtual libraries are designed to be user friendly; the records produced by basic and advanced searches are filtered through librarian checks for authenticity, currency, and impartiality of content. Teachers should encourage students to use virtual libraries because of their reliability.

A **digital library,** digital collection, or digital image collection uses electronic-information technologies to digitize primary source documents, assemble them into collections, and present them online. The Digital Library Federation (DLF) is a consortium of libraries and related agencies that are pioneering the use of electronic-information technologies to extend their collections and services. The DLF promotes sustainable, scalable digital collections and encourages the development of new collections and collection services. The DLF website at http://www.diglib.org/ provides links to over 30 DLF partners. Some examples of digital libraries include the following:

- The National Science Digital Library (NSDL; http://nsdl.org) is a digital library of resource collections and services in support of science education at all levels. NSDL is a comprehensive, online source for science, technology, engineering, and mathematics education. Its purpose is to extend science literacy through access to materials and methods that reveal the nature of the physical universe and the intellectual means by which it is discovered and understood. A partnership of NSDL-funded projects, the NSDL is a center of innovation for digital libraries and a virtual community center for groups focused on digital-library-enabled science education.

- The Library of Congress (http://memory.loc.gov/) features a digital library with over 100 collections, as well as a section for teachers (i.e., The Learning Page) that provides lesson plans, interactive puzzles, learning games, classroom projects, and professional development activities.

- Exploratorium (http://www.exploratorium.edu) is a virtual museum. The bricks-and-mortar Exploratorium is a museum of science, art, and human perception located in San Francisco, California. In 1993 it became one of the first science museums to build a site on the World Wide Web, which now includes more than 12,000 Web pages and many sound and video files exploring hundreds of different topics. Many of the resources on the website are simple uses of information technology. For example, the site presents over 500 simple experiments, for which instructions can be viewed on any type of Web browser and easily printed out. The website extends the educational experiences available on the museum's floor.

## Professional and Standards-Oriented Organizations

Professional and standards-oriented organizations publish curriculum standards, teaching resources, and lesson plans on the Web. The following professional organizations cover almost all of the national curriculum standards in various subject areas:

- National Council of Teachers of Mathematics (NCTM; http://illuminations. nctm.org/) provides Internet resources to improve the teaching and learning of mathematics, including ready-to-use, interactive multimedia math lessons, lessons developed by expert math teachers, interactive programs to demonstrate math concepts, video vignettes, research reports, and articles.

- National Council for the Social Studies (http://www.socialstudies.org/) provides teaching resources categorized by the 10 themes of the curriculum standards for social studies, lists of online classes and learning opportunities, forums to discuss social studies education, classroom tips, general topics related to the education of effective citizens, listings of organizations, article citations, and resources related to social studies education.

- National Council of Teachers of English (NCTE; http://www.ncte.org/) provides links to teaching ideas selected from NCTE publications or submitted directly by teachers and organized according to ESL, journalism, literature, reading, technology, writing, and vocabulary, as well as a forum where teachers share ideas, strategies, problems, and solutions. The NCTE and the International Reading Association (IRA) sponsor a website called Read•Write•Think (http://www.readwritethink.org/), which provides educators and students with access to teaching practices and resources in reading and language arts instruction, including a collection of lessons, a description of IRA/NCTE standards, and Web resources reviewed by an expert panel to ensure selection of the best resources for English language arts teachers.

- American Association for the Advancement of Science (AAAS; http://www.aaas.org/) sponsors an educational website, Science NetLinks (http://www.sciencenetlinks.org/), which provides Internet-based learning activities for the classroom, Web resources reviewed by a panel of editors and supportive of standards-based teaching and learning, and the benchmarks for science literacy established by an AAAS initiative addressing K–12 science education.

- National Geographic Society (http://www.nationalgeographic.com/) sponsors a website, Xpeditions (http://www.nationalgeographic.com/xpeditions/), which describes U.S. geography standards and provides forums to discuss geography education, an interactive learning museum, online and off-line learning activities, and lesson plans written by educators and tested in the classroom. In addition, the National Geographic Society website provides an education section (http://www.nationalgeographic.com/education/) with lesson plans, online adventures, and online mapping, including dynamic maps, atlas maps, country profiles, printable maps with black-line masters optimized for overhead transparencies, and star charts.

- National Council on Economic Education (NCEE; http://www.ncee.net/) sponsors a website called EconEdLink (http://www.econedlink.org/), which provides classroom-tested, Internet-based economics lesson materials for K–12 teachers and their students. The materials are centered on curriculum standards and the essential principles of economics.

National standards and examples for arts education are provided by the ArtsEdge website (http://artsedge.kennedy-center.org/). ArtsEdge includes teaching materials focused on national art education standards and provides K–12 teachers with curriculum units, lesson plans, activities and other ideas for integrating the arts into classroom teaching, a directory of instructional Web resources, and a lesson submission and exchange system.

## Government Resources

Federal and state government departments and agencies publish a considerable amount of information on the Internet. Most online government publications, books, articles, statistics, and releases are authored by specialists and scholars and are closely reviewed by field experts. In general, teachers can encourage students to utilize electronic government resources with little concern over quality or authorship. Most of these resources are available at no charge and without subscription requirements.

The information available at specific departments or agencies is probably the most useful information resource for students. For example, the U.S. government sponsors a website with health and nutrition information at http://www.nutrition.gov/. And the National Archives and Records Administration provides excellent history and social studies resources, including document-based lesson plans and student research activities, in its digital classroom at http://www.archives.gov/. In addition, the U.S. Department of Justice sponsors a website called Justice for Kids and Youth (http://www.justice.gov/kidspage/), which provides information on safety, substance abuse prevention, criminology, current events, technology, science, and history.

The FirstGov for Kids website (http://www.kids.gov) is an interagency portal for children that provides links to U.S. government children's sites and some of the best children's sites from other organizations. Further, federal agencies and institutions like the National Aeronautics and Space Administration (http://www.nasa.gov/), the Smithsonian Institutes (http://www.si.edu/), the National Weather Service (http://www.weather.gov/), and the U.S. Geological Survey (http://www.usgs.gov/) maintain websites that are rich in educational resources and suitable for use in developing Web-enhanced learning activities. Several agencies, such as the Bureau of Labor Statistics at http://www.bls.gov/ and the Census Bureau at http://www.census.gov/, produce student-friendly materials relevant to multiple curriculum themes and career information.

Much of the content contained on these governmental websites can help students obtain data and information for project-based learning activities. However, these sites also provide numerous documents intended for an advanced audience, which may require instructor intervention and guidance to prevent students from becoming overwhelmed with massive amounts of information not intended for educational purposes.

## Regional Technology in Education Consortia

Regional Technology in Education Consortia (R*TECs) help states, schools, teachers, school library and media personnel, school administrators, and other education personnel and entities successfully integrate technologies into K–12 classrooms, library media centers, and other educational settings, including adult literacy centers. The Office of Educational Research and Improvement of the U.S. Department of Education funds 10 R*TECs (http://www.rtec.org) to establish and conduct regional activities that address professional development, technical assistance, and information resource dissemination to promote the effective use of technology in education. R*TECs put special emphasis on meeting the documented needs of educators and learners in the region they serve and foster regional cooperation and resource sharing. They provide a number of Web tools and resources that are useful for creating Web-enhanced learning activities.

## Encyclopedias

Online encyclopedias are a good place to begin research on a topic that may be unfamiliar to a student, especially a younger student. Some useful online encyclopedias include the following:

- *Encyclopedia.com* (http://www.encyclopedia.com/) is a good place to start a research activity. It is a free Internet service that provides more than 57,000 frequently updated articles from the *Columbia Encyclopedia* (sixth edition). Each article is enhanced with links to newspaper and magazine articles as well as pictures and maps. Each entry is short but includes hyperlinked references to other encyclopedia articles, as well as links to periodicals and images in the fee-based e-Library. A Search Encarta button in each article performs a related search of Encarta.

- *Encyclopedia Britannica* (http://www.britannica.com/) provides free access to condensed articles by keyword search, by browsing alphabetically, or by subject, with access to the full text of the hard-copy *Encyclopedia Britannica* available only to paying subscribers.

- *Encarta* (http://encarta.msn.com/) offers thousands of articles from the CD-ROM encyclopedia, hundreds of related multimedia clips, a talking dictionary, a world atlas, and a resource for educators. The Web pages do contain a fair number of advertisements.

- *Encyclopedia Smithsonian* (http://www.si.edu/resource/faq/start.htm) features answers to frequently asked questions about the Smithsonian Institution and links to

Smithsonian resources on subjects from art to zoology. Because there is no search function, A-to-Z the only way to navigate is to browse through a topic listing.

- Information Please (http://www.infoplease.com/) is an encyclopedia, dictionary, and almanac that integrates the various *Information Please Almanacs* on sports, entertainment, and general knowledge with *Random House Webster's College Dictionary* and the *Columbia Encyclopedia*. It can be navigated by an integrated search function, and the almanacs can be browsed by topics.

## Educational Content Sites

Educational content sites on the Internet can provide high-quality content for use in lesson building, primarily lesson plans and curriculum resources. Some of the most popular Internet content sites include the following:

- Blue Web'n (http://www.kn.pacbell.com/wired/bluewebn/) is an online library of hundreds of Internet sites categorized by subject, grade level, and format (i.e., lessons, activities, projects, resources, references, and tools). You can search by grade level, subject area, or specific subcategories. New sites are added regularly, and you can receive a list and description of these additions by e-mail by registering with the website.

- DiscoverySchool.com Lesson Plans Library (http://school.discovery.com/lessonplans/) provides innovative teaching materials for teachers, useful and enjoyable resources for students, and advice for parents about how to help their kids enjoy learning and excel in school. A link to Teaching Tools gives access to Puzzlemaker, Lesson Planner, Quiz Center, and Worksheet Generator. The site is constantly reviewed for educational relevance by practicing classroom teachers in elementary school, middle school, and high school.

- Education World (http://www.educationworld.com) is designed as a kind of Web portal for educators, a place for teachers to gather and share ideas, as well as a complete online resource where educators can find lesson plans and research materials. Website resources include a search engine for educational websites only, lesson plans, practical information for educators, information on how to integrate technology in the classroom, articles written by education experts, website reviews, daily features and columns, teacher and principal profiles, chats with important individuals in education, and employment listings.

- Educator's Reference Desk Lesson Plans (http://www.eduref.org/Virtual/Lessons/index.shtml) is a collection of more than 2,000 unique lesson plans that have been written and submitted by teachers from all over the United States and the world.

- EduScapes (http://www.eduscapes.com) is designed to work with teachers, parents, and children around the world to effectively integrate technology into teaching and learning environments. The website includes a weekly project section that contains a thematic topic with selected Web resources, ideas and activities, vocabulary, lesson plans, WebQuests, and student-produced materials.

- Federal Resources for Educational Excellence (FREE) (http://www.ed.gov/free/) provides easy, one-stop access to learning resources from dozens of federal organizations, including the Library of Congress, National Aeronautics and Space Administration (NASA), National Archives and Records Administration (NARA), National Endowment for the Humanities (NEH), National Gallery of Art, National Park Service, National Science Foundation (NSF), Peace Corps, and Smithsonian Institution. Resources include teaching ideas, learning activities, photos, maps, primary documents, data, paintings, sound recordings, and more—on thousands of topics.

- Gateway to Educational Materials (GEM; http://www.thegateway.org/) provides educators with quick and easy access to thousands of educational resources found on various federal, state, university, nonprofit, and commercial websites. GEM is a consortium of over 400 organizations and individuals providing substantial but un-catalogued collections of Internet-based educational materials.

- MarcoPolo Internet Content for the Classroom (http://www.marcopolo-education. org/) provides high-quality educational resources for teachers and students: lessons plans, student materials, reviewed Web resources, primary source materials, interactive learning activities, and assessments. All are developed by world-renowned organizations that are experts in their fields. MarcoPolo content covers arts integration, economics, geography, the humanities, mathematics, reading, language arts, and science; and all lessons are developed to support, align with, or extend national standards. Classroom-ready lesson plans and other teaching materials make it easy to begin integrating Internet resources into the classroom. And grade-specific research lists help teachers customize materials to teaching style and needs.

- PBS TeacherSource (http://www.pbs.org/teachersource/) provides educational resources by curricular subject, topic, and grade level; in-depth professional development services; tips on how to effectively teach with technology; best practices information from other teachers; tools for teaching, such as recommended books and websites; and much more.

## Electronic and Online Journals

**Electronic journals** include journals, magazines, e-zines or webzines, newsletters, and any other type of serial publication that is available on the World Wide Web. There are many electronic journals currently available, and new ones are always being added, so it is best to use a directory to locate electronic journals in a particular field. Many different libraries, consortia, and organizations have developed lists and guides. Some of the better and more comprehensive sites with directories of electronic journals are listed here:

- Electronic Journal Miner (http://ejournal.coalliance.org/) is sponsored by the Colorado Alliance of Research Libraries. This site includes primarily e-journal sites as they are offered by the publishers, accessed through a series of indexes. No evaluation of the titles is provided, but a unit record that gives some information about scope and content must be viewed before launching to a title of interest. New titles are added as they are discovered.

- New Jour: Electronic Journals & Newsletters (http://gort.ucsd.edu/newjour/) is the Web archive of the New Jour discussion list for new journals and newsletters available on the Internet. The website provides a daily listing of new serial publications. This website is located at the University of California, San Diego but is actually a collaborative effort of many librarians at different institutions.

- University of Pennsylvania Library E-Resources (http://www.library.upenn.edu/ and then select E-Resources > È-Journals) allows a search of electronic journals by title and more than 70 broad subject categories. It also has a listing of newspapers and other electronic journal sites.

## Searchable Databases

**Searchable databases** are useful for organizing large amounts of disparate information; most search engines like Google contain searchable databases. For many of these databases the search results are dynamically generated and then virtually delivered in Web pages associated with a specific search. Such pages are not stored anywhere because it is easier and cheaper to generate the answer page for each query than to store all the possible pages containing all the possible answers to all the possible queries.

The visible Web refers to the links listed on the results pages from general search engines and in directories. The → **invisible Web** refers to what is not returned with the search results, that is, the contents of thousands of specialized searchable databases. You can

Go
to the Companion Website
and browse *Chapter 5 Lesson Links:*
*The Invisible Web* to learn more
about this topic.

find searchable databases and other invisible Web content in the course of routine searching in most Web directories:

- Direct Search (http://www.freepint.com/gary/direct.htm) consists of several long pages listing and describing searchable databases on many academic topics.

- Profusion (http://www.profusion.com/) from Intelliseek is a Yahoo-like directory with a large collection of searchable databases, including many academic subjects. It is a high-quality, human-edited and indexed collection of highly targeted databases that contain specific answers to specific questions.

- The Big Hub (http://www.thebighub.com/) maintains a directory of over 1,500 subject-specific searchable databases in over 300 categories. Listings for each database feature both annotations and search forms to directly access the database. However, these search forms do not include most advanced searching features offered by each database on its own site.

- Web Lens (http://www.weblens.org/invisible.html) provides a collection of research tools for mining the invisible Web.

## Building Your Toolkit:
### Building a Classroom List of Educational Resources on the Internet

You should start building a list of Internet resources that are appropriate for the grade level and/or subject you teach. You can create your list by browsing through the Internet resources that were discussed in this lesson; and if a particular resource (or some part of it) seems appropriate for use in your classroom, you can include the title, URL, and a short description on your list.

| STEP | PROCEDURE |
|------|-----------|
| 1. | Open your Web browser and browse through several of the Internet resources discussed in this lesson. |
| 2. | A virtual library: Librarian's Index to the Internet at **http://lii.org/**. |
| 3. | A digital library: National Science Digital Library at **http://nsdl.org/**. |
| 4. | A virtual museum: Exploratorium at **http://www.exploratorium.edu/**. |
| 5. | Curriculum standards: National Geographic Society Xpeditions at **http://www.nationalgeographic.com/xpeditions/**. |
| 6. | Government resources: FirstGov for Kids Web at **http://www.kids.gov**. |
| 7. | Regional Technology in Education Consortia: High Plains R*TEC at **http://www.hprtec.org/**. |
| 8. | Online encyclopedia: Encyclopedia.com at **http://www.encyclopedia.com/**. |
| 9. | Educational content: Gateway to Educational Materials at **http://www.thegateway.org/**. |
| 10. | Online journals: Electronic Journal Miner at **http://ejournal.coalliance.org/**. |
| 11. | Searchable databases: The Big Hub at **http://www.thebighub.com/**. |

Go
to the Companion Website
and browse *5.1 Building Your Toolkit
Enrichment Activity: U.S. Government and
R*TEC Online Resources.* Use the Web
resources listed in the enrichment activity
to create learning activities that specify
information resources on the
Internet.

Go
to the Companion
Website and browse *5.1 Project
Sample: Planning a Research Project
Using an Online Encyclopedia.* Use the
project sample as the foundation for a
learning activity that builds skills for
conducting Internet-based research.
Adapt the project sample to the
subject area and/or grade level
that you teach.

## Lesson 5.2 Searching for and Researching Information on the Internet

### FOCUS QUESTIONS

- What types of search engines are available to search the Internet, and how are they used?
- What are the advantages of using Google as a search engine in the classroom?
- How are Internet search engines used as part of a general research strategy?

## ■ USING COMMERCIAL SEARCH ENGINES

Commercial search engines are usually employed to support project-based learning activities. To perform productive searches, teachers and students should be skilled in using search engines effectively. Internet searches can be as much about eliminating inappropriate sources as about locating appropriate ones. Well-known, commercially backed search engines are usually the best choice because they are more likely to be well-maintained and upgraded, producing more dependable results. And because search engines do not cover every Web page published on the Internet, you should use more than one. The website SearchEngineWatch.com (http://www.searchenginewatch.com/) provides an online guide to the major search engines.

Search engines are most useful when you first begin a research task. The main rule to remember is that it is important to be specific because of the vast quantity of information available. You usually go through several trials to refine your search for more specific and appropriate information.

### Types of Search Engines

Search engines have a variety of ways to refine and control searches. Some use menu systems, whereas others require special commands as part of the query; some use a combination of approaches. Some search engines provide filtering settings to control searches; children's search engines can filter results and/or search criteria. As a consequence of the → Children's Internet Protection Act, most public schools run filters that prevent students from accessing inappropriate links as the result of a search. Because there are numerous Internet search engines and various ways in which they perform searches, it is important to understand how they work.

*Go to the Companion Website and browse Chapter 5 Lesson Links: Children's Internet Protection Act to learn more about this topic.*

#### Search Directories

**Search directories** are hierarchical databases with references to websites. The websites that are included are handpicked by real people and classified according to the rules of that particular search service. Yahoo! is an example of a search directory. Directories are useful when you have only a general idea about how to search. The first page normally gives you the most general categories, and then you click down through the hierarchy to the appropriate category and select a website. If you use the search form with a search directory, you are not searching the text of actual Web pages but are searching the text of the site title and the site description, as composed by the directory editors. Most directories also search the words contained in category titles and descriptions.

#### Search Engines

**Search engines** use programs that *crawl*, or *spider*, the Web. The spider visits a Web page, reads the information in it, and then follows links to other pages within that site.

The spider returns to each website periodically to look for changes. Everything the spider finds goes into a catalog, or index. Much like the index of a book, the search index contains a reference to every Web page the spider finds. If a Web page changes, the index is updated with new information. Search engines then examine the millions of pages referenced in the index to find matches to the search subject and rank them by relevancy. Search engines should be your first choice when you know how to search for your topic because they cover a much larger part of the Web than do the directories.

### Hybrid Search Engines

**Hybrid search engines** use both crawler-based results and human-powered listings. The distinction between search engines and search directories is not always clear because all the major search directories provide results from a search engine if they cannot find the subject in their own directory. For example, Yahoo! uses the search engine Google for this purpose. Hybrid search engines may provide information from search directories before data from the search engine's database and may even favor one type of listing over another. For example, MSN Search is more likely to present human-powered listings although it also presents crawler-based results.

### Metasearch Engines

**Metasearch engines** search several search engines and directories at the same time and extract the most relevant hits, or results, from all of them. Metasearch engines are useful for gaining a general understanding of what information is available on a topic. Examples of metasearch engines are Vivisimo (http://vivisimo.com) and Ixquick (http://www.ixquick.com). Sherlock is a metasearch engine on Macintosh. For complex searches you should use the relevant search engine because metasearch engines provide only a small number of the results from each individual search engine. Metasearch engines send queries to multiple search engines and other data sources and then collate the results and format them together into a single hit list for display. (Metasearch engines do not search Google.) The data sources used by metasearch engines may include internal indexes, associated-text search engines, database search engines, message archives, and Web search engines. Like single search engines, metasearch engines generate lists of documents that must be evaluated, but they do provide a quick way to determine which engines are retrieving the best results for a search.

## Searches with Google

**Google** (http://www.google.com) is a widely used search engine that provides dependable search results and will be used for many of the examples in this textbook. Google ranks Web pages based on algorithms that examine the entire link structure of the Web and determine the importance of a Web page based on which other Web pages link to it and how often. Google then determines which pages are relevant to the specific search being conducted. Although Google runs related ads above and next to its results, it does not sell placement within the results themselves; thus, no one can buy a higher page ranking. Google searches are an easy, honest, and objective way to find websites with information relevant to a specific search.

To learn more about Google features, services, and tools, browse the following pages on the Google site:

- Google Web search features at http://www.google.com/help/features.html
- Benefits of a Google search at http://www.google.com/technology/whyuse.html
- Google services and tools at http://www.google.com/options/index.html

## Building Your Toolkit:
## Search Engine Basics

The following exercise demonstrates techniques that increase the precision of search criteria to produce more relevant and useful search results with Google.

| STEP | PROCEDURE |
|------|-----------|
| **1.** | Open your Web browser and then the Google search engine at **http://www.google.com**. A Web page similar to that shown in Figure 5–1 should be displayed. |

**FIGURE 5–1:  Google Search Screen**

*Source:* Retrieved September 30, 2003, from http://www.google.com. Reproduced with permission.

| | |
|------|-----------|
| **2.** | The plus (+) symbol is useful when you do a search and are overwhelmed with information. To ensure that a search engine finds pages that contain all the keywords you enter, use the + symbol. For example, to find information about the English colonization of North America, enter **Pilgrims** and notice that you obtain more than a half-million hits. To refine your search by locating references to both Pilgrims and Plymouth, enter **+Pilgrims +Plymouth**, using a space before the plus sign (case does not matter). Because the number of results is still substantial, try to refine your search further by entering **+Pilgrims +Plymouth +Mayflower**. |
| | *NOTE:* Google ignores common words and characters such as *where* and *how* and certain single digits and single letters that can slow down a search without improving the results. Google indicates such an exclusion by displaying details on the results page below the search box. If a common word is essential to a search, you should put a + in front of it. Another method is to conduct a phrase search by putting quotation marks around two or more words (see Step 4). |
| **3.** | The minus (–) symbol is also useful when you get too many hits that are unrelated to your topic. To ensure that a search engine finds pages that contain one keyword but not another, use the – symbol. To find information about the pilgrims in relation to the colonization of American, enter **+pilgrims –pilgrimage**, again using a space before the minus sign. Continue to subtract terms until you get better results. Most major search engines allow you to exclude certain words to narrow a search. If you want to locate information about Baron Manfred von Richthofen, Germany's greatest WWI fighter pilot, but do not know his name or even how to spell it, enter **red baron**. Your hit list includes references to a well-known comic strip, so enter **red baron –peanuts –snoopy**. Your hit list still includes many irrelevant hits, so enter **red baron –peanuts –snoopy –game –pizza –motorcycle**. |
| **4.** | A phrase search is a good way to obtain specific results, words enclosed in double quotation marks appear together in all results. Phrase searches are especially useful when searching for famous sayings or proper names (e.g., "to be or not to be"). Enter **"Pilgrims at Plymouth"** to locate pages about the settlement of Plymouth by the English colonists. |

*(Continued)*

**Building Your Toolkit:**
**Search Engine Basics (Continued)**

| STEP | PROCEDURE |
|------|-----------|
| **5.** | Once you have mastered adding, subtracting, and "multiplying," you can combine symbols to easily create targeted searches. For example, the Red Baron search would be better conducted as a phrase search. Enter **"red baron"** and then combine it with other search criteria, using both addition and subtraction. Enter each of the following terms, one at a time, and check the number of hits as you include each term: **"red baron" –peanuts –snoopy –game –pizza –motorcycle +war**. |

**Go to the Companion Website and browse 5.2 Building Your Toolkit Enrichment Activity: Google Advanced Search Features. Practice the skills presented in the enrichment activity to perform advanced searches with Google.**

## ■ USING RESEARCH STRATEGIES

Information that is relevant to a learning task can have a direct effect on search performance (Spilker & Barrick, 2001); therefore, teachers may need to advocate different research strategies for different learning tasks. The San Diego State University (SDSU) library and information-access website suggests the following strategy to provide a benchmark for teaching search and research techniques to students. This resource is located at http://infodome.sdsu.edu/research/guides/strategy.shtml.

1. *Analyze your research problem.* What do you need to know about the topic of your research? What do you already know about this topic? What do you need to learn about the topic?

2. *Determine your information requirements.* What types of information do you need to find—brief or thorough, scholarly or popular, factual or descriptive, historical or current, primary or secondary?

3. *Identify your information source needs.* What sources of information do you need to search—books, periodical articles, Web documents? What library resources will help you fulfill your information needs? Are these resources accessible electronically or in print or both?

4. *Conduct your information search.* Translate your research topic into phrases or keywords. Gather relevant information using appropriate resources.

5. *Critically interpret, evaluate, and synthesize your information search results.* Conduct additional information searches if necessary.

You can adapt this research strategy to your own classroom by focusing or broadening its scope to support a specific learning activity in a way that is appropriate for your specific grade level or subject matter.

Researchers have provided insight into factors influencing the search process that ultimately affect decisions. For example, Spilker and Barrick (2001) considered the effects of **task-relevant knowledge** and decision aids. They maintained that task-relevant knowledge affects the search strategy, which affects search performance. Specifically, they analyzed the extent to which decision makers implemented *directed* search strategies (searching for specific information) and *sequential* search strategies (searching available data according to its presentation order). The researchers found that in an unaided search more knowledgeable subjects implemented more directed search strategies than less knowledgeable subjects did. They also concluded that the presence of a keyword(s) helped less knowledgeable subjects locate relevant resources to a greater extent than it helped more knowledgeable subjects.

Go to the Companion Website and browse *Chapter 5 Lesson Links: Differentiated Classrooms* to learn more about this topic.

In planning Web-enhanced learning projects, Ms. Alarcon takes into account the search strategies that students will use. Understanding the influence of search strategy on search performance is not only important in improving the efficiency and effectiveness of search processes, but it also allows teachers to support students at their varied points of readiness to learn. In → **differentiated classrooms** teachers can provide mechanisms that allow students at multiple knowledge levels to optimize their search for relevant information and thus their achievement of learning objectives.

## Building Your Toolkit: An Online Research Strategy

It is important to establish a procedure for conducting Internet searches that is appropriate for the grade level and subject you teach. You may want to present a lesson about searching. The library at the University of California, Berkeley provides an online tutorial that features the latest searching strategies and tools.

| STEP | PROCEDURE |
|------|-----------|
| 1. | Open your Web browser and then the University of California, Berkeley library tutorial. "Finding Information on the Internet" at **http://www.lib.berkeley.edu/TeachingLib/Guides/Internet/FindInfo.html**. |
| 2. | On the tutorial page browse each of the following topics:<br>• **Things To Know before you begin searching. . . .**<br>• **Recommended Search Strategy: Analyze Your Topic & Search with Peripheral Vision**<br>• **Three Families or Types of Search Tools** |
| 3. | Choose a topic such as a hobby or an interest to use for an Internet search. |
| 4. | Open the Recommended Search Engines and Recommended Directories at **http://www.lib.berkeley.edu/Help/search.html**. Use the search engines and directories to conduct a comprehensive search of your topic. |

Go to the Companion Website and browse *5.2 Building Your Toolkit Enrichment Activity: Developing a Comprehensive Research Strategy*. Practice the skills presented in the enrichment activity to develop a comprehensive search strategy for your classroom.

## Lesson 5.3   Evaluating the Quality of Internet Information

### FOCUS QUESTIONS

■ What criteria are used to evaluate the quality and credibility of websites?

■ How can a URL be examined to provide information about the quality and credibility of a website?

■ What procedure should be used to evaluate websites?

### ■ A SOURCE OF GOOD AND BAD INFORMATION

While two middle-school students were researching the Holocaust together as part of a unit on World War II, they located information on the Internet that contradicted their textbooks' and their teacher's versions of events. A website claimed that Nazis had not really murdered millions of Jews, as falsely reported elsewhere. The students also read on the website that these false reports were the result of a worldwide conspiracy, and the website listed numerous national governments, religions, industries, and ethnic groups that were participating in this conspiracy. The students began to think that their teacher and the school might be part of the conspiracy and, at first, were afraid to ask about their new information. In this case a website not only misinformed these students but generated mistrust and suspicion as well.

Information searches on the Web are essential to Web-enhanced learning activities. Unfortunately, the wealth of information on the Internet presents teachers and students with the enormous challenge of determining when information is accurate and credible and when it is incorrect and unreliable. Students can participate safely in the many benefits of the Internet if they are taught to protect themselves from misinformation. Thus, the evaluation of information published on the Web is an important aspect of information collection.

Unlike information published in textbooks and journals, which have usually undergone a rigorous procedure called *peer review,* the information published on Web pages may not have been subjected to the scrutiny of anyone knowledgeable of the topic. There are no universal quality controls for Internet publication. Consequently, a person browsing a particular Web page who is unfamiliar with the content presented may have difficulty distinguishing between accurate and inaccurate, reliable and questionable, current and outdated, or authoritative and fallacious information.

## ■ STRATEGIES FOR EVALUATING INFORMATION QUALITY

The evaluation of websites is an important skill for both teachers and students. Not only do they need to find information on the Internet, but they also need to utilize it appropriately and effectively. Both teachers and students should learn to judge the value of any facts, figures, reports, or other information found on the Internet, much as they evaluate what they hear on the radio, see on television, or read in newspapers and books.

Although there is no single set of criteria to be applied to Internet information, the **evaluation criteria** of accuracy, authority, objectivity, currency, and coverage that are applied to other media can also apply to the Internet. Appropriate evaluation criteria also depend on the needs of the user and the purposes of the information. For example, the criteria applied by researchers to online articles used in scholarly research would differ from the criteria applied by a librarian developing a subject guide or a teacher developing a lesson plan. There can even be differences in the evaluation criteria applied by elementary and secondary classrooms. Kathy Schrock's Guide for Educators provides evaluation guides for elementary-, middle-, and high-school levels (http://school.discovery.com/schrockguide/eval.html).

Alan November (2001) contends that an examination of the uniform resource locator (URL) can be the first step in determining whether an online resource is credible. Much can be learned from deconstructing a URL into its component parts, removing one element at a time from right to left. Thus, students should be taught the general structure of URLs, which are composed of words separated by dots (.) and slashes (/). Table 5–1 describes the component parts of the URL just presented for Kathy Schrock's evaluation guides.

Once credible URLs have been identified, further evaluation is still necessary. The Web document and the home page of the website publishing it should be evaluated using one of several protocols or procedures. November (2001) recommends the following plan:

1. Examine the structure of the URL, and know how different search engines order their results.

2. Identify the sponsor of the website, and/or investigate the credentials of the website author.

3. Determine the purpose of the website, whether to present objective information, or to advocate for a cause or an issue.

| TABLE 5–1 | The Components of the URL for Kathy Schrock's Evaluation Guides—http://school.discovery.com/schrockguide/eval.html—Deconstructed from Right to Left |
|---|---|

| Component | Description |
|---|---|
| eval.html | The name of the Web page, or file, containing the evaluation guides (html is the file name extension) |
| shrockguide | The name of the folder containing the Web pages |
| com | The domain, or Internet classification, of this website (*com* suggests a commercial enterprise) |
| discovery | The name of the primary Web server for the domain (similar to a family's last name) |
| school | The name of a secondary Web server or a location on a Web server (similar to the first name of a family member) |
| www | Indicates a location on the World Wide Web (included in some URLs but not in others, like this one) |
| http | Indicates the protocol the browser will use to load the Web page (most modern versions of browsers default to http) |

The evaluation of websites is important in determining the authority, authenticity, and applicability of information located on the Internet. You should adopt, adapt, or develop an evaluation procedure that is appropriate for the grade level that you teach and that your students can use easily as part of their Internet research strategy.

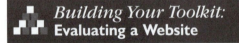

## Building Your Toolkit:
## Evaluating a Website

Kathy Schrock's Guide for Educators (http://school.discovery.com/schrockguide) is a website started in June, 1995, to help teachers identify curriculum-related Web resources to enhance teaching and learning in the classroom. In 1999 Schrock partnered with Discovery Channel School to provide a well-rounded and robust site. Schrock is the technology administrator of the Nauset Public Schools in Orleans, Massachusetts, but is well known for her website, which provides tools and advice for integrating technology in the classroom. In the following exercise you will use some of Kathy Schrock's tools for evaluating websites.

| STEP | PROCEDURE |
|---|---|
| 1. | Open your Web browser and then Kathy Schrock's home page at **http://www.KathySchrock.net**. |
| 2. | Click on the **Support for Presentations** tab, and on the next page select the text link that says **Web Evaluation** to open **The ABC's of Website Evaluation** page (http://www.kathyschrock.net/abceval/). |
| 3. | In the bulleted list after the first paragraph, click on the link to **Classroom Connect** (or **Updated 7/15/02** for the most recent version). Read (or print and read) "The ABC's of Website Evaluation" article. Go **Back** to **The ABC's of Website Evaluation** home page. |
| 4. | The sites listed below the bulleted list are useful for viewing pages with a specific critical purpose in mind. Several questions are asked about each site to cause you to reflect on the appropriateness of the website. If available, work with a partner or a small group, click the links to some of the sites, and answer the questions about the sites. |
| 5. | In the bulleted list after the first paragraph, click on **Links** to critical evaluation sheets and other articles, and then click on the **Critical Evaluation Survey** for the grade level you teach (HTML or PDF version). Review and print the evaluation survey. Go **Back** to **The ABC's of Website Evaluation** home page. |

*(Continued)*

## Building Your Toolkit:
### Evaluating a Website (Continued)

| STEP | PROCEDURE |
|------|-----------|
| **6.** | Scroll down the page to the list of links under the heading **Sites to Use for Demonstrating Critical Evaluation** near the bottom of the page. Use this tool to evaluate the **Aluminum Foil Deflector Beanies**, **Burmese Mountain Dog**, **Feline Reactions to Bearded Men**, and **Oklahoma Association of Wine Producers**. If available, work with a partner or a small group to evaluate the example websites. |

**Go to the Companion Website** and browse *5.3 Building Your Toolkit Enrichment Activity: Online Evaluation Resources and Tutorials.* **Use the Web resources listed in the enrichment activity to create learning activities that evaluate information resources on the Internet.**

**Go to the Companion Website** and browse *5.3 Project Sample: Just Because It's on the Internet Doesn't Mean It's True: Critically Evaluating Web Pages.* **Use the project sample as the foundation for a learning activity to build skills to evaluate information resources on the Internet. Adapt the project sample to the subject area and/or grade level that you teach.**

# REFLECTIONS

The sociologist Robert Merton (1968) defined the Matthew effect—the phenomenon of allocating more credit or recognition for scientific work to well-known scientists, particularly Nobel laureates, than to their lesser known colleagues. The term was taken from a passage in the Gospel of Matthew: "For unto every one that hath shall be given, and he shall have abundance: but from him that hath not shall be taken away even that which he hath" (Matthew 25:29, KJV). This passage has been loosely paraphrased to mean, "The rich get richer and the poor get poorer," and it is commonly used in the field of education to describe what happens when children fail to develop foundational reading skills in the early grades.

The term *Matthew effect* was originally applied to reading acquisition by Herbert Walberg (Walberg & Tsai, 1983), but Keith Stanovich (1986) popularized the concept with his research describing the relationship between frequent reading and reading achievement. According to Stanovich, frequent reading leads to higher achievement, which leads to more frequent reading, and thus the gap between more and less frequent readers grows over time—that is, the Matthew effect.

Now, educational researchers tell us that what was true for reading literacy is also true for **information literacy.** Those who know how to locate and use information to build knowledge that is immediately useful to themselves and the community have an advantage over those who do not (Scardamalia & Bereiter, 2002). Thus, approaches that allow students to pursue knowledge that is of value to them in making sense of their world hold out the possibility of developing skills and habits of mind that facilitate lifelong learning. The Matthew effect suggests, "The more you know about how to know and learn, the more you can learn," making knowledge building a promising foundation for education in the information age (Scardamalia & Bereiter, 2002).

With the wealth of information resources available on the Internet, it is necessary for students to develop information literacy skills so that they can properly interpret and use information for constructing knowledge. Information literacy refers to information-processing skills, which are learned while students complete projects that are relevant and can be related to almost any subject in the curriculum and any grade level (Jukes, Dosaj, & Macdonald, 2000). Students need to develop information fluency in using Internet technologies, tools, and resources for learning.

The American Association for School Librarians (AASL), in partnership with the American Library Association (ALA), has developed standards for information literacy. According to the AASL/ALA definition, information literacy calls for students to access information efficiently and effectively and evaluate and use it critically and competently. Information literacy is not the same as computer literacy, which refers to the technical or technological expertise to operate computer hardware and software. Technology alone does not guarantee that students will engage in high-quality learning experiences. The ALA (2003) lists the following teaching practices that support information literacy:

- Supports diverse approaches to teaching
- Incorporates appropriate information technology and other media resources
- Includes active and collaborative activities
- Encompasses critical thinking and reflection
- Responds to multiple learning styles
- Supports student-centered learning
- Builds on students' existing knowledge
- Links information literacy to ongoing coursework and real-life experiences appropriate to program and course level

Web-enhanced learning provides the means of giving students the information literacy skills they need to be successful in the information age.

# EXERCISES TO REVIEW AND EXPAND YOUR SKILLS

### Set 1: Reflecting on Practice

- *Closing the Case.* Ms. Alarcon says that her students need to know whether information located on the Internet is good and how to use the information appropriately. At the beginning of each school year she presents an orientation on using the Internet. What are the most important principles or procedures that should be included in a classroom Internet orientation? What would you say about each of these points in the orientation?

- *Closing the Case.* Two middle-school students located information on the Internet that contradicted their textbooks' and their teacher's versions of events regarding the Holocaust. How should the teacher convince these students that the information on the website is incorrect? What would you tell your students about why people publish false information on the Internet?

- *Children's Internet Protection Act.* Conduct searches on the Web to find more information on the following topics related to protecting children from offensive websites:

  - Rules and guidelines for Internet safety (see http://www.fbi.gov/publications/pguide/pguide.htm). Develop your own list of dos and don'ts.

  - Ratings systems for Web pages. Create your own rating system. How would you want it displayed on Web pages?

  - Filtering and blocking mechanisms. How do they work? What is the difference between filtering and blocking?

- *Invisible Web.* One of the advantages of using databases to generate Web page content is that it is easier to update information in a database than it is to edit, reformat, and republish a Web page. Thus, information that often changes is more appropriate for databases, whereas information that is relatively static is more appropriate for a Web page. Begin the design of a classroom website by making a list of the kinds of information you would store in databases to display on dynamic Web pages (e.g., assignment schedules) and a list of the kinds of information that would be appropriate for static Web pages. As you create these two lists, remember that the information contained in the databases (i.e., the invisible Web) would not be found by search engines, whereas the information on static pages would be.

■ *Differentiated Classrooms.* Write a short position paper on one or more of the following issues related to the role of technology in differentiating instruction in the classroom:

- Is differentiating instruction feasible in the typical one-teacher classroom? Why or why not?
- In what ways can technology support differentiated classrooms?
- What roles do intelligence, meaning, and challenge play in differentiating instruction in the classroom?

## Set 2: Expanding Your Skills

*Advanced Searching Techniques.* You can increase the power and accuracy of a search by including some operations that refine the searching capability of your keywords.

| Step | Procedure |
| --- | --- |
| 1. | One of the powerful features of a search engine is the ability to control which sites are included in or excluded from a search. If you want to limit your search to a particular website, you can use Google to search only that domain by using the site command. For example, if you wanted to prepare a lesson on nutrition, you might want to see all the pages on the U.S. Department of Agriculture website that reference the word *nutrition.* You could enter nutrition site:www.usda.gov. *NOTE:* There is no space between *site:* and the domain. |
| | You could also place the search criteria at the end of the search command: site:www.usda.gov nutrition. |
| | To obtain all pages about nutrition from any U.S. government website, you would enter nutrition site:gov. |
| | You can also use the plus (+) and minus (−) symbols to further refine your search. For example, to search the USDA website for the food guide pyramid for children only, you would enter +children −adults site:www.usda.gov "food guide pyramid". *NOTE:* You can place the search criteria at either end of the search command or at both. |
| 2. | Several search engines offer the ability to search within the text of a URL. If you start a search with *inurl:*, Google will restrict the results to those pages with the search criteria in the URL. For example, to find any Web page that contains *nutrition* in the URL, you should enter **inurl:nutrition.** |
| | If you start a search with *allinurl:*, Google will restrict the results to pages containing those words in the URL. For example, to find Web pages with the words *nutrition* and *children* in the URL, you should enter **allinurl:nutrition/children**. *NOTE:* Use a slash between the search criteria. Google will return results with the search criteria in any order in the URL. In this example the search could return Web pages with URLs in which *children* comes before *nutrition.* |
| 3. | You can search for variations of words using a wildcard character, which is useful when you do not know the spelling of a word. The asterisk (*) symbol is used as the wildcard symbol in most major search engines. For example, to find Web pages that have *nutrition* and *child* or *children* on the Web page, you would enter **+nutrition +child\***. |
| 4. | Boolean search commands are also useful for refining a search. The Boolean *OR* command is used to allow any of the specified search terms to be present on the Web pages listed in the results. Some search engines perform an *OR* search by default. Google supports the use of the *OR* operator if you include an uppercase *OR* between search criteria. To locate pages with either *nutrition* or *healthy* on the Web page, you should enter **nutrition OR healthy.** |

| Step | Procedure |
|------|-----------|
|      | The Boolean *AND* command is used to require that all search terms be present on the Web pages listed in the results. For example, to retrieve pages that contain both *nutrition* and *healthy* on the Web page, you should enter **nutrition AND healthy.** |
|      | *NOTE:* Some search engines such as Google perform an *AND* search by default so that you obtain the same results by entering **+nutrition +healthy** or simply **nutrition healthy** as the search criteria. |
|      | The Boolean *NOT* command is used to require that a keyword not be present on Web pages listed in the results. The *NOT* operator is the same as an exclude search. You would use the command like this: **nutrition children NOT adult.** |
|      | *NOTE:* You could accomplish the same search by entering **+nutrition +children –adult.** The plus, minus, and phrase searches you learned earlier in this chapter provide most of the same basic functionality as Boolean commands and are also supported by all the major search engines. |
| 5.   | Nesting allows you to build a complex search by using parentheses. For example, to search for Web pages containing *nutrition* and either *fast food, junk food,* or *snack food* on the Web page, you should enter **nutrition AND ("fast food" OR "junk food" OR "snack food").** |

## Set 3: Using Productivity and Web-Authoring Tools

■ *Develop a Research Strategy.* Use a graphic organizer program such as Inspiration to create a research protocol that can be used by students in your classroom for collecting and evaluating Internet resources.

■ *Develop a Web Evaluation Tool.* From Kathy Schrock's Guide for Educators (http://school.discovery.com/schrockguide/eval.html), download the document version of the evaluation survey that is appropriate for the grade level you teach, and modify it for use in your classroom.

## Set 4: Creating Your Own Web-Enhanced Lesson

■ *A Project for Internet Searching and Researching.* When designing WEL lesson plans, you should perform the procedures specified in the lesson plan prior to using it in the classroom. The following WEL lesson plan uses the Berkeley library Web tools and resources presented earlier in this chapter, as well as other search tools and resources, to identify an Internet search strategy. Use this WEL lesson plan as an example for developing your own project lesson plan for searching and researching strategies.

| Title Topic | Simply Searching the Internet |
|-------------|-------------------------------|
| Problem task | Productive searches require an established search procedure using efficient and effective search strategies and appropriate Internet and Web resources. |
| Curriculum area | Information technology |
| Grade level | 6–12 |
| Standards of learning | ISTE NETS•S: Technology research tools |
|  | • Students use technology to locate, evaluate, and collect information from a variety of sources. |
|  | • Students use technology tools to process data and report results. |
|  | • Students evaluate and select new information resources and technological innovations based on the appropriateness for specific tasks. |

| **Title Topic** | **Simply Searching the Internet** |
| --- | --- |
| Objectives | Students will<br><br>• use basic and advanced features of common search engines<br>• identify different types of search engines and explain how they work<br>• develop effective and efficient Internet search strategies<br>• locate appropriate Internet and Web information resources |
| Background information | Because the Internet and the Web allow for relatively inexpensive access to large volumes of information, it is important to become skillful and efficient in locating appropriate sources of information. A variety of Internet search technologies, content-related websites, and Web databases are available to facilitate searches. Commercial search engines also provide a useful and practical means of locating information. |
| Scenario | Students will conduct a Web search of a hobby or an interest, answering the following questions as they conduct their search:<br><br>Which search engine(s) did you use?<br><br>What keywords did you use to find your information?<br><br>What other resources or tools did you discover or use for your search? |
| Procedures | 1. Students should individually complete the following online tutorials and exercises:<br><br>    • "What Is the Internet, the World Wide Web, and Netscape?"<br>    • "Things to Know Before You Begin Searching"<br>    • "Noodle Tools: Choose the Best Search Strategy for Your Information Need"<br><br>2. In small groups students should use the resource "Recommended Search Strategy: Analyze Your Topic & Search with Peripheral Vision" to conduct their search of a hobby or an interest. Each group should keep a record or notes of its search strategy, including keywords, search results, and resources.<br><br>3. Each small group should create a graphic organizer representing the steps of the search process it used and should then present it to the whole class.<br><br>4. The class should select the best graphic organizer (or should synthesize all into one) and should then develop a high-quality version to be posted in the classroom. |
| Resources | • "What Is the Internet, the World Wide Web and Netscape?" from http://www.lib.berkeley.edu/TeachingLib/Guides/Internet/ WhatIs.html<br>• "Things to Know Before You Begin Searching" from http://www.lib.berkeley.edu/TeachingLib/Guides/Internet/ ThingsToKnow.html<br>• "Noodle Tools: Choose the Best Search Strategy for Your Information Needs" from http://www.noodletools.com/debble/ literacies/information/5locate/adviceengine.html<br>• "Recommended Search Strategy: Analyze Your Topic & Search with Peripheral Vision" from http://www.lib.berkeley.edu/Help/search. html |
| Teaching learning strategies | • Uses individual, small-group, and whole-class learning activities<br>• Uses several Internet search engines and information resources |

| Title Topic | Simply Searching the Internet |
|---|---|
| Assessment | • A written record of search engines, keywords, results, and resources used |
| | • Participation in small-group and class discussions about search strategies and techniques |
| | • A graphic representation of effective search strategies (developed in small groups) |

■ *WEL Lesson Plans.* Expand one of the project samples presented on the Companion Website for this chapter—Planning a Research Project Using an Online Encyclopedia or Just Because It's on the Internet Doesn't Mean It's True: Critically Evaluating Web Pages—into a WEL lesson plan that is appropriate for the grade level and/or subject that you teach.

# REFERENCES

American Library Association. (2003). *Characteristics of programs of information literacy that illustrate best practices.* Retrieved May 6, 2003, from http://www.ala.org/aasl/ip_nine.html

Jukes, I., Dosaj, A., Macdonald, B. (2000). *NetSavvy: Building information literacy in the classroom.* Thousand Oaks, CA: Corwin Press.

Merton, R. K. (1968). Matthew effect in science. *Science, 159*(3810), 56–62.

November, A. (2001). *Empowering students with technology.* Arlington Heights, IL: Skylight Professional Development.

Scardamalia, M., & Bereiter, C. (2002). Knowledge building. In *Encyclopedia of education* (2nd ed.). New York: Macmillan Reference.

Spilker, B. C., & Barrick, J. A. (2001, August). *The effect of knowledge and decision aids on information search strategy and performance.* Paper presented at the annual meeting of the American Accounting Association, Atlanta, GA.

Stanovich, K. E. (1986). Matthew effects in reading: Some consequences of individual differences in the acquisition of literacy. *Reading Research Quarterly, 21*(4), 360–406.

Walberg, H. J., & Tsai, S. L. (1983). Matthew effects in education. *American Educational Research Journal, 20*(3), 359–373.

# CHAPTER 6

# Publishing Information on the Internet

Mrs. Bogucki is a third-grade teacher at Anne E. Moncure Elementary School, Stafford, Virginia. She publishes a highly informative, content-rich website for her classroom at http://www.mrsbogucki.com. Before creating her first classroom home page in 1997, she did not think she had the time or inclination to develop one. Then, when she finally decided to do it, she wanted just to highlight her classroom and its activities. However, she soon changed her mind. "As a new teacher, I found that the Internet has plenty of information to offer, but finding what was useful and what was not took a lot of time. The same was true when I decided to put a classroom page together. I searched the Net to get an idea of what was out there. I hit schools from all over the country and, in many cases, was not impressed with what I saw; pages that just kept saying over and over again, 'Hi, here we are!' Search the Net and you will see the same. 'Hi, we are the [select a grade] class at [select a school name] school. See what we've done.' Or 'Come see [select a teacher's name] class!' So what! What were these pages trying to say, or better yet, what did they have to offer? Usually you hit them once, or maybe twice, to give them the benefit of the doubt, that perhaps they had only recently joined the Internet and were just getting started. But after that, you usually end up just forgetting them."

Mrs. Bogucki decided to publish a website that offered useful information, not only for her students and their parents, but also for teachers and students in other classrooms. She didn't have a good idea of what she wanted, but she was interested in various topics, such as activities scheduled for the upcoming week, homework the students would be doing, and pages to demonstrate student work. Soon she began to add links to other sites. As the website grew, it began to take on a life of its own and required more of her time to support it. Mrs. Bogucki offers some guidelines for creating and supporting a classroom website later in this chapter.

## NEW TERMS

| | |
|---|---|
| aggregator | filamentality |
| blog | GIF |
| e-zines | hotlist |

HTML tags                         PNG
JPEG                              RSS
multimedia scrapbook              subject sampler
PDF                               treasure hunt
plug-in                           WebQuest

## National Educational Technology Standards for Teachers

The following NETS•T are addressed by the lesson content and learning activities in this chapter:

**I.  Technology Operations and Concepts**

   **A.** Demonstrate understanding of technology concepts and skills

   **B.** Demonstrate continual growth in technology knowledge and skills

**V.  Productivity and Professional Practice**

   **A.** Use technology for ongoing professional development

   **B.** Continually evaluate and reflect on professional practice

   **C.** Apply technology to increase productivity

   **D.** Use technology to communicate and collaborate

**VI. Social, Ethical, Legal, and Human Issues**

   **A.** Model and teach legal and ethical practice related to technology use

   **B.** Enable and empower diverse learners

   **C.** Identify and use technology resources that affirm diversity

   **D.** Promote safe and healthy use of technology resources

   **E.** Facilitate equitable access to technology resources

## National Educational Technology Standards for Students

The following NETS•S are addressed by the lesson content and learning activities in this chapter:

**1. Basic Operations and Concepts**

- Demonstrate sound understanding of technology
- Be proficient in the use of technology

**2. Social, Ethical, and Human Issues**

- Understand ethical, cultural, and societal issues related to technology
- Practice responsible use of technology
- Develop positive attitudes toward technology

**3. Technology Productivity Tools**

- Use technology to enhance learning, increase productivity, and promote creativity
- Use tools to collaborate, prepare publications, and produce creative works

**4. Technology Communications Tools**

- Use telecommunications to collaborate, publish, and interact with others
- Use varied media and formats to communicate information and ideas

**5. Technology Research Tools**

- Use technology to locate, evaluate, and collect information
- Use technology tools to process data and report results
- Evaluate and select new information resources and technology

# OVERVIEW

As teachers begin to incorporate Web-enhanced learning activities into classroom projects, they want students to use the communication features of the Internet to publish results and reports in a multimedia or Web-based format. Publishing information on the Web is an exciting way for students to present their ideas to others in their classroom and beyond. It engages students in learning and encourages creativity in problem solving and decision making. It also opens the doors of the classroom to an audience in the outside world and provides opportunities for students to interact with that audience.

It is useful for students to learn to publish information as Web documents that can be read by a Web browser but stored on a classroom computer, rather than on a school or a district Web server. The Web documents or products developed from the tutorials, exercises, and other activities in this and other chapters can be stored on classroom computers and loaded with a Web browser or the application that created the document, or they can be posted to a Web server.

Teachers and students do not have to know HTML to publish Web pages; they can be created using word processing, spreadsheets, or other desktop applications that directly save and publish documents as Web pages. Desktop applications such as Microsoft Office allow Web documents to be created and published using familiar applications. Desktop applications also make it easy to embed images, create hyperlinks, format tables, and accomplish many other functions. In addition, there are several Web-based tools that teachers and students can use; filamentality is one that allows teachers to create Web-based learning activities through a fill-in-the-blank process without knowing anything about HTML.

## Lesson 6.1 Using Web Page Authoring Tools

### FOCUS QUESTIONS

- How can productivity applications such as word processing and electronic spreadsheets be used to publish documents on the Internet?
- What is the difference between interactive and noninteractive Web documents?

## ■ WEB PAGE EDITORS

Web page editors are the most common approach to developing and publishing Web pages. These products are like a word processor for Web pages. Two leading products are Microsoft FrontPage and Macromedia DreamWeaver. FrontPage is often included as part of the Microsoft Office Suite but can be purchased as a stand-alone product as well. These products are the preferred way to create Web pages because they assist the author in creating standard HTML code, rather than the nonstandard code generated with tools such as word processors and spreadsheets.

Text-editing programs are often used to edit Web pages. For example, if you use the editing function of a Web browser to edit a Web page, it may default to a text-editing program on your computer. The Mozilla Suite provides an open-source solution for editing Web pages; it includes the Mozilla browser, an e-mail program, and an HTML editing program called Mozilla Composer. With Composer you can create, edit, and publish your own Web pages, adding tables and pictures, changing font styles, and easily performing other creative functions.

## ■ WORD PROCESSING AND SPREADSHEET PROGRAMS

Word processing documents can be created in their original format—for example, as a DOC file using Microsoft Word—and then published to the Web in HTML. Word includes features that allow documents to be saved as HTML, which others can access using a Web browser. The text formatting included in a Word document usually translates easily into HTML. Once a Word document is saved and published as a Web page, the HTML file can be edited using Web page authoring programs, such as FrontPage or DreamWeaver.

Like word processing applications, spreadsheet applications usually include features that allow documents to be saved as HTML. For example, Microsoft Excel provides features to save a spreadsheet or part of one as a Web page that others can access using a Web browser. Excel also allows a spreadsheet document to be saved in either interactive or noninteractive form. In interactive form Microsoft Office users can work with the worksheet data and make changes to it by using Microsoft Internet Explorer (4.01 or later), much as one would use Excel to work with the data. In noninteractive form others can view but not edit worksheet data using a Web browser. Once an Excel document is saved and published as a Web page, the HTML file can be edited using Web page authoring programs, such as FrontPage or DreamWeaver.

## ■ MULTIMEDIA PRESENTATION PROGRAMS

Multimedia presentation files, such as those created with Microsoft PowerPoint, can also be saved as Web pages. PowerPoint provides a simple way to create Web pages from one or more slides in a presentation. However, unlike word processing or spreadsheet documents, presentation documents are published as multiple Web pages, with a single Web page corresponding to a single slide in the presentation document. But PowerPoint automatically links multiple Web pages and builds navigation mechanisms into the pages to permit the Web surfer to move sequentially through the presentation.

### ◢◣ *Building Your Toolkit:*
### Using Productivity Tools to Create Web Documents

Microsoft Office offers many ways to publish documents on the Web; the productivity software provides several tools to help students publish documents on the Web, edit and update them, and share Web-based information with others. Microsoft Office can also make it easier to publish results or solutions in a report or multimedia format or on Web pages. Tutorials can be found in Technology Tools for Teachers: A Microsoft Office Tutorial (2nd ed.) by Mills and Roblyer (2005). The tutorials that follow here help you create hyperlinks and then publish Web pages using Microsoft Word and Microsoft Excel. Figure 6–1 gives an example of the Web page you will create with Microsoft Word.

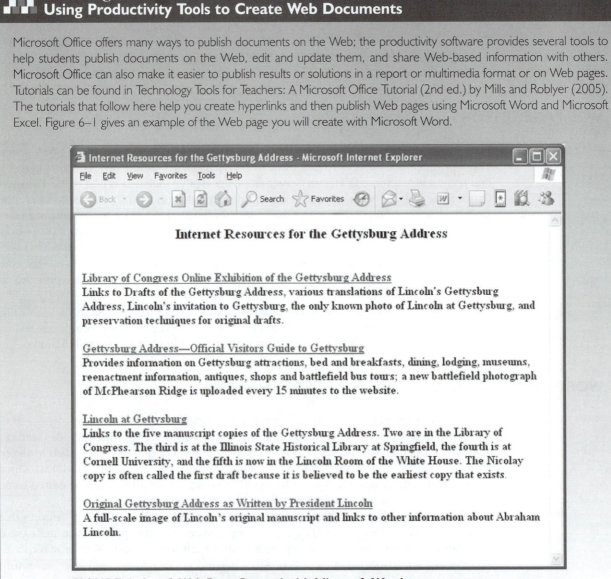

**FIGURE 6–1:   A Web Page Created with Microsoft Word**

*(Continued)*

## Building Your Toolkit:
## Using Productivity Tools to Create Web Documents (Continued)

| STEP | PROCEDURE |
|------|-----------|
| **1.** | Open Microsoft Word on your computer. |
| **2.** | Open a new Word document, and insert and center the heading **Internet Resources for the Gettysburg Address.** |

- Two or three lines below the heading and aligned left, enter this website title—**Library of Congress Online Exhibition of the Gettysburg Address**—and bold it.
- Now highlight that title and select **Insert > Hyperlink,** or click on the **Insert Hyperlink** button. Type the URL **http://www.loc.gov/exhibits/gadd/** in the address box, and click **OK.** The title thus becomes a hyperlink (i.e., text color is changed to blue, the text is underlined, and you can click it to link to the website).
- Starting on the line below the linked title, enter this description of the website: **Links to drafts of the Gettysburg Address, various translations of Lincoln's Gettysburg Address, Lincoln's invitation to Gettysburg, the only known photo of Lincoln at Gettysburg, and preservation techniques for original drafts.**
- Repeat for the following websites to create a document with a list of preferred Web resources:
- **Gettysburg Address—official Visitor's Guide to Gettysburg**
  **http://www.gettysburgaddress.com/**
  **Provides information on Gettysburg attractions, bed and breakfasts, dining, lodging, museums, reenactment information, antiques, shops, and battlefield bus tours; a new battlefield photograph of McPhearson Ridge is uploaded every 15 minutes to the website.**
- **Lincoln at Gettysburg**
  **http://www.virtualgettysburg.com/exhibit/lincoln/feature.html**
  **Links to the five manuscript copies of the Gettysburg Address. Two are in the Library of Congress. The third is at the Illinois State Historical Library at Springfield, the fourth is at Cornell University, and the fifth is now in the Lincoln Room of the White House. The Nicolay copy is often called the first draft because it is believed to be the earliest copy that exists.**
- **Original Gettysburg Address as Written by President Lincoln**
  **http://www.cybernation.com/lincoln/gettyaddressoriginal.php**
  **A full-scale image of Lincoln's original manuscript and links to other information about Abraham Lincoln.**

| STEP | PROCEDURE |
|------|-----------|
| **3.** | To prepare a Word document for posting as a Web page, you must save it as an HTML document. Before you save or publish data on a Web page, you should be certain that you have saved your document as a Word document file (.doc). |

- To save the list of Web resources as a Web page, select **File > Save as type > Web Page** (some versions of Word may say **File > Save as Web Page**).
- Name the file—for example, **GettysburgAddressWebResources**—and save it to a desired location on a disk or hard drive. The Save as Web Page option saves a document file as an HTML document and so adds the .htm extension. Thus, your file name becomes GettysburgAddressWebResources.htm. Any graphic images contained in the document are stored in a folder named GettysburgAddressWebResources_file. (Saving in the Web page, Filtered format removes tags specific to Microsoft Office from the HTML so that you can use a Web page editing program other than Microsoft Word to edit it.)
- The resulting file may look different from the original one because HTML formatting is different from word processing formatting. HTML pages can be edited with Word and then posted to the Internet, using an FTP (file transfer protocol) program.
- You can browse the Web page you just created by starting your browser program and using **File > Open** to access **GettysburgAddressWebResources.htm.** If your computer is connected to the Internet, you can select one of the hyperlinks and review that website.

*(Continued)*

## Building Your Toolkit:
## Using Productivity Tools to Create Web Documents (Continued)

Figure 6–2 gives an example of the Web page you will create with Microsoft Excel.

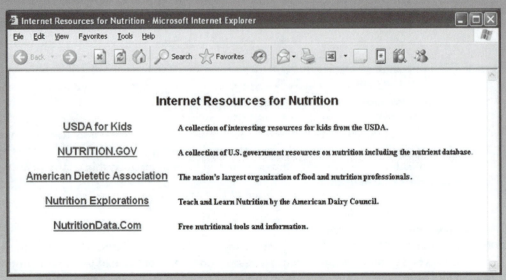

**FIGURE 6–2:    A Web Page Created with Microsoft Excel**

### STEP    PROCEDURE

1.    Open the Microsoft Excel program on your computer.

2.    Open a new Excel spreadsheet, or workbook, and format the width of column **A** to **36** and column **B** to **68.**

- In cell **A1** enter this title for the worksheet—**Internet Resources for Nutrition**—and press **ENTER.** Highlight cells **A1** and **B1,** and click the **Merge and Center** button in the toolbar to center the heading over columns A and B.

- To enter a hyperlink, select **A3** and **Insert > Hyperlink.** Under **Link to:** select **Existing File or Web Page** to create a link to a Web page. Click in the **Text to display** box, and type **USDA for Kids.** Type the URL **http://www.usda.gov/news/usdakids/** in the address box, and click **OK.** The title thus becomes a hyperlink.

- To include a short description of the website, in **B3** enter **A collection of interesting resources for kids from the USDA.**

- Repeat for the following websites to create a worksheet document with a list of preferred Web resources:

- **A5: NUTRITION.GOV**
  **http://www.nutrition.gov/**
  **B5: A collection of U.S. government resources for nutrition, including the nutrient database**

- **A7: American Dietetic Association**
  **http://www.eatright.org/Public/**
  **B7: The nation's largest organization of food and nutrition professionals**

- **A9: Nutrition Explorations**
  **http://www.nutritionexplorations.org/**
  **B9: Teach and learn nutrition by the American Dairy Council**

- **A11: NutritionData.Com**
  **http://www.nutritiondata.com/**
  **B11: Free nutritional tools and information**

*(Continued)*

## *Building Your Toolkit:*
## Using Productivity Tools to Create Web Documents (Continued)

| STEP | PROCEDURE |
|------|-----------|

- Select cells **A3–A11,** and format as **Arial, 12, Bold,** and **Center.**
- Select cells **B3–B11,** and format as **Arial, 9,** and **Left.**

**3.** To prepare an Excel document for posting as a Web page, you must save it as an HTML document. The Excel data you publish in a Web page are usually static or noninteractive data, which means that you want others to view the data without making changes. Before you save or publish data on a Web page, you should be certain that you have saved your spreadsheet as an Excel workbook file (.xls).

- To save your Excel worksheet of Web resources in a noninteractive form, select **File > Save as Web Page.**
- In the **Save As** dialog box, select the radio button **Selection:Sheet,** and enter an appropriate file name—for example, **NutritionWebResources.**
- Click on the **Publish** button to display **Publish as Web Page** on the screen. In the **Choose** box make sure that **Items on Sheet1** is selected and **Sheet** is selected in the list.
- Because you placed a title on the worksheet, it is not necessary to publish a title on the Web page. In the **File name** box, make sure that the appropriate location and file name are displayed.
- Save the file to a desired location on a disk or hard drive. The Save as Web Page option saves a worksheet file as a Web page (HTML document) and adds the .htm extension so that your file name becomes, for example, NutritionWebResources. htm.
- To view the Web page in your browser after you publish it, check the **Open published web page in browser** check box, and click the **Publish** button. The Web page created with Excel should now be displayed in the browser. Some formatting and other features of your worksheet may not have been retained when you saved it as a Web page.
- If your computer is connected to the Internet, select one of the hyperlinks and review that website.

**4.** If you want students to be able to add to the Web page you have created with Excel, you can produce a worksheet that is interactive. With interactive worksheets Web surfers can perform such operations as filtering, entering new values for calculations, or summarizing and analyzing data. Before you save or publish data on a Web page you should be certain that you have saved your spreadsheet as an .xls file.

- To publish the Web resources worksheet in an interactive form so that additional resources can be added to it, select **File > Save as Web Page.**
- In the **Save As** dialog box, select the radio button **Selection:Sheet,** check the **Add Interactivity** check box, and enter an appropriate file name—for example, **NutritionWebResources.**
- Click on the **Publish** button to display the **Publish as Web Page** dialog box on the screen. In the **Choose** box make sure that **Items on Sheet1** is selected and **Sheet** is selected in the list.
- Under **Viewing options** make sure that the **Add interactivity with** check box and **Spreadsheet functionality** are selected.
- Because you placed a title on the worksheet, it is not necessary to publish a title on the Web page. In the **File name** box, make sure that the appropriate file name is displayed.
- Save the file to a desired location on a disk or hard drive. The **Save as Web Page** option saves a worksheet file as a Web page (HTML document) and adds the .htm extension so that your file name becomes, for example, NutritionWebResources.htm.
- To view the Web page in your browser after you publish it, check the **Open published web page in browser** check box, and click the **Publish** button. The Web page created with Excel should now be displayed in the browser. Some formatting and other features of your worksheet may not have been retained when you saved it as a Web page.
- From your Web browser navigate the active cell up and down in the worksheet; notice that you have Excel functionality. If your computer is connected to the Internet, select one of the hyperlinks and surf that website.

**Go to the Companion Website and browse 6.1 Building your Toolkit Enrichment Activity: Publishing a Multimedia Presentation on the Web. Practice the skills presented in the enrichment activity to publish a multimedia presentation on the Internet.**

### FOCUS QUESTIONS

- What online tools allow publication of information on the Internet without using HTML?
- What is Filamentality, and how is it used to create Web documents?
- What kinds of Web documents can be created with Filamentality, and how is each kind used?

## ■ CREATING ONLINE LEARNING ACTIVITIES WITH FILAMENTALITY

Teachers most often create Web pages to present (a) information with links to relevant websites, (b) exercises and student assignments to support classroom learning activities, and (c) project solutions or findings. One easy-to-use publishing tool called filamentality allows teachers who do not know anything about HTML, Web pages, or Web servers to develop online learning activities. **Filamentality** is an interactive website that allows teachers to create Web-based learning activities through a fill-in-the-blank process; it combines the "filaments" of the Web with a learner's "mentality." The teacher can pick a topic, search the Web to gather websites, and then transform these Web resources into learning activities, guided by Mentality Tips.

Filamentality (http://www.kn.sbc.com/wired/fil/) helps design, develop, and publish five types of Web documents, called activity formats: hotlist, multimedia scrapbook, subject sampler, treasure hunt, and WebQuest. Subject samplers, treasure hunts, and WebQuests work best online, but hotlists and multimedia scrapbooks can be used effectively as either an off-line or an online activity. Figure 6–3 shows the different kinds of learning activities targeted. The following discussion describes the structure and application of each format; lesson examples can be found on the Filamentality website.

### Assembling Information

#### Hotlists

A **hotlist** is a list of websites that a teacher finds useful for completing one or more specific learning activities. Creating a hotlist can spare students a lot of time in aimless searching.

**FIGURE 6–3:** Learning Goals and Activities Linked to Filamentality Activity Formats

The links in a hotlist can be developed as a paper list of locations on the Web, an electronic file (such as a word processing document), bookmarks in the Web browser, or a Web page created by a Web page authoring program or Filamentality. When a hotlist is published as a Web page, the collection of links is available to everyone in the classroom and on the Internet. When teachers want students themselves to search and evaluate websites as part of the learning process, hotlists can be a useful tool for students to publish their findings.

### Multimedia Scrapbooks

A **multimedia scrapbook** is used with a subject or a topic of which students already have a general understanding from classroom instruction and/or textbooks. Multimedia scrapbooks are useful as a beginning activity for exploring the Web and collecting and publishing information located on the Internet. With multimedia scrapbooks students surf a collection of Internet sites organized around specific categories, such as photographs, maps, stories, facts, quotations, sound clips, videos, or virtual reality tours. Students collect important items by downloading or copying and pasting them into a newsletter, presentation program, word processing document, or Web page.

## Achieving Learning

### Treasure Hunts

Like multimedia scrapbooks **treasure hunts** are useful learning activities for generating knowledge on a subject or a topic. However, multimedia scrapbooks support generative or exploratory learning, whereas treasure hunts are more structured and use a problem-solving approach. The basic strategy of treasure hunts is to find Web pages that contain multimedia information—text, graphics, audio, and video—that contributes to a basic understanding of a topic. For example, a teacher might provide a set of URLs for Web pages where students could obtain information and then pose a key question for each Web resource. A treasure hunt can be used as the first phase of a project, helping students develop factual knowledge about a subject. Filamentality suggests including a culminating "big question" so that students can synthesize what they have learned and shape it into a broader understanding of the problem or concept being explored. Treasure hunts also structure and facilitate student efforts to collect and publish information found on the Internet.

### Subject Samplers

A **subject sampler** presents a small number of websites organized around a main topic and offering something interesting to do, read, or see. Students are asked to respond to the Web-based activities from a personal perspective and participate in a community of learners relating to the topic. Subject samplers are useful for connecting students to a topic and developing an awareness or understanding of its importance or relevance.

### WebQuests

A **WebQuest** presents teams of students with a challenging task, scenario, or problem connected to a current event or a controversial social or environmental concern. Students explore a wide variety of Web resources to make sense of the issue. With a WebQuest all students begin by learning some common background knowledge and then divide into groups in which each student or pair of students takes on a particular role, task, or perspective. Students effectively become experts on some aspect of the topic and then come together to synthesize their learning, completing a summarizing task such as presenting their interpretation to a real expert on the topic. WebQuests take advantage of the wide range of perspectives available on the Web to address complex topics. They are discussed in more detail in chapter 8.

## Building Your Toolkit:
## Using Filamentality to Publish Educational Web Pages

In the following tutorial you will create a hotlist Web page using Filamentality. You can use a topic of your own and enter associated links for it, or you can enter the information presented here on the topic of the American Southwest. If you use your own topic, Filamentality will give you an opportunity to perform a Web search, but it is best to establish your links ahead of time.

| STEP | PROCEDURE |
|------|-----------|
| 1. | Open the Filamentality website at **http://www.kn.sbc.com/wired/fil/**. Your screen should look similar to that in Figure 6–4. |

**FIGURE 6–4:    Filamentality Home Page**

*Source:* © 2004 SBC Knowledge Ventures, L.P. All rights reserved. Portions of this page have been copied and distributed with the permission of the copyright owner, SBC Knowledge Ventures, L.P. SBC Knowledge Ventures, L.P. is not responsible for and assumes no liability for any loss, injury, or damage which may be incurred by persons or entities using this page. Any person or entity using this page does so at its own risk.

2.    Select **Start a New Page** from the Filamentality home page. You will be prompted to enter the following information:
   • **What's the topic you're making a page for?**
     Enter **American Southwest.**
   • **Type your name as you want it to appear on your finished product:**
     Enter your first and last name.
   • **Type a password. Each topic needs a different password, so pick something you'll remember.**
     Enter a password to use for Filamentality.
   • **Enter your e-mail address:**
     Enter your e-mail address.
   • **What's your school or library name?**
     Enter the name of your school or library.
   • **Your schools Internet location:**
     Enter your school or library URL.
   • **Your Personal Homepage location:**
     Enter URL for your home page if you have one.
   Click the **Spin this Thing** icon to begin adding links related to your topic.

*(Continued)*

## Building Your Toolkit:
## Using Filamentality to Publish Educational Web Pages (Continued)

| STEP | PROCEDURE |
|------|-----------|
| **3.** | On the next screen Filamentality gives you an opportunity to change your basic information. Make any needed corrections, and then print the information page so that you will know your log-in information the next time you use Filamentality. Then click **Add Links** at the bottom of the page. |
| **4.** | The collection of links you gather here will form the basis of the hotlist, scrapbook, hunt, sampler, and/or WebQuest that you create later. To get started, scroll down to add your first link, or read the Mentality Tips. You can enter the link information that follows or information for a topic of your own choosing. Although it is best to have had your links prepared before beginning this process, you can use the links to the search engines at the bottom of the page to locate links. Be sure to click an item on the menu at the bottom of the page to save your information. You will be prompted to enter the following types of information for each link: location, title, and description (recommended). |

- Location: **http://www.state.az.us**
  Title: **Arizona Home Page**
  Description:  **Nicknamed the Grand Canyon State, Arizona was the 48th state in the Union. With a population of over 5 million residents, it is the 20th most populous state and the 6th largest state in land area with 113,642 square miles.**
- Location: **http://www.state.nm.us**
  Title: **New Mexico Home Page**
  Description: **Nicknamed the Land of Enchantment, New Mexico was the 47th state in the Union. With a population of almost 2 million residents, it is the 36th most populous state and the 5th largest state in land area with 121,359 square miles.**
- Location: **http://www.state.ok.us**
  Title: **Oklahoma Home Page**
  Description: **Nicknamed the Sooner State, Oklahoma was the 46th state in the Union. With a population of almost 3.5 million residents, it is the 27th most populous state and the 20th largest state in land area with 69,903 square miles.**
  Click **Add Links** and then add the following link information:
- Location: **http://www.state.tx.us**
  Title: **Texas Home Page**
  Description: **Nicknamed the Lone Star State, Texas was the 28th state in the Union. With a population of almost 21 million residents, it is the 2nd most populous state and the 2nd largest state in land area with 261,914 square miles.**

| | |
|------|-----------|
| **5.** | Click on **Hotlist** on the menu at the bottom of the page to create a hotlist online activity. |
| **6.** | You can add a title and an introduction to your hotlist by entering the information in the associated form fields, or you can use the default information entered by Filamentality. Leave the title as shown, but enter the following information for the **Introduction: The American Southwest states of Arizona, New Mexico, Oklahoma, and Texas form a geographically diverse region of the United States. The Southwest has various landforms, including deserts, mesas, and high plains in the west and rolling hills and deciduous forests in the east. The climate is arid in most of the Southwest although it is humid on the eastern edge of the Southwest. Some of the major landforms of the American Southwest include the Colorado Plateau, the Great Plains, the Grand Canyon, the Rocky Mountains, the Painted Desert, Carlsbad Caverns, and the Gulf Coastal Plain.** |
| **7.** | If you have more than 10 links, you may want to categorize them. If not, you can skip this step. |
| **8.** | To post your hotlist on the Web, click **Hotlist** on the menu at the bottom of the page. Filamentality builds the hotlist for you and puts it on the Web, but you will get to review and proof your page. Your hotlist Web page should look similar to that in Figure 6–5: |
| **9.** | From here you can go back and change your hotlist or the links, or you can move on to another activity format. Filamentality provides a URL for your hotlist. You should bookmark it in your browser using the Favorites or Bookmark feature, so that you can provide the URL to your students. |

*(Continued)*

*Building Your Toolkit:*
**Using Filamentality to Publish Educational Web Pages (Continued)**

## A Hotlist on the American Southwest

### Introduction

The American Southwest states of Arizona, New Mexico, Oklahoma, and Texas form a geographically diverse region of the United States. The Southwest has various landforms including deserts, mesas, and high plains in the west and rolling hills and deciduous forests in the east. The climate is arid in most of the Southwest although it is humid on eastern edge of Southwest. Some of the major landforms of the American Southwest include the Colorado Plateau, the Great Plains, the Grand Canyon, the Rocky Mountains, the Painted Desert, Carlsbad Caverns, and the Gulf Coastal Plain.

### The Internet Resources

- Arizona Home Page - Nicknamed the Grand Canyon State, Arizona was the 48th state in the Union. With a population of over 5 million residents it is the 20th most populous state and the 6th largest state in land area with 113,642 square miles.
- New Mexico Home Page - Nicknamed the Land of Enchantment, New Mexico was the 47th state in the Union. With a population of almost 2 million residents it is the 36th most populous state and the 5th largest state in land area with 121,359 square miles.
- Oklahoma Home Page - Nicknamed the Sooner State, Oklahoma was the 46th State in the Union. With a population of almost 3.5 million residents it is the 27th most populous state and the 20th largest state in land area with 69,903 square miles.
- Texas Home Page - Nicknamed the Lone Star State, Texas was the 28th State in the Union. With a population of almost 21 million residents, it is the 2nd most populous state and the 2nd largest state in land area with 261,914 square miles.

Created by SBC

http://www.kn.sbc.com/wired/fl2/pages/artamericasw3.html
Last revised Thu Jun 30 21:42:33 US/Pacific 2005

**FIGURE 6–5:   A Hotlist Created with Filamentality**

| STEP | PROCEDURE |
|------|-----------|
| 10. | If you provided a correct and complete e-mail address, you can send yourself an e-mail reminder with your password and hotlist location by selecting the **Send Reminder** button. |
| 11. | From the Filamentality website you can obtain a number of printed guides on using Filamentality: The Filamentality fact sheet (http://www.kn.sbc.com/support/filtrain/filfact.doc) provides a quick introduction to Filamentality and the various formats. The flow chart (http://www.kn.sbc.com/support/filtrain/filflow.doc) provides a graphic outline of the steps used in creating learning activities with Filamentality. You can also print a comprehensive training guide for Filamentality at http://www.kn.sbc.com/support/filtrain/filtour.pdf. |

**Go to the Companion Website and browse *6.2 Building Your Toolkit Enrichment Activity: More Online Design Tools for Teachers and Students*. Use the information in the enrichment activity to create learning activities for publishing findings and results on the Internet.**

## Lesson 6.3 Publishing Student Work on the Web

### FOCUS QUESTIONS

- What resources and tools allow students to publish information on the Internet?
- What are Web logs, and how do they work?
- How are Web pages created, and how do they work? What kinds of multimedia files can be used in Web pages?

# ■ RESOURCES AND TOOLS FOR STUDENT PUBLICATION

### Publishing Creative Works Online

The various opportunities to publish on the Web can engage students in learning and encourage their creativity in problem solving and decision making. A number of websites permit students to submit their work, such as poetry, essays, research reports, and school articles. Some websites publish only selected student submissions, some publish all the student work that is submitted, and others even offer prizes and incentives for students who submit their work. The WWW4teachers website presented in the 6.2 Companion Website enrichment activity permits students to publish their work using the project poster tool.

Journals or magazines that can be delivered by e-mail or read online are called **e-zines,** or web-zines. E-zines often provide websites where students can publish stories, poems, articles, or outstanding individual work and classroom projects, as well as read the work of other student authors. Generally, students can submit an article or project for review and receive feedback on their submission. Some e-zine sites are focused on specific types of work, like poetry or science projects, whereas others publish creative writing and stories. KidAuthors.com (http://www.kidauthors.com) is a creative place for young children to share stories and poems with people around the world. And International Kids Space (http://www.kids-space. org) includes monthly stories, picture prompts, and international folktales.

Publishing the school newspaper on the Web, as well as in print, allows others in the community and around the world to stay informed about what is happening at the school. In addition, online newspapers allow students to cover more activities and give more students writing experience. The High School Journalism website at http://highschool-journalism. org/students/SchoolInf_index.cfm has compiled a database of many high school newspapers that can be searched and viewed on the Web.

Publishing information on the Web to present the results of or solutions to projects or problems is another exciting way for students to share their work with others. Students often like to create their own pages and learn to organize and structure information in the process. Creating Web pages can also be a collaborative experience when teams of students demonstrate their collective knowledge from a learning activity.

### Self-Publishing with Web Logs

One of the most flexible and easy-to-use resources for Web publishing is Web logs, which are easily created and easily edited. A Web log, or **blog,** is a Web page made up of short, frequently updated posts, which are arranged chronologically like a journal. The content and purpose of blogs vary greatly, from Web links and commentary about other websites to news about a company, person, or idea. Blogs often take the form of a digital diary (Kennedy, 2003) but can contain photos, poetry, miniessays, project updates, and even fiction. A blogger is a Web-based tool that helps individuals publish to the Web immediately, an example is located at http://www.blogger.com/.

Web logs are a powerful teaching and learning tool in the classroom because they offer students the advantage of writing and publishing for a real audience in a collaborative environment in which they can give and receive feedback. Such feedback can function as scaffolding, which helps students refine and transfer knowledge. In addition, Web logs provide a more sophisticated learning environment than discussion forums (Ferdig & Trammell, 2004), which are shared by many participants. A blog gives individual students control over their own online content.

Web logs also have several advantages over Web pages because they are as easy to use as a word processing application and do not require either an understanding of HTML or the uploading of files to Web servers. Web logs are accessible and can be updated from any Internet connection. And they encourage the evaluation of information, as well as participation and collaboration, as readers offer alternate or supportive points of view and express those views freely.

Thus, Web logs offer numerous benefits for classroom learning (Richardson, 2002):

1. Virtual spaces for feedback from and collaboration with parents, community members, and professionals; easy storage and organization of student work; and easy tracking of student progress and learning

2. Digital portfolios that enable peer coaching and mentoring from outside school walls

3. Online portals for posting notes, homework assignments, links, schedules, policies, forms, and other classroom information

4. More collaboration among learners

5. An easy way for parents and community members to enter the discussion

6. Virtual spaces for school groups to communicate, share ideas, and work collaboratively

7. A collection of hypertext links to references and sources

8. Virtual spaces for schools to share successes, experiences, and goals

## Creating Web Pages with HTML

Hypertext markup language, or HTML, is the language in which Web pages are written. HTML is a document-structuring language to organize information on a Web page and control some of its appearance. An HTML file contains all the writing that will appear on the Web page and instructions to the browser about where that writing should go and how it should look. HTML defines the structure and layout by using a variety of tags and attributes; **HTML tags** such as <h1>, <p>, and <li> structure text into headings, paragraphs, and lists. Tags are also used to specify hypertext links and to include graphics in a document. An HTML file is just a page of text, like an e-mail message or a word processor document. In fact, you can use a word processor to write HTML code, or you can use any other program that allows you to enter and save text in a file.

Creating Web pages with HTML can be as simple or complex as you want it to be. Because Web pages, or HTML files, are basically text, the only tool you really need is a text editing program, such as Simpletext on Macintosh or Notepad on Windows computers. However, Web page editing tools, such as Microsoft FrontPage or Macromedia Dreamweaver, make it possible to create more sophisticated Web pages. Teachers who allow students to create classroom Web pages should provide them with some guidance. Mrs. Bogucki, the teacher highlighted in the opening scenario, offers teachers some advice and →guidelines for creating and supporting classroom Web pages.

> **Go**
> to the Companion Website and browse *Chapter 6 Lesson Links: Teacher's Guide to Creating Classroom Web Pages* to learn more about this topic.

## Using Multimedia Files

Creating multimedia products or adding multimedia elements to a Web page or a Web log usually involves the creation of specialized multimedia files, which provide graphics, audio, or video effects. Several multimedia file formats are commonly used, and special authoring or development tools or programs are required to create these files. Multimedia files are viewed with a Web browser using → **plug-ins,** which are self-contained programs that can be inserted into a main program to expand its capabilities. For example, a plug-in can enable a Web browser to play music or video files. The following discussion describes the most common multimedia file formats and their purposes and capabilities.

> **Go**
> to the Companion Website and browse *Chapter 6 Lesson Links: Browser Plug-Ins* to learn more about this topic.

### Graphics and Images

Written and oral communication can be enhanced by photographs, illustrations, maps, charts, and other graphics. Sources for graphics include digital cameras, scanners, and painting programs. Although graphics can be saved in many different file formats, three are typically used on the Web: graphics interchange format (GIF), joint photographic experts group (JPEG), and portable network graphics (PNG).

The **GIF** format is limited to 256 colors and is best used for graphics with areas of solid color. GIFs are saved with a .gif file extension. The **JPEG** format is best for continuous-tone photographs or other graphics requiring more than 256 colors. JPEG files are compressed; that is, a large amount of graphic detail is compressed into a small file. Image-generating tools usually permit a choice in the amount of compression to be used for a JPEG file. A JPEG with very little compression will look good but will have a larger file size and consequently take longer for a Web browser to load. A JPEG with a greater amount of compression will have a much smaller file size, but the image quality will diminish. JPEGs usually have a .jpeg or a .jpg file name extension.

The **PNG** format provides a patent-free, well-compressed, well-specified standard so that no image quality is lost when an image file is compressed. PNG files are saved with a .png extension. The initial motivation for developing PNG was to replace GIF, but the PNG design provided some useful new features not available in GIF. PNG is designed to work well in online viewing applications, such as the World Wide Web, although some older browser versions may not work well with PNG files.

### Animation

Animation is a useful tool for showing processes. A series of drawings or photographs can be turned into an animation and added to a Web page. Animations work by creating a series of images, with each one in the sequence showing the next step in the motion being depicted. These separate images can be transformed into an animated GIF using any number of inexpensive graphic programs. The file extension for animated GIFs is also .gif. Macromedia Flash is a program commonly used to create animations for the Web. Flash animations are vector-based, which means that the file size can be fairly small even though the animation is complex. The file extension for Flash animation is .swf.

### Audio

Even though audio files can be a powerful enhancement to a Web page or a slide presentation, poor-quality audio effects can also detract. Audio files should complement a multimedia presentation and should always be able to be turned off. It is relatively simple to create digital voice recordings using programs that come with the computer. Digital audio files are usually saved as .au, .wav, or .aif files, depending on the capability of their sound editing program. Sound files containing music are often saved as MIDI files and can be used as background music in a Web-based multimedia project. MIDI music files are saved as .mid or can be imported into QuickTime and saved as .mov. Movie files can have sound only without pictures.

### Digital Video

Digital video, or desktop movies, can add effects to multimedia presentations and Web pages that are motivating and engage students in learning. Movies can also incorporate still pictures, artwork, text, and audio. And they can be created and edited in a wide variety of software applications, ranging from the professional to simple programs suitable for elementary students. File formats for video include .mov (used by QuickTime), .avi (Audio Visual Interleave), and .mpg (Motion Picture Experts Group).

### Portable Document Format

Portable document format, or **PDF,** is a file format that captures all the elements of a printed document as an electronic image that can be viewed, navigated, printed, and easily transferred from one computer to another. PDF files are created using Adobe Acrobat, Acrobat Capture, or similar products, but many word processing and layout programs have the capacity to save information as a PDF file. PDF files ensure that Web pages will display text and graphic information exactly as it was created. To display a PDF, a Web page links to the PDF file, and the Adobe Acrobat Reader plug-in displays the PDF in the browser. PDF files are especially useful for highly formatted documents in which you want to preserve the original graphic appearance online. A PDF file contains one or more page images, each of which can be zoomed in or out. PDF files can also page and scroll forward and backward.

## Guidelines for Student Publication Online

When publishing student work on the Internet, it is important to post information in such a way that students' privacy is protected. For example, when publishing student work, you should never post students' last names or other identifying material, such as personal phone numbers, home addresses, personal e-mail addresses, or individual pictures with names. And the contact person for student products posted on the Internet should always be the instructor, not the student.

Furthermore, information that is published by students should offer some interaction with users so that the learning activity becomes a richer experience. For example, instead of having students post just digital pictures about a topic, they might also post information about what they have learned and provide an e-mail link for others to comment on the topic.

Student work products that are published on the Internet should also include background color or a background image, text and hyperlink colors that can be easily read against the background, a banner or a heading that identifies the content, and at least navigational buttons to move forward or backward through the project pages and to link to the home page.

Students should be selective in choosing and using graphics and should include a text alternative for each image. The size of the images should be as small as possible for reasonable viewing.

Finally, student projects should include a home page that is an introduction to their content or activity. Credibility can be established on the home page by including a contact person (i.e., the instructor) and an e-mail address to which visitors can respond. The name of the school and a link to the school's home page should be included on one of the navigational buttons. In addition, student projects should always include a bibliography, which lists the resources used to collect the information—links to Web-based resources and citations for print-based resources.

---

### *Building Your Toolkit:* **Publishing Web Logs**

Web logs are fully functional websites that are updated directly in the Web browser. SchoolBlogs are Web logs for education set up by Peter Ford, a former teacher at the British School of Amsterdam, and Adam Curry, an ex–MTV video jockey and cofounder of the United Resources of Jamby. The aim of SchoolBlogs is to make available the potential of Web logs to the educational world. Thus, anyone involved in education can create and maintain an individual SchoolBlog at that site free of charge by simply registering.

| STEP | PROCEDURE |
|------|-----------|
| 1. | Open the SchoolBlogs Web log site at **http://www.schoolblogs.com/**. Click the button **Create a New Weblog** on the left side of the window. |
| 2. | Read the information screen about creating a SchoolBlog, and then click the link to the **Site Request Form**. A registration screen should be displayed that is similar to that shown in Figure 6–6. Enter a name for your blog in the first form field, but do not use any of the reserved words that were listed on the previous screen. The name you enter will have spaces removed and will be shortened to 19 characters. Because it becomes part of |

*(Continued)*

## Building Your Toolkit:
## Publishing Web Logs (Continued)

| STEP | PROCEDURE |
|------|-----------|
| | the URL, after www.schoolblogs.com, it is good to use a short name, such as wel, to decrease the possibility of misspellings when students type the Web address (http://www.schoolblogs.com/wel). Then enter your user name, e-mail, and password, and click the **Submit** button. |

**SchoolBlogs**

- Home
- What are School Blogs?
- Terms of Service
- Create a New Weblog
- View Updated School Blogs
- Connection Refused?
- Contact System Administrator
- Manila (documentation and info)
- Support School Blogs

### Site Request

http://www.schoolblogs.com/ [_____]

Name: [_____]

Email: [_____]

Password: [_____]

[ Submit ]

( Discuss )   ( Print )   ( Email This Page )

This Page was last update: Monday, August 23, 2004 at 6:39:15 PM
This page was originally posted: 8/23/04; 6:39:15 PM.
Copyright 2005 SchoolBlogs

**FIGURE 6–6:   Registration Screen to Create a SchoolBlog**

**3.** Once you have completed the registration for your blog, a confirmation page will be displayed. To start editing, you must log in, using the e-mail address and password entered in the previous step.

**4.** After logging in, click the **Edit this Page** button, and enter a title and text for your Web log home page. Then click the **Post Changes** button to save that information.

**5.** You can change almost everything about the site, including its name, appearance, membership, and bulletin features. Explore the various features of this website, which are listed across the top of the page: **Stories, Pictures, Gems, Shortcuts, Discuss, Prefs, Admin, Bulletins,** and **Help.** Use **Logoff** or **Sign Out** to exit your Web log.

**Go to the Companion Website and browse 6.3 Building Your Toolkit Enrichment Activity: Designing a WEL Lesson Plan Using Web Logging.** Use the information in the enrichment activity to create lesson plans that involve Web logging to publish student work.

**Go to the Companion Website and browse 6.3 Project Sample: Publishing an Online Review.** Use the project sample as the foundation for a learning activity to build writing skills through Internet publishing. Adapt the project sample to the subject area and/or grade level that you teach.

# REFLECTIONS

The Internet has provided almost unlimited possibilities for collecting and publishing information. The multiple venues for publishing Web documents include online magazines, newspapers, journals, Web pages, Web logs, and e-mail. To integrate multimedia content into a Web-based format, that content must be in HTML format. There are several Web authoring and publishing tools that teachers and students can use to create Web documents easily. One that is designed for teachers who do not know anything about HTML, Web pages, or Web servers is called Filamentality. It is an interactive website that allows teachers to create Web-based learning activities using a fill-in-the-blank process.

Educators are finding out that when students are involved with their learning, that learning can be enhanced. Publishing information on the Internet is an easy way to actively involve students in learning. The various opportunities to publish on the Web can engage students and encourage their creativity in problem solving and decision making.

# EXERCISES TO REVIEW AND EXPAND YOUR SKILLS

## Set 1: Reflecting on Practice

- *Closing the Case.* Mrs. Bogucki decided to publish a website that offered useful information not only for her students and their parents but also for teachers and students in other classrooms. Soon she began to add more information activities, as well as links to other sites that she had collected. As the website grew, it began to take on a life of its own. List the advantages and disadvantages of having a classroom website. Do you plan to have a classroom website? Why or why not? If yes, what information will be published on your classroom website?

- *Teacher's Guide to Creating Classroom Web Pages.* Is the creation of Web pages using HTML something that teachers should learn? Why or why not? Is it something that students should learn? Why or why not?

- *Plug-ins.* If you could create your own plug-in module to facilitate Web publishing, what would it do? Which features of a Web browser would you like to extend, or which new features would you like to add? Give your new plug-in a name, and describe the functions it will perform. Also describe what the Web browser will do when you use the plug-in; that is, explain how your plug-in will facilitate Web publishing.

## Set 2: Expanding Your Skills

***RSS Aggregators for Web Logs.***   Many Web logs now have an RSS feed. A rich site summary **RSS** is a type of Web document used to share news headlines and other types of Web content. RSS feeds have been adopted by news syndication services, Web logs, and other online information services. Because an RSS file is simple and easy to use, it has become widely adopted by content developers to create a description of a website. It can include a logo, a site link, an input box, and multiple news items. Each news item in the RSS file consists of a URL, a title, and a summary. Content developers make their RSS files available by placing them on their Web server.

RSS **aggregators** are programs that read RSS files from multiple sources, collect them into an index, and then provide customized feeds of topic-specific news headlines. Even though aggregator programs are often downloaded to your desktop computer, Bloglines (http://www.bloglines.com/) is an online RSS aggregation system that allows you to subscribe to blogs and RSS feeds. Once you have subscribed, Bloglines periodically checks the feed for changes or additions. And because a Bloglines account is accessible through a Web browser, you can access your account from any Internet-connected machine. Bloglines uses

**FIGURE 6–7:   A Personal Bloglines Page**

*Source:* Retrieved from http://www.Bloglines.com. ©Copyright 2003–2005. Ask Jeeves, Inc. All rights reserved. Reproduced with permission.

a two-part screen for easy viewing (see Figure 6–7) and provides notification when blogs to which you are subscribed have been updated.

Subscribe to the Bloglines website by completing the registration page; you will need to provide an e-mail address and a password. Respond to the confirmation e-mail to complete the registration. Then click on the **My Blogs** button to enter your online account. With Bloglines you can subscribe to blogs and news feeds in a number of ways:

- *Keyword search.* The Bloglines keyword search is a good way to find blogs and entries that might interest you. If you subscribe to a search, Bloglines will automatically notify you when new items matching your keyword(s) are published. Simply use the search box at the top of your personal Bloglines page to define your search. When viewing the results, click on the **Subscribe To This Search** button, and you will be notified when new entries are received that match your search.

- *Easy subscribe.* Click on the **Easy Subscribe Bookmarklet** link; when the page is loaded, follow the instructions for your browser to install. Your browser may give you a security warning, but Bloglines says that it is safe to ignore the warning. Then, when you are visiting a site to which you would like to subscribe, click on the bookmark (by clicking on the **Links** bar on your browser and then clicking on the **Sub with Bloglines** link on the drop-down menu), and Bloglines will subscribe you to the site.

- *Subscribe with URL.* You can also subscribe to blogs and news feeds directly by entering the URL of the website to which you want to subscribe.

## Set 3: Using Productivity and Web-Authoring Tools

- *Developing a Classroom Hotlist with Productivity Tools.* Use a word processing or spreadsheet application to create a hotlist document consisting of useful websites (include a title, URL, short description, and rating). Don't forget to create a hyperlink for each website so that students can link directly to it from the hotlist.

- *Creating Web Pages with HTML.*
  - Create a Web page in HTML with a text editor or a Web-authoring program. Use the information and links you included in the hotlist of Gettsyburg Address Web Resources in Lesson 6.1: *Building Your Toolkit* (first tutorial).
  - Create another Web page in HTML with a text editor or a Web-authoring program. Use the information and links you included in the hotlist of Nutrition Web Resources in Lesson 6.1: Building Your Toolkit (second tutorial).
  - Create a set of linked Web pages in HTML with a text editor or a Web-authoring program. Use the information and links you included in the interactive instructional presentation created in Lesson 6.1: Building Your Toolkit Enrichment Activity on the Companion Website.

- *Designing a Classroom Website.* Use Mrs. Bogucki's guidelines for creating a classroom website. In narrative and outline form describe the function and the content of the pages on your website; describe the background, graphics, and layout of the website; and identify the structure of the pages (i.e., the sequence of presentation and the links to each other.) You might want to use a design/outline tool such as Inspiration for this activity. Use a Web-authoring tool or a word processing application to create the home page.

### Set 4: Creating Your Own Web-Enhanced Lesson

- *Using Web Tools to Publish Project Solutions.* Create either a project sample or a WEL lesson plan for a curriculum-based project (i.e., in math, science, social studies, or language arts) that provides students with opportunities for Web publishing. In completing the project, students should not only complete the curricular objectives, but also experience the use of software productivity tools, Web-based development tools, Web logs, and/or HTML.

- *WEL Lesson Plan.* Expand the project sample presented on the Companion Website for this chapter—Publishing an Online Review—into a WEL lesson plan that is appropriate for the grade level and/or subject that you teach.

- *Creating Web Pages with HTML.* Create a Web-enhanced project for students to learn the basics of HTML through an online tutorial and examples. Prepare a project sample (see Figure 1–5) appropriate for the grade level you teach. The project should allow students to reference student-developed Web pages, complete an online interactive HTML tutorial, and then work in teams to create a simple Web page on subject matter of their own choosing.

## REFERENCES

Ferdig, R. E., & Trammell, K. D. (2004, February). Content delivery in the "Blogosphere." *T.H.E. Journal*, 12–20.

Kennedy, K. (2003, February). Writing with Web logs. *Technology & Learning*, 11–14.

Mills, S. C., & Roblyer, M. D. (2005). *Technology tools for teachers: A Microsoft Office tutorial* (2nd ed.). Upper Saddle River, NJ: Merrill/Prentice Hall.

Richardson, W. (2002). *Weblogs in the classroom* [Online PowerPoint presentation]. Retrieved March 24, 2002, from http://journalism.hcrhs.k12.nj.us/journ/web2/web/weblogs_files/frame.htm

# CHAPTER 7

# Using the Internet for Information Problem Solving

Media and technology programs are at the center of instruction at Timber Drive Elementary School in Garner, North Carolina (see the school website at http://timberdrivees.wcpss.net). Information literacy is a part of each child's education, and teachers and students work together to answer educational questions, with help from library media coordinators and instructional technology facilitators. Timber Drive Elementary School uses an information and technology team and the Big6 information problem-solving model to integrate information literacy into classroom teaching and learning. The school uses two full-time media specialists, a technology resource teacher, and a network administrator who is also a certified teacher to support the grade-level teachers. The Big6 model is used in thousands of K–12 schools, institutions of higher education, and corporate and adult training programs to teach information and technology skills. The information problem-solving model is applicable to almost any situation in which people need to locate and use information. It integrates information search and application skills with technology tools in a systematic process to find, use, apply, and evaluate information for specific needs and tasks.

## NEW TERMS

| | |
|---|---|
| authentic assessment | Big6 |
| electronic portfolios | problem-based learning |
| rubrics | transfer |

### National Educational Technology Standards for Teachers

The following NETS•T are addressed by the lesson content and learning activities in this chapter:

**III. Teaching, Learning, and the Curriculum**

   **A.** Facilitate technology-enhanced experiences to address standards

   **B.** Use technology to support learner-centered strategies

   **C.** Apply technology to develop students' higher order skills

   **D.** Manage student learning activities

**IV. Assessment and Evaluation**

   **A.** Apply technology in assessing student learning

   **B.** Use technology resources to collect and analyze data, interpret results, and communicate findings

   **C.** Apply multiple methods of evaluation

### National Educational Technology Standards for Students

The following NETS•S are addressed by the lesson content and learning activities in this chapter:

**3.  Technology Productivity Tools**

   • Use technology to enhance learning, increase productivity, and promote creativity

   • Use tools to collaborate, prepare publications, and produce creative works

**6.  Technology Problem-Solving and Decision-Making Tools**

   • Use technology to solve problems and make decisions.

   • Employ technology to develop real-world problem-solving strategies

## OVERVIEW

Information literacy occurs when computer and Internet technologies are utilized in the context of solving a problem. Because the features of the Internet make it a unique educational resource, it is important for students to become fluent in using Internet technologies and resources for information problem solving.

Problem-based learning is focused on solving a realistic problem, which promotes a deep understanding of a topic or subject related to the curriculum. The problem is often unstructured and/or ambiguous, reflecting real-world situations. Students take an active role in solving the problem and develop problem-solving strategies while constructing knowledge about the problem. Students are encouraged to tackle the problem, construct an individual understanding, and find and present a solution while teachers model, coach, support, and provide resources.

A number of information problem-solving models describe the processes people use to solve problems. Problem-solving models can provide metacognitive scaffolds to support students in locating and using information. The Big6 is one information problem-solving process that guides students through the steps of solving a problem or making a decision and also provides a basic framework for teaching and promoting information literacy. Many adaptations are available for using the Big6 with multiple age groups or grade levels. The model provides students with a structure for answering questions, completing assignments, and creating work products.

Authentic assessment is a testing or evaluation methodology that is intended to correspond to real-world experiences. Authentic assessment supports a student-centered approach to teaching and learning because it supports the learning needs of students. Using authentic tasks and assessments can improve teaching and learning because students have a clear understanding of learning outcomes and are required to master relevant tasks. In addition, teachers can be confident that assessment results are meaningful and useful for improving instruction.

Rubrics are assessment tools that describe the various permutations of task performance when students are engaged in solving real-world problems. Rubrics assist teachers in scoring or grading student performance; they are effective with Web-enhanced learning activities. Using rubrics for assessment supports a student-centered learning approach because it involves students in both peer and self-assessment. Rubrics allow assessment to be more objective and consistent because they clearly indicate what is expected from students and how they will be assessed.

## Lesson 7.1   Problem-Solving Models for Web-Enhanced Learning

### FOCUS QUESTIONS

- Why is problem solving a useful approach to teaching and learning in today's classrooms?
- What are the components of a problem-solving model?
- Which problem-solving models are used for Internet research? Describe them.

## ■ PROBLEM-BASED LEARNING FOR INFORMATION PROBLEM SOLVING

**Problem-based learning** is focused on solving a realistic problem in order to promote a deep understanding of a topic or a subject. Such a problem is often unstructured and/or ambiguous and reflects real-world situations. Students take an active role in solving the problem and thus develop problem-solving strategies while constructing knowledge about the problem.

Problem-based learning always begins with the curriculum; the real-world problem must be related to a curriculum topic. Students are encouraged to tackle the problem, construct an individual understanding, and find and present a solution while teachers model, coach, support, and provide resources and guidance (Barrows, 1985; Stepien, Gallagher, & Workman, 1993).

Information problem-solving models describe the processes people use to solve problems; models can provide scaffolds to support students in locating and using information. That structure permits learners to regulate their own learning processes. For example, the Big6™ information problem-solving model (Eisenberg & Berkowitz, 1990), which is discussed later in this chapter, is comprised of a number of steps with tasks for each step that guide students in using and applying information across multiple content areas.

For students to be effective learners, they must have the ability to regulate their own learning while locating, selecting, organizing, analyzing, evaluating, and applying relevant information to the completion of learning tasks and activities. Problem-based learning can help students acquire these information literacy skills to become proficient in handling information and creating useful knowledge.

Internet technologies provide excellent tools for developing information literacy skills. For example, the Web can provide learning environments that simulate real-world situations and provide the context for a problem. The Web can also provide the information necessary to understand the problem, and the Internet can help students communicate with outside experts or peers to gain multiple perspectives.

With problem-based learning, the teacher guides students through a problem-solving process. Students can first apply the knowledge they already have, which helps them understand what information they need to acquire. As students begin to research and acquire that information and contemplate possible solutions, they are developing the information literacy skills they need to become self-directed learners.

Problem-based learning can be considered a type of project-based learning (Moursund, 1999), focused on a challenging problem or task that requires higher order thinking skills.

Usually a student working independently does not possess the knowledge, skills, or time to perform complex tasks or solve ambiguous problems. Consequently, problem-based learning can help students learn to work together collaboratively and cooperatively.

**Transfer** of learning occurs when a learner applies knowledge or skills associated with one task to the completion of another task. Basically, this is the goal of learning—to transfer knowledge and skills from one context to another. Problem-based learning promotes transfer, and Web-enhanced learning can establish contexts that create opportunities for transfer to occur.

## ■ INFORMATION PROBLEM-SOLVING MODELS

LaDonna Washington is a library media specialist in an elementary school. You can usually find her sitting among clusters of students working at computers in the library media center or in classrooms. The teams of students Ms. Washington helps are engaged in locating information on the Internet. She is a new breed of school librarian, who frequently joins students and teachers in their classrooms to help them learn to locate information on the Internet. Ms. Washington provides leadership in instructional technology by teaming with classroom teachers to present technology-enhanced lessons and assist them in helping students acquire the information literacy skills they need for the 21st century workplace.

Problem solving is the process of designing and executing a series of steps to reach a goal (Moursund, 1999). There are a number of problem-solving strategies, some of which are domain specific and some of which use general approaches. Ms. Washington uses several problem-solving models that focus on skills related to the appropriate use of information for problem solving and research using the Internet. All are applicable to Web-enhanced learning activities.

### InfoSavvy

One general problem-solving strategy is InfoSavvy by Ian Jukes (Jukes, Dosaj, & Macdonald, 2000), which considers a problem to be an information need and identifies five basic steps to solve that need:

1. *Asking*—clearly defining the problem and its context in question format
2. *Accessing*—determining where information is and what skills are needed to locate it
3. *Analyzing*—identifying missing information, managing incomplete information, separating facts from opinions, and establishing the authenticity and credibility of the data
4. *Applying*—creating products, taking actions, solving problems, and/or satisfying information needs
5. *Assessing*—asking questions about the process used and the information obtained, reflecting on the process, and transferring the learning to other situations

When these steps are applied to problem solving on the Internet, Jukes et al. call it NetSavvy. The NetSavvy model helps students develop information-processing skills while completing relevant student projects and using Internet technologies.

### The Research Cycle

The Research Cycle by Jamie McKenzie (2000) differs from some other problem-solving models because its focus is on essential and subsidiary questions early in the problem-solving process. The Research Cycle rejects the use of topical research because it puts students in the role of information consumers and demands little thought, imagination, or skill. There may be

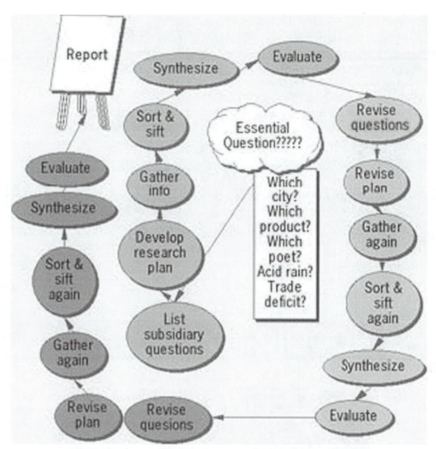

**FIGURE 7–1:    The Research Cycle Problem-Solving Model**

*Source:* From *The Research Cycle* by J. McKenzie. Retrieved September 25, 2003, from http://www.questioning.org. Copyright by Jamie McKenzie. Reproduced with permission.

information that students do not know about when they first plan their investigations. Therefore, they may start gathering information without carefully determining the many questions they should be examining.

**Go to the Companion Website and browse *7.1 Building Your Toolkit Enrichment Activity: Using the Research Cycle to Develop Information Literacy.* Practice the skills presented in the enrichment activity to create learning activities using information problem solving.**

In contrast, the Research Cycle puts students in the role of information producers and requires them to make up their own minds, create their own answers, and show independence and judgment. Because students are actively revising and rethinking their research questions and plans throughout the process, they are forced to cycle back repeatedly through the steps or stages of the cycle. Thus, the more skill they develop, the less linear the process.

The Research Cycle (see Figure 7-1) is a recursive process: Students move repeatedly through each of the steps—questioning, planning, gathering, sorting and sifting, synthesizing, and evaluating. Reporting occurs after several repetitions of the cycle create sufficient insight on the part of students (McKenzie, 2000).

## The Big6

The Big6 model by Michael B. Eisenberg and Robert E. Berkowitz (1990) is a widely used, general problem-solving model that includes these steps: task definition, information-seeking strategies, location and access, use of information, synthesis, and evaluation (see Figure 7–2). This model's application for Web-enhanced learning is discussed in the next lesson in this chapter.

### Building Your Toolkit:
## Using NoodleTools to Develop Information Literacy

NoodleTools is a suite of interactive tools designed to help students and professionals with online research. NoodleBib 5 is a tool that allows you to generate, edit, and publish a reference list that conforms to the style of the current *MLA Handbook* or the *Publication Manual of the American Psychological Association*. NoodleBib 5 takes care of punctuation, alphabetization, and formatting, producing a polished reference list for import into Word. NoodleQuest is a wizard to help you find information about a research topic by identifying some of the best search strategies and search engines to use. NoodleLinks helps you find resources for your research topic. You can browse by category or search by keyword for bibliographies produced by researchers around the world on hundreds of topics. NoodleBoard is an online moderated discussion board available to NoodleTools subscription users, which allows you to talk to the NoodleTools community. And NoodleTeach introduces teachers to 21st Century Literacies, a Web project that investigates how we read and understand the world around us.

**STEP    PROCEDURE**

1.    Open your Web browser and then the NoodleTools website at **http://www.noodletools.com/**. On the NoodleTools home page select the link for **21st Century Literacies** (see Figure 7–3).

**FIGURE 7–3:    The NoodleTools Home Page**

*Source:* Retrieved from http://www.noodletools.com. © Copyright 1999–2005 NoodleTools, Inc. Reproduced with permission.

2.    On the 21st Century Literacies page scroll down to the **Information Literacy** heading, and select the link for **Building Blocks of Research**.

*(Continued)*

| STEP | PROCEDURE |
|------|-----------|
| 3. | The Building Blocks of Research (see Figure 7–4) describe the process for developing information literacy. Select and browse each of the building blocks pages and their links to learn more about information literacy: **Engaging** the Searcher; **Defining** the Search; **Initiating** the Search; **Locating** Materials and Resources; **Examining, Selecting, Comprehending, Assessing; Recording, Sorting, Organizing, Interpreting; Communicating** and **Synthesizing;** and **Evaluating** the Process and the Product. |

 ENGAGING

 DEFINING

 INITIATING

 LOCATING

 EXAMINING, SELECTING, COMPREHENDING, ASSESSING

 RECORDING, SORTING, ORGANIZING, INTERPRETING

 COMMUNICATING, SYNTHESIZING

 EVALUATING

**FIGURE 7–4: The Building Blocks for Research from NoodleTeach**

*Source:* Retrieved from http://www.noodletools.com. © Copyright 1999–2005 NoodleTools, Inc. Reproduced with permission.

| | |
|------|-----------|
| 4. | How could you use the Building Blocks in developing Web-enhanced learning activities? How would your students use the Building Blocks? Write an information-seeking and problem-solving procedure appropriate for the grade level and/or subject you teach. |

| FIGURE 7–2 | The Big6 Information Problem-Solving Model |
|---|---|

1. Task definition
   - Define the information problem
   - Identify information needed

2. Information-seeking strategies
   - Brainstorm all possible sources
   - Select the best sources

3. Location and access
   - Locate sources
   - Find information within sources

4. Use of information
   - Engage in the source (read, hear, view, touch)
   - Extract relevant information

5. Synthesis
   - Organize information from multiple sources
   - Present the information

6. Evaluation
   - Judge the process (efficiency)
   - Judge the product (effectiveness)

*Source:* From *Information Problem Solving: The Big Six Skills Approach to Library & Information Skills Instruction* by M. Eisenberg and R. Berkowitz, 1990, Norwood, NJ: Ablex. Copyright 1990 by Ablex. Reprinted with permission.

## Lesson 7.2   Information Problem Solving Using the Big6

### FOCUS QUESTIONS

- What are the steps of the Big6 information problem-solving model?
- How can the Big6 be used to support Internet-based research and problem solving?

## ■ USING THE BIG6 FOR WEB-ENHANCED LEARNING

Sara Conley believes that the school librarian should teach students how to find the information they need to solve educational problems. She also believes that the Internet can expand the depth and breadth of information resources available for the classroom. As a school librarian, Ms. Conley has spent many years teaching students how to locate and use information resources. She teaches them how to use the Big6 as an information problem-solving strategy, usually in collaboration with the classroom teacher. Ms. Conley says that using an information problem-solving strategy such as the Big6 for locating and using information on the Internet can help students better achieve information literacy.

The **Big6** is an information problem-solving process to guide students through the steps of solving a problem or making a decision. The Big6 model is comprised of six stages, each with two substages (see Figure 7–2). The six stages do not necessarily have to be completed in the recommended sequence, and some stages may be completed more than once during the problem-solving process. The Big6 model provides students with a structure for answering questions, completing assignments, and creating work products. Many adaptations are available for use with multiple age groups or grade levels.

The task definition step defines both the task and the final product. At this stage students identify what types of information are needed to accomplish the task and are encouraged to ask their own questions. A Web-enhanced learning project might be posted on a Web page or in an online class discussion area, and students might reply to a class bulletin board, send an e-mail message, or discuss the assignment in a chat session with peers or the teacher.

The information-seeking strategies identify what sources of information students need and how they should search for the information. Students should consider all possible sources of information that are available and feasible, including textbooks, encyclopedias, library reference books, CD-ROM databases, experts, and the Internet. The Internet dramatically increases the available resources. For Web-enhanced learning projects, a worksheet might be provided that requires students to formulate a search strategy, listing keywords and synonyms, a general subject, a phrase, and a combination of words and phrases for performing Internet searches.

If Steps 1 and 2 are performed properly, the location and access step is easily accomplished. In this step students conduct searches and investigations by accessing each source (in person or electronically) and determining what information is relevant. Students might start with Internet dictionaries and encyclopedias to find an overview of a concept. Searches can then be refined to locate the most relevant sources. Subscription and online databases can provide scholarly journal articles, and students can e-mail experts and others interested in a topic or use designated chat rooms, listservs, or newsgroups. Different search engines can also be helpful.

Use of information is the stage in the research process when a theme or focus emerges and students can determine how best to use each source of information. Students need to evaluate the relevancy and validity of their information sources, deciding what information fits their focus and comes from a documented source. Students should be aware of plagiarism, copyright laws, and citation guidelines.

In the synthesis step students organize the information they have collected and integrate it with their prior knowledge and experiences. Students must make decisions about how to present solutions and how to shape the final product, based on the intended audience. Students can publish their results electronically using PowerPoint, Hyperstudio, or other multimedia presentation software programs. In addition, Internet technologies such as HTML, e-mail, and online publication tools permit students to publish graphics, text, video, photographs, and audio files on the Internet.

The evaluation step measures how well the final product matches the original task (i.e., effectiveness) and how efficient students were in performing the information problem-solving process. At this stage students can still examine and refine their information sources and solutions. In the final editing of a product, students should evaluate the technical and visual aspects as well as the content.

The ability to recognize an information need and apply a structured process to find, use, and evaluate that information is an important skill in the school curriculum. The teaching of information literacy skills should be coordinated within the curriculum and reinforced within the educational setting. K–12 teachers should develop high-quality classroom activities that allow students to practice and master information technology skills in the context of curriculum-based lessons.

The Big6 is a useful framework for integrating information literacy across the curriculum because it establishes a common terminology that fits many subject areas and also provides a mechanism for finding, filtering, and using many types of information. Furthermore, because the Big6 is widely used in K–12 education, many examples and lesson plans are available on the Web. In addition, the Big6 website provides guidance on how each step of the model can be applied across the curriculum (see Table 7–1).

Ms. Conley uses the steps of the Big6 model in lesson plans to describe the step-by-step procedures the learner should follow to complete the project. When using the Big6 model in Web-enhanced learning lesson plans, the steps are incorporated into the procedures section. You can also include Step 1 in the problem/task section and Step 2 in the resources section.

| TABLE 7–1 | Application of Big6 Skills to Curriculum Areas | | | | |
|-----------|-----------|---------|------|----------------|---------|
| | **Curriculum Area** | | | | |
| **Big6 Skill** | **Reading** | **Writing** | **Math** | **Social Studies** | **Science** |
| **1. Task Definition** | Read the selection and read the questions | Develop ideas and content for audience, purpose, and occasion | Understand the problem | Identify issue or problem situation for investigation | Recognize and define the problem |
| **2. Information-seeking strategies** | Outline key terms and concepts | Continue developing ideas and content for audience, purpose, and occasion; find voice; choose organization | Choose an appropriate problem-solving strategy | Develop a plan for undertaking the investigation | Design a problem-solving strategy |
| **3. Location and access**<br>**4. Information use** | Choose appropriate information sources, words, and sentences | Refine the voice, including appropriate strategy flow, and proofread for conventions | Implement a problem-solving strategy | Acquire and organize information | Implement a problem-solving strategy |
| **5. Synthesis** | Apply appropriate information sources to answer questions or solve problems | Submit to editor; revise for appropriate audience, purpose, and occasion | Find and report conclusion | Choose and justify a position on the issue; present results of the investigation | Interpret and communicate findings and conclusions |
| **6. Evaluation** | Check response for understanding, accuracy, and completeness | Publish and evaluate for audience reception and logic | Evaluate conclusion for reasonable results | Evaluate process and product of the investigation | Evaluate findings for clarity, accuracy, and real-life applications |

*Source:* From "Information Literacy in All Subject Areas" by Tami J. Little. Retrieved September 30, 2003, from http://www.big6.com/showarticle.php?id=40. Reprinted with permission.

## ■ ENGAGING PARENTS WITH THE BIG6

Parents can play an important role in helping their children learn, but they need an effective approach. Mike Eisenberg and Bob Berkowitz (1996) explain how parents can incorporate the Big6 skills into their support of their children's homework assignments. The Big6 skills can be applied to any homework assignment that requires a solution or a result based on information. Parents can assume the role of a coach, guiding their students through all the necessary steps to complete a school assignment.

For example, parents might first ask their children to explain an assignment in their own words, much like task definition. And parents can brainstorm with their students to determine possible sources of information, similar to the information-seeking strategies. Parents can then help their children find those resources, as in location and access. Using the Internet, students can connect to many nontraditional sources of information and are not limited to information contained on library shelves or in the classroom. Parents can also discuss whether the information that is located is relevant and, if so, how their child might decide to use it—that is, use of information. In addition, parents can ask their students to summarize the information in their own words and tell whether it meets the requirements identified in the task definition, much like synthesis. Finally, parents can help their children with evaluation by discussing whether the product answers the original question, whether it meets the teacher's expectations, and whether the assignment could have been done more efficiently.

Thus, parents can be useful partners in their children's education by modeling the steps of a problem-solving strategy to guide their children through assignments and to help them become independent learners and users of information. Teachers should be sure to share problem-solving strategies and models with parents and enlist their help applying these strategies at home as students complete classroom projects and homework assignments.

---

### Building Your Toolkit:
## Information Problem Solving with the Big6

The Big6 integrates information searching skills and technology tools into a systematic process to find, use, apply, and evaluate information to meet specific needs.

| STEP | PROCEDURE |
|------|-----------|
| 1. | Open your Web browser and then the Big6 website at **http://www.big6.com/**. Click on the **Overview** link, and a Web page similar to the screen shot in Figure 7–5 should be displayed. |

**The Big6™ Skills**

1 task definition
2 information seeking strategies
3 location and access
4 use of information
5 synthesis
6 evaluation

### A Big6™ Skills Overview
by: Mike Eisenberg

Developed by Mike Eisenberg and Bob Berkowitz, the Big6 is the most widely-known and widely-used approach to teaching information and technology skills in the world. Used in thousands of K-12 schools, higher education institutions, and corporate and adult training programs, the Big6 information problem-solving model is applicable whenever people need and use information. The Big6 integrates information search and use skills along with technology tools in a systematic process to find, use, apply, and evaluate information to specific needs and tasks.

The six basic steps of the Big6™ model and components of each step commonly referred to as "the little twelve." read more...

### An Introduction: Big6™ Information Problem-Solving With Technology
by: Ann B. Canning

This PowerPoint slide show presents the Big6 process within the context of an assignment. Learn how to integrate technology tools with each Big6 step. read more...

### Big6™ History

We are often asked about how we got started—how we met and how we developed the Big6. So, at the urging of our readers and

**FIGURE 7–5:   An Overview of the Big6 Process**

*Source:* Retrieved September 30, 2003, from http://www.big6.com/showcategory.php?cid-6. Reproduced with permission.

*(Continued)*

## Building Your Toolkit:
### Information Problem Solving with the Big6 (Continued)

| STEP | PROCEDURE |
|------|-----------|
| 2. | Under the section titled **A Big6™ Skills Overview,** click the **read more…** text link, and read the description of each of the six steps in the information problem-solving model. |
| 3. | Return to the Big6 Skills Overview page, and under the section titled **An Introduction: Big6™ Information Problem-Solving With Technology,** click the **read more…** text link. Review the online PowerPoint presentation by clicking on the **Next Page** text link near the bottom of each page. |
| 4. | Return to the Big6 home page and click on **Lessons.** Under **Banana Splits** click on the **read more…** text link, and review that application of the Big6 model. |
| 5. | How could you use the Big6 in developing Web-enhanced learning activities? How would your students use the Big6 for learning? Write an information-seeking and problem-solving procedure appropriate for the grade level and/or subject you teach. |

**Go to the Companion website and browse 7.2** *Building Your Toolkit Enrichment Activity: Using the Big6 to Develop Metacognitive Skills.* **Use the information in the enrichment activity to create learning activities using information problem solving.**

## Lesson 7.3    Authentic Assessment for Information Problem Solving

### FOCUS QUESTIONS

- What is authentic assessment, and what learning strategies support it?
- How does authentic assessment support Web-enhanced learning?
- How can authentic assessment be implemented with rubrics?

## ■ AUTHENTIC ASSESSMENT

**Authentic assessment** is an evaluation methodology that is intended to correspond to real-world experiences. Its purpose is to provide an opportunity for students to produce an authentic performance. Thus, authentic assessment is sometimes called performance assessment because it has long been used in training and apprenticeship programs in which assessment is based on the successful or appropriate performance of a task. With performance assessment an instructor observes a student working on a real task, provides feedback, monitors the student's application of the feedback, and adjusts instruction and evaluation accordingly. Authentic assessment applies the principles of performance assessment to the evaluation of realistic work products in all areas of the curriculum.

Authentic assessment supports the differing learning needs of students and thus makes teachers confident that assessment results are meaningful and useful for improving instruction. Students also gain a clearer understanding of learning outcomes and are involved in far more engaging tasks. Figure 7–6 explains the differences between authentic and traditional assessment methods (Wiggins, 1990).

Authentic assessment uses learning activities that encourage students to use higher order thinking skills. Because authentic assessment emphasizes process and performance, it

| FIGURE 7–6 | A Comparison of Authentic and Traditional Methods of Assessment (Wiggins, 1990) |
|---|---|

- **Transfer versus recall.** Authentic assessments require students to be effective users of acquired knowledge, whereas traditional tests primarily reveal whether the student can recall out of context what was learned.
- **High order versus low order.** Authentic assessments present students with challenging instructional activities—such as conducting research, writing, discussing, analyzing, or collaborating—whereas conventional tests are limited to paper-and-pencil, single-answer questions.
- **Understanding versus remembering.** Authentic assessments focus on whether a student can create appropriate products and performances, whereas conventional tests typically ask the student only to select or write correct responses.
- **Real-world versus artificial.** Authentic assessment involves unstructured tasks that better prepare students for the complexities of the real world, whereas traditional tests assess static and simplistic elements of intellectual skills and abilities.

encourages students to practice critical-thinking skills and to become motivated about learning. The Pearson Education Development Group (2003) describes five types of authentic assessments:

1. **Performance assessment**—Performance assessments test students' ability to use skills in a variety of authentic contexts—for example, solving complex problems or working collaboratively. Performance assessments may include activities such as writing, revising, and presenting a report to the class; conducting a science experiment and analyzing the results; and working with a team to prepare a position for a classroom debate.

2. **Short investigations**—Short investigations assess how well students have mastered basic concepts and skills. Most short investigations begin with a task, like a math problem, a map, or an excerpt from a primary source, which the teacher asks students to calculate, explain, interpret, describe, or predict. Short investigations might use enhanced multiple-choice questions or concept mapping, a technique that assesses how well students understand relationships among concepts.

3. **Open-response questions**—Open-response questions present students with a stimulus and ask them to respond. Responses can include brief written or oral answers, mathematical solutions, drawings, diagrams, charts, or graphs.

*Go to the Companion Website and browse Chapter 7 Lesson Links; Electronic Portfolios to learn more about this topic.*

4. **Portfolios**—Student portfolios document learning over time and teach students the value of self-assessment, editing, and revision. Portfolios can include journal entries and reflective writing, peer reviews, group reports, artwork, diagrams, charts and graphs, student notes and outlines, and rough drafts and polished writing. **Electronic portfolios** use computer and Internet technologies to maintain and publish this information.

5. **Self-assessment**—Self-assessment requires students to evaluate their own participation, process, and products. Evaluative questions are posed, to which students give written or oral responses.

## ■ USING RUBRICS FOR ASSESSMENT

**Rubrics** are assessment tools that are useful for assessing criteria that are complex and subjective. A rubric describes the various performance permutations of a task or activity in which students are engaged. A rubric for a project would list the components the student should include to receive a certain score or rating. Rubrics help students figure out how their projects will be evaluated and assist teachers in scoring or grading student performance.

Using rubrics for assessment supports student-centered learning because it involves students in the assessment process through both peer and self-assessment. In addition, students can assist in the rubric design, which can help them become self-directed, self-regulated learners; they assume more responsibility for their own learning and have a clearer idea of what is expected of them in a learning activity.

Rubrics allow assessment to be more objective and consistent because they clearly indicate how students will be assessed. Rubrics are also useful in providing feedback on the effectiveness of instruction and benchmarks for student progress.

Although rubrics can take a variety of forms, they all contain several common features: Rubrics measure stated learning objectives, use a scale to rate performance, and contain specific criteria that indicate the degree to which a goal or objective has been met. Rubrics set standards for performance levels and include examples or descriptions of expected behaviors. Rubrics can use different types of scales; for example, they might employ a simple checklist or a two-dimensional table or matrix. Teachers determine the grade equivalents for each level of the rubric.

Effective assessment rubrics are essential for project-based learning and information problem-solving activities. Whether general or task specific, a good rubric will provide accurate and appropriate information about students' skills. The following procedure will help you create an authentic assessment rubric:

1. Determine the essential learning objectives for the project.
2. Identify the criteria or standards of performance for each learning objective, and specify the evidence to be produced.
3. Develop a rubric matrix, and insert the criteria for product and process in the leftmost column.
4. Determine levels of competence or expertise, and enter labels for those levels in the topmost row.
5. Describe expected student performance for each of the criteria, and enter that information in the appropriate cell for each level.
6. Share the rubric with students before they begin the project.

Rubrics can apply the same scoring weight to all criteria or different weights for different criteria. Weighted rubrics indicate those criteria that have priority over others for certain activities and permit teachers to apply a greater value to some criteria than to others. To create a weighted rubric, you can use a proportional method with cumulative weights summing to 100% or a multiples method (e.g., .5x, 1x, 1.5x, 2x, 3x). However, weighted rubrics should not specify meaningless details, such as the number of pages written.

Table 7–2 is a rubric template that identifies broad educational categories and performance levels. Although it does not necessarily represent a working model for rubric creation, it does demonstrate the use of levels of performance. Those levels are arranged in descending order from left to right. The rubric template describes specific behaviors and examples of performance for each level of performance, with each being inclusive of the lower levels. For example, Level 4 performance presumes that students are competent in performing Levels 3, 2, and 1 as well. Examples of broad educational criteria and corresponding weighting are also included in the template, as is a space for self-evaluation.

Rubrics are an effective assessment tool with Web-enhanced learning activities and should be incorporated into the assessment section of the WEL lesson plan. The rubric should state what the learner will do to demonstrate understanding and mastery of objectives and should describe the assessment process.

| TABLE 7–2 | A Rubric Template for Authentic Assessment | | | | | |
|---|---|---|---|---|---|---|
| **Criterion/ Standard/ Objective** | **4 Expert/ advanced** | **3 Proficient/ intermediate** | **2 Emerging/ competent** | **1 Novice/ beginner** | **0 Incorrect/ no attempt** | **Self- evaluation** |
| Mastery of subject or content 30% | Completes all important components of the task and communicates ideas clearly, demonstrates an in-depth understanding of the relevant concepts or process, and/or makes insightful interpretations or extensions. | Completes most important components of the task and communicates those ideas clearly and/or demonstrates understanding of major concepts but may over-look or misun-derstand some less important ideas or details. | Completes some important components of the task and communicates those clearly but exhibits gaps in understanding. | Shows minimal understanding and/or addresses only a small number of the required tasks. | Response is incorrect or irrelevant. | |
| Process: Ability to investigate and research (20%) | Identifies multiple, valid, authoritative sources of information that clearly relate to the topic and includes supporting details or examples. | Identifies multiple sources of information that relate to the topic, some of which are authoritative, and provides some details or exam-ples for impor-tant concepts. | Identifies multiple sources of information that relate to the topic and includes supporting details or examples. | Identifies multiple sources of information that relate to the topic. | Does not identify sources of information or identifies sources that are irrelevant. | |
| Product: Ability to reflect and apply (40%) | Covers topic in depth with details and examples, demonstrates in-depth understanding of the subject, and makes full use of printed, visual, or audio effects to enhance the product presentation. | Covers most important components of the topic with some details and examples, demonstrates understanding of the subject, and makes use of some printed, visual, or audio effects to enhance the product presentation. | Covers some important components of the topic, demonstrates some understanding of the subject, and makes use of printed, visual, or audio effects for product presentation. | Demonstrates only a minimal understanding of the topic and does not use multimedia to enhance product presentation. | Produces no product or one that is inappropriate or irrelevant. | |
| Team work and/ or collaboration (10%) | Each student on the team can explain what information is needed, what tasks he or she is responsible for performing, and when the infor-mation is needed. | Each student on the team can clearly explain what tasks he or she is responsible for performing. | With some prompting from peers, each student can explain what tasks he or she is responsible for performing. | Each student cannot clearly explain what tasks he or she is responsible for performing. | No effort is made to work cooperatively or participate. | |

### Building Your Toolkit:
## Using RubiStar to Create Rubrics for Assessment

In this exercise you will first complete a tutorial for using an online rubric-creation tool called RubiStar. Then you will create your own rubric for assessing student performance on your own topic. RubiStar is a tool to help teachers create rubrics more quickly and efficiently. It creates rubrics that can be printed and used for projects and research assignments. RubiStar provides sample rubrics that permit teachers to modify the suggested text in the rubric to make it fit the requirements of a particular project.

| STEP | PROCEDURE |
|------|-----------|

**1.**   Open your Web browser and then the RubiStar website at **http://rubistar.4teachers.org/.** Scroll down the page until you see the section labeled **Start Here,** and select the link for **Make a New Rubric** (see Figure 7–7).

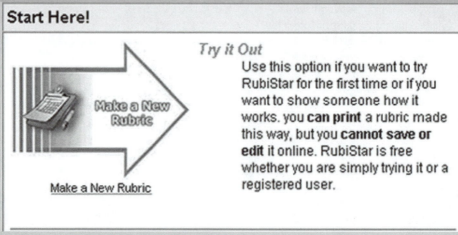

**FIGURE 7–7:    RubiStar Home Page**

*Source:* Development of this resource was supported, in part, by the U.S. Department of Education awards to ALTec (Advanced Learning Technologies) at the University of Kansas Center for Research on Learning. These include Regional Technology in Education Consortium 1995–2002 awards #R302A50008 and #R302A000015. This resource does not necessarily reflect the policies of the U.S. Department of Education.

**2.**   Select a student performance you would like to evaluate. RubiStar provides templates for many topics in the following categories:

- Art
- Math
- Multimedia
- Music
- Oral projects
- Products
- Reading
- Research and writing
- Science
- Work skills

Select a topic that is appropriate for the subject and/or grade level you teach.

**3.**   Enter the following information for your rubric:

- **Your Name**
- **Rubric Project Name**
- **Zip Code**
- **Demonstration Rubric:** Select **Yes, my rubric is a temporary rubric.**

**4.**   Scroll down the page to the **Category** section; RubiStar provides a drop-down list of categories from which to select. Use the pull-down menu in the first row to select the category you want to appear first in your rubric. When you select a category, RubiStar automatically displays assessment information for each permutation in the

*(Continued)*

## Building Your Toolkit:
## Using RubiStar to Create Rubrics for Assessment (Continued)

| STEP | PROCEDURE |
|---|---|

rubric. You can customize the rubric content or keep the default content provided. Next, use the pull-down menu in the second row to select the second category, and then a third or fourth. You do not have to use all the categories; if you do not use some, there should be blank rows at the bottom of your rubric. If you want to have your own customized row, simply leave the drop-down menu at "Please Choose" and enter your own words in the text field. You can then supply the content in each of the text boxes for that particular row.

**5.** You can edit the rating scale (4, 3, 2, 1) by entering your values or descriptors for each column heading.

**6.** When you are finished customizing your rubric, scroll down and click on the **Submit** icon at the bottom of the form to preview your rubric.

**7.** When the preview page is displayed, you can click the **Modify This Rubric** link at the top of the page to make changes to your rubric (see Figure 7–8).

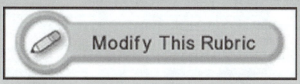

**FIGURE 7–8:   A Link to Modify the Rubric**

*Source:* Development of this resource was supported, in part, by the U.S. Department of Education awards to ALTec (Advanced Learning Technologies) at the University of Kansas Center for Research on Learning. These include Regional Technology in Education Consortium 1995–2002 awards #R302A50008 and #R302A000015. This resource does not necessarily reflect the policies of the U.S. Department of Education.

**8.** You are able to print, download, or make your rubric available online. If you decide to save it, you will be asked to register or log in. There is no fee for doing so.

**9.** If you simply wish to create a paper copy of your rubric or save it on your computer, choose the option **Print or Download** (see Figure 7–9). The saved rubric will be in a format that can be viewed off-line, but it will not be saved in the Rubistar database.

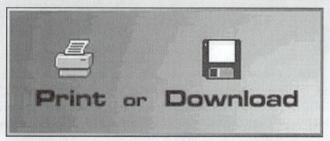

**FIGURE 7–9:   An Option to Print or Download the Rubric**

*Source:* Development of this resource was supported, in part, by the U.S. Department of Education awards to ALTec (Advanced Learning Technologies) at the University of Kansas Center for Research on Learning. These include Regional Technology in Education Consortium 1995–2002 awards #R302A50008 and #R302A000015. This resource does not necessarily reflect the policies of the U.S. Department of Education.

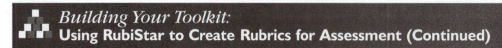

## Building Your Toolkit:
## Using RubiStar to Create Rubrics for Assessment (Continued)

| STEP | PROCEDURE |
|---|---|
| 10. | If you choose the option **Make Available Online,** RubiStar will save your rubric data in its online database (see Figure 7–10). Rubrics that are saved online can be modified at a later date and will be viewable online. Users who choose this option must have an existing account or create a new, free RubiStar account. |

**FIGURE 7–10:    The Option to Make the Rubric
Available Online**

*Source:* Development of this resource was supported, in part, by the U.S. Department of Education awards to ALTec (Advanced Learning Technologies) at the University of Kansas Center for Research on Learning. These include Regional Technology in Education Consortium 1995–2002 awards #R302A50008 and #R302A000015. This resource does not necessarily reflect the policies of the U.S. Department of Education.

> **Go
> to the Companion Website
> and browse *7.3 Building Your
> Toolkit Enrichment Activity:
> More Online Rubric-Building Tools.*
> Practice the skills presented in
> the enrichment activity to create
> rubrics for Web-enhanced
> learning activities.**

| 11. | Share your completed rubric with another person to obtain feedback. |
|---|---|

## REFLECTIONS

Information problem solving can provide positive, engaging learning experiences for students. Using Internet technologies to enhance that problem solving is an essential skill for today's student. Library media specialists, computer teachers, and classroom teachers should work together to develop lessons that include information skills, technology skills, and content-area curriculum outcomes. Information problem-solving models can be used effectively to design learning activities for the classroom. These models include strategies that help students systematically define, investigate, and solve a real-world problem. Information problem-solving models that are useful for planning web-enhanced learning activities include InfoSavvy, the Research Cycle, and the Big6.

Alternative assessment methodologies are needed to evaluate problem-solving activities. Using rubrics to assess students' problem-solving skills allows teaches to be consistent and objective in measuring student achievement.

# EXERCISES TO REVIEW AND EXPAND YOUR SKILLS

## Set 1: Reflecting on Practice

- *Closing the Case.* Timber Drive Elementary School uses an information and technology team comprised of two full-time media specialists, a technology resource teacher, and a network administrator who is also a certified teacher to support the grade-level teachers. How much technology support should schools provide to assist teachers in teaching with technology? How is this support provided in most schools?

- *Closing the Case.* LaDonna Washington and Sara Conley are library media specialists who help students develop information literacy by teaching them how to locate and use information resources. These specialists use an information problem-solving process and partner with classroom teachers. What is the role of the library media specialist in the classroom? How do you want a library media specialist to support teaching and learning in your classroom?

- *Problem-Solving Models.* Several problem-solving models were mentioned in this chapter. What elements do they have in common? Create a table or a matrix that lists the models mentioned in this chapter (as well as others you may find on the Web) across the top row and all the different elements of these models down the leftmost column. Then mark the elements characteristic of each model. Develop your own problem-solving model or research cycle, based on this synthesis.

- *Electronic Portfolios.* Imagine that you have decided that the best way to evaluate student progress in your classroom is to have your students keep portfolios of their learning products. Design a plan that is appropriate for the grade level and/or subject you teach.

  - Will your student portfolios be electronic, print, or both? Explain your choice.

  - How will students create and manage their portfolios? If they are electronic, what software will students use to submit contributions to their portfolios?

  - What artifacts do you want to be included in the portfolios? List the work products and other components, and state the reason for including each artifact.

  - How will you provide feedback for the portfolios? What role will that feedback play in evaluating the portfolios? What role will the portfolios play in student grades?

  - What will you do with the portfolios at the end of the school year?

## Set 2: Expanding Your Skills

- *Graphic Organizers.* The K-W-H-L technique is a good method to help students activate prior knowledge. It is an instructional strategy developed by Donna Ogle (1986) that serves as a model for active thinking. The strategy was originally called the K-W-L because of three questions designed to engage readers in nonfiction texts: What do I **know**? What do I **want** to know? What have I **learned**? The questions were meant to elicit children's prior knowledge and motivate them to learn about a new topic and find answers for their questions. Other educators have added the *H* so that students will also consider **how** they will go about the learning. The how question is intended to prompt students to think of information-gathering ideas, such as browsing and searching the Internet, interviewing an expert, planning a survey, or conducting an experiment.

  A K-W-H-L chart is a simple and effective organizer for planning and gathering information. It can be used to access prior information on a topic or a theme, identify primary and secondary resources to access, develop a plan for accessing those resources, and identify attributes and characteristics to research. The K-W-H-L chart is an excellent tool with which to plan an investigation, it can include questions about predictions and implications. It can also be used to formulate a hypothesis, or research question, with confirmation or refutation emerging as the research progresses. Throughout the process information can be added to the K-W-H-L chart.

The Big6 website and the Graphic Organizer website (**www.graphic.org**) both provide information about K-W-H-L charts. After reviewing that information, prepare your own K-W-H-L chart, using one of the lessons on the Big6 website or a topic of your own choosing.

■ *Scoring Guides.* Another Web tool that is designed to assist teachers in assessing content knowledge and effective use of technology in communicating ideas and information is the Scoring Guide for Student Products. Its developers, the North Central R*TEC and the North Central Regional Laboratory, maintain that a scoring guide is different from a rubric, which is also an instructional tool, whereas a scoring guide primarily focuses on student products and provides an objective assessment based on predetermined standards. Teachers may want to use scoring guides as a basis for developing rubrics.

To create a scoring guide, open the website **http://www.ncrtec.org/tl/ sgsp/** and select **Scoring Guide** from the navigation bar on the left side of the Web page.

- Choose one type of student product to be scored, and click the **Continue** button.
- Select descriptor information for scoring student products, and click the **Generate Preview and Customize Your Guide** button.
- Review the scoring guide you have just created, and then select the **Submit and generate PDF** link to produce a PDF version of your scoring guide. You can display and print your scoring guide by selecting **Your PDF report is ready**.
- Use the scoring guide to create a rubric for a corresponding lesson or project.

## Set 3: Using Productivity and Web-Authoring Tools

■ *Develop an Information Problem-Solving Strategy.* Use a graphic organizer program, such as Inspiration, to create a graphic representation of an information problem-solving strategy that is based on the models presented in this chapter. Create the model as a handout that can be used by students in your classroom for collecting, evaluating, and applying Internet information resources to educational problems.

■ *Write a Parent Letter About an Information Problem-Solving Strategy.* Use word processing to write a letter to parents, explaining your overall information problem-solving strategy. (You may want to include the graphic representation created in the previous exercise.) The letter should include specific strategies parents can use to assist their students in completing classroom projects and homework assignments.

■ *Create a Problem-Solving Template.* With a word processing or a spreadsheet program, create a table template: In the first column name the steps of an information problem-solving strategy, and in the second column describe the tasks to be accomplished at each step. In the third column have each student describe the information-searching and -evaluating tasks he or she will perform for that step of the problem-solving strategy. At the top of your template document, describe an educational problem that students can solve using Internet information resources (see the following example).

**PROBLEM: Find out the nutritional value of a fast food meal.**

| Information problem-solving step (Big6) | Description of task | How I plan to do this task |
|---|---|---|
| Step 1: Task definition | Define the problem and identify the information needed | |
| Step 2: Information-seeking strategies | Brainstorm all possible sources and select the best | |
| Step 3: Location and access | Locate sources and find information within sources | |

## Set 4: Creating Your Own Web-Enhanced Project

- *WEL Lesson Plan Using the Big6.* The Big6 integrates information-searching skills and technology tools into a systematic process to find, use, apply, and evaluate information to meet specific needs. You can use the Big6 model to support Web-enhanced learning, incorporating the steps into the procedures section of the lesson plan. Using the Big6 steps and the lesson plan template, design a WEL lesson plan for a project called "A Nutritious Meal." Modify the components in Figure 7–11 to be appropriate for the grade level you teach.)

- *Rubrics.* Use the following template to develop a rubric for the assessment of the nutritious meal project. Use the objectives to help you develop the rubric.

| Competency | Superior | Good | Satisfactory | Unsatisfactory |
|---|---|---|---|---|
| Accuracy | | | Substantiates opinion based on information found in solving the problem; provides a reasonable solution | |
| Appearance | | | Readable and neat | |
| Mechanics | | | Uses correct punctuation, spelling, grammar, paragraph formation | |
| Organization | | | Organized and coherent | |

| **FIGURE 7–11** | **A Lesson Plan for Web-Enhanced Project** |
|---|---|
| Title/topic | A Nutritious Meal |
| Problem/task | • To find out how nutritious a fast food meal is<br>• To develop a menu for a nutritious meal<br>   (Use information from Step 1 of the Big6.) |
| Curriculum area | Science/health |
| Grade level | 6–8 |

(Contiuned)

| FIGURE 7–11 | A Lesson Plan for Web-Enhanced Project (Continued) |
|---|---|

**Standards of learning**

Benchmarks for Science Learning from the American Association for the Advancement of Science state: Students should extend their study of the healthy functioning of the human body and ways it may be promoted or disrupted by diet, lifestyle, bacteria, and viruses. Students should consider the effects of tobacco, alcohol, and other drugs on the way the body functions. They should start reading the labels on food products and considering what healthful diets could be like. By the end of the 8th grade, students should know that

- The amount of food energy (calories) a person requires varies with body weight, age, sex, activity level, and natural body efficiency. Regular exercise is important to maintain a healthy heart/lung system, good muscle tone, and bone strength.
- Toxic substances, some dietary habits, and some personal behavior may be bad for one's health. Some effects show up right away; others may not show up for many years. Avoiding toxic substances, such as tobacco, and changing dietary habits to reduce the intake of such things as animal fat increase the chances of living longer.

**Objectives**

- Describe the nutritional content of a typical fast food meal.
- Plan a menu for a healthy meal that includes nutritional information.

**Procedures**

[Use the Big6 steps here.]

**1. Task definition:**
Identify the information requirements of the problem.

_____
_____
_____

**2. Information-seeking strategies:**
Determine the range of possible sources.

_____
_____
_____

Evaluate the different possible sources to determine priorities.

_____
_____
_____

**3. Location and access:**
Locate sources.

_____
_____
_____

Find information within sources.

_____
_____
_____

**4. Use of information:**
Engage the information in a source.

_____
_____
_____

Extract relevant information from a source.

_____
_____
_____

| FIGURE 7–11 | A Lesson Plan for Web-Enhanced Project (Continued) |
|---|---|

**5. Synthesis:**

Organize information from multiple sources.

_____

_____

_____

Present the information.

_____

_____

_____

**6. Evaluation:**

Judge the product (effectiveness).

_____

_____

_____

Judge the information problem-solving process (efficiency).

_____

_____

_____

| | |
|---|---|
| Resources | • USDA website: http://www.usda.gov<br>• USDA Nutrition website: http://www.nutrition.gov<br>• USDA Nutrient Data Laboratory: http://www.nal.usda.gov/fnic/foodcomp/<br>  [Use information from Step 2 of the Big6 here.] |
| Teaching/learning strategies | This project can be performed through independent learning or within small groups. |
| Assessment | Students should identify the nutritional values of typical fast food items and should plan a menu that includes healthy foods. |
| Credits/references | Reprint by permission from the Project 2061 website: www.project2061.org/tools/benchol/ch6/ch6.htm# PhysicalHealth_6_8 © 2003 by the American Association for the Advancement of Science. |

Alternate version for K–2 teachers (Super3 is early childhood version of Big6):

| | |
|---|---|
| Procedures | **1. Beginning** [corresponds to Steps 1 and 2]:<br>When students get an assignment or a task, they should stop and think before they start doing anything:<br>• What am I supposed to do?<br>• What will it look like if I do a really good job?<br>• What do I need to find out to do the job?<br><br>**2. Middle** [corresponds to Steps 3 and 4]:<br>Here students do the activity; they read, view, tell, make a picture.<br>**3. End** [corresponds to Steps 5 and 6]:<br>Before finishing and turning in the product, students should stop and think:<br>• Is this done?<br>• Did I do what I was supposed to do?<br>• Do I feel OK about this?<br>• Should I do something else before I turn it in? |

# REFERENCES

Barrows, H. S. (1985). *How to design a problem-based curriculum for the preclinical years*. New York: Springer.

Dabbagh, N. (2003). Scaffolding: An important teacher competency in online learning. *Tech Trends, 47*(2), 39–44.

Eisenberg, M., & Berkowitz, R. (1990). *Information problem-solving: The Big Six skills approach to library & information skills instruction*. Norwood, NJ: Ablex.

Eisenberg, M., & Berkowitz, R. (1996). *Helping with homework: A parent's guide to information problem-solving*. Syracuse, NY: ERIC Clearinghouse on Information & Technology.

Jukes, I., Dosaj, A., Macdonald, B. (2000). *NetSavvy: Building information literacy in the classroom*. Thousand Oaks, CA: Corwin Press.

Mayer, R. E. (2001). *Multimedia learning*. Cambridge, UK: Cambridge University Press.

McKenzie, J. (2000). Beyond technology: Questioning, research, and the information literate school. Bellingham, WA: FNO Press. Also available at http://www.fnopress.com/

Moursund, D. (1999). *Project-based learning using information technology*. Eugene, OR: International Society for Technology in Education.

Ogle, D. (1986). The K-W-L: A teaching model that develops active reading of expository text. *The Reading Teacher, 39,* 564–570.

Pearson Education Development Group. (2003). *Authentic assessment overview*. Retrieved April 28, 2003, from http://www.teachervision.com/lesson-plans/lesson-4911.html

Stepien, W. J., Gallagher, S. A., & Workman, D. (1993). Problem-based learning for traditional and interdisciplinary classrooms. *Journal for the Education of the Gifted, 4,* 338–345.

Wiggins, G. (1990). The case for authentic assessment. *Practical Assessment, Research & Evaluation, 2*(2). Also available at http://PAREonline.net/getvr.asp?v=2&n=2

# CHAPTER 8

# Using the Internet for Cooperative Problem Solving

High-school students at Monticello High School recently used the Internet to go back in history and become participants in the Constitutional Convention, explorers on the Lewis and Clark expedition, Civil War soldiers, and astronauts preparing to make the first trip to the moon. The project, Back to America's Future, was designed to give ninth graders the opportunity to research historical events and to analyze and reflect on their impact in view of current developments.

The project was a collaboration between ninth-grade English teacher Jennifer Allison and American history teacher David Chang. They designed a WebQuest that allowed ninth graders in their classes to use computers and the Internet to develop creative writing and research skills. The project was intended to help students identify, analyze, and synthesize historically accurate information and create a work product from their research.

Using the computer lab in the library, students worked in cooperative groups, searching websites and reading at least five stories or articles about their event. Student teams then wrote a diary from the perspective of a character in the event they were researching. And they diagrammed a concept map to illustrate the impact of their historical event on certain current developments. Student projects were posted on the school's website so that other teachers and students could view them. The project went so well that Ms. Allison and Mr. Chang plan to do a second project, in addition to working with other teachers to create multidisciplinary WebQuests.

## NEW TERMS

cooperative learning                                    Web inquiry project
WebQuest

| National Educational Technology Standards for Teachers | National Educational Technology Standards for Students |
|---|---|
| The following NETS•T are addressed by the lesson content and learning activities in this chapter: | The following NETS•S are addressed by the lesson content and learning activities in this chapter: |

**National Educational Technology Standards for Teachers**

The following NETS•T are addressed by the lesson content and learning activities in this chapter:

**II. Planning and designing**

  **A.** Design technology-enhanced learning opportunities to support diverse needs

  **B.** Apply current research on teaching and learning with technology

  **C.** Identify, locate, and evaluate technology resources

  **D.** Plan for the management of technology resources

  **E.** Manage student learning in a technology-enhanced environment

**III. Teaching, Learning, and the Curriculum**

  **A.** Facilitate technology-enhanced experiences to address standards

  **B.** Use technology to support learner-centered strategies

  **C.** Apply technology to develop students' higher order skills

  **D.** Manage student learning activities

**National Educational Technology Standards for Students**

The following NETS•S are addressed by the lesson content and learning activities in this chapter:

**3. Technology Productivity Tools**

- Use technology to enhance learning, increase productivity, and promote creativity
- Use tools to collaborate, prepare publications, and produce creative works

**5. Technology Research Tools**

- Use technology to locate, evaluate, and collect information
- Use technology tools to process data and report results
- Evaluate and select new information resources and technology

**6. Technology Problem-Solving and Decision-Making Tools**

- Use technology to solve problems and make decisions
- Employ technology to develop real-world problem-solving strategies

## OVERVIEW

Cooperative learning activities are the key to effective Web-enhanced learning in the classroom. Cooperative problem solving can utilize teams or groups of students within the same classroom or in classrooms in multiple locations. Synchronous and asynchronous communication tools can facilitate the exchange of ideas among distant participants or even among students in the same classroom.

WebQuests are a widely used teaching and learning tool to create cooperative problem-solving activities. WebQuests are inquiry-oriented activities in which most or all of the information used by learners is acquired from the World Wide Web. WebQuests focus on using information to create knowledge. Their educational rationale is to engage learners in real-world learning activities, develop critical-thinking skills, and support teamwork and cooperation.

The WebQuest instructional model is comprised of several components: an introduction, a task, the process for accomplishing the task, the resources (usually Web-based) used to accomplish the task, an evaluation, and a conclusion. Before trying to create a new WebQuest for a particular lesson, you should search through the thousands of WebQuests already available on the Web and see whether any existing ones are appropriate for your use. If not, several design tools are available on the Web to help you in adapting or creating your own WebQuests, and this chapter discusses several of them.

## Lesson 8.1   Understanding the WebQuest Model

### FOCUS QUESTIONS

- What is a WebQuest, and how is it used in the classroom?
- What is the educational rationale for WebQuests?
- What are some of the instructional features of cooperative learning?
- What are the instructional components of the WebQuest model?

## ■ A BRIEF HISTORY OF WEBQUESTS

**WebQuests** are inquiry-oriented activities in which most or all of the information used by learners is acquired from the World Wide Web (Dodge, 1997). WebQuests focus on using information to create knowledge, rather than just looking for information; thus, they support the development of higher level thinking skills. According to Tom March (1998b), WebQuests were designed to bring together the most effective instructional practices in one integrated student activity, maximizing student learning in a most efficient way.

A WebQuest is an interactive learning activity that uses a variety of Internet resources and guides students through a sequence of steps to organize their learning. The WebQuest model was developed in early 1995 at San Diego State University by Bernie Dodge with Tom March. Dodge, a professor of educational technology, developed the concept of WebQuests while teaching a class for preservice teachers in the spring of 1995. He wanted to provide his student teachers with a format for online lessons that would make the best use of student time, while fostering higher level thinking skills. Soon thereafter, Tom March, a Pacific Bell Fellow at San Diego State at the time, constructed the first fully developed WebQuest as part of PacBell's Knowledge Network (now SBC Knowledge Network).

Dodge wrote a paper on the topic, "Some Thoughts About WebQuests," which was widely read (see http://webquest.sdsu.edu/about_webquests.html). Many teachers started to adopt the technique, and both staff development coordinators and teacher educators began using the WebQuest site as a source of training and course materials. As the Website grew, it developed links to WebQuests created all over the world.

## ■ EDUCATIONAL PRINCIPLES OF WEBQUESTS

Tom March (1998b) explained the threefold rationale behind the instructional features of a WebQuest: engaging learners in real-world learning activities, developing critical-thinking skills, and supporting teamwork and cooperation.

- *Real-world learning*—WebQuests use several strategies to increase student motivation. They pose a central question based in the real world, thereby presenting students with authentic tasks. That relevance can motivate students, as does their use of real resources as they access online information and experts.
- *Higher-order thinking*—WebQuests use the rich resources of the Web to provide a large amount of information and multiple perspectives, which students must filter through until they have constructed a deep understanding of the issue. WebQuests break learning tasks into meaningful chunks and ask students to undertake specific subtasks, requiring them to transform information into useful knowledge.
- *Teamwork*—Because a WebQuest targets a complex or controversial topic, no student is expected to master all of its aspects. However, when students take on roles within a cooperative group or team, they must develop expertise on one particular

aspect or perspective, and each student's participation in the cooperative learning process has a direct impact on the collective understanding of the group, which is expressed through the final product. The answer or the solution a student team develops becomes an authentic assessment that can be posted, e-mailed, or presented to real people for feedback and evaluation. And authentic assessment motivates students to develop a real answer, not just something that fulfills an assignment.

Christie (2002) identified several of the same and several additional features of WebQuests:

- WebQuests encourage students to use reasoning skills in a problem-solving process that promotes deep understanding and meaningful learning.
- WebQuests require students to use critical-thinking skills to interpret, analyze, evaluate, and draw inferences from the information obtained.
- WebQuests use a collaborative process of discovery to facilitate learning.
- WebQuests promote the development of social skills, such as listening, cooperating, affirming others, giving constructive criticism, and accepting multiple perspectives. Participation can also promote multiculturalism and appreciation of diversity.
- WebQuests facilitate reflection as students analyze and evaluate their own thinking and problem-solving processes.
- WebQuests foster interdisciplinary learning by making connections across content areas in the curriculum.

WebQuests provide a methodology for connecting Web-enhanced learning activities to the curriculum. In addition, students can internalize the WebQuest model of cooperative problem solving and apply it as a learning strategy to guide their own independent studies.

## ■ COOPERATIVE LEARNING

**Cooperative learning** is the instructional use of small groups to maximize individual and group learning (Johnson, Johnson, & Holubec, 1990). It is a set of processes that help people interact to accomplish a specific goal or end product. Compared to collaborative learning, cooperative learning entails more structure and teacher direction and is more appropriate with well-defined, well-structured problems. Many structured, technology-based activities are easily performed with cooperative learning groups—for example, research projects that involve the use of online resources and the development of multimedia products (Roblyer, 2003).

WebQuests are generally conducted with cooperative learning groups. In the opening scenario of this chapter, Ms. Allison and Mr. Chang used cooperative learning groups to organize their historical WebQuest project; students conducted their research and prepared their writing projects in teams. Figure 8–1 lists several features of effective cooperative learning groups, as identified by Johnson and Johnson (1999).

## ■ WEBQUEST COMPONENTS

The WebQuest site defines a WebQuest as a "constructivist lesson format used widely around the world" (see http://www.webquest.org). Bernie Dodge (1997) called the WebQuest model a lesson with several components, or building blocks, which can be reconfigured in many ways to accomplish a broad range of learning goals. As was mentioned earlier, the original WebQuest model had six components: an introduction, a task, the process for accomplishing the task, the resources (usually Web-based) to accomplish the

| **FIGURE 8–1** | **Elements of Cooperative Learning Groups (Johnson & Johnson, 1999)** |
| --- | --- |

1. **Positive interdependence.** Group members work together to accomplish a common goal, understanding that they need each other for support, explanations, and guidance.

2. **Individual accountability.** Individual performance is assessed against a standard, and members are held responsible for their contributions to achieving group goals.

3. **Face-to-face communication.** Group members interact face-to-face in ways that promote each other's learning.

4. **Interpersonal skills.** Interpersonal skills—such as giving constructive feedback, reaching consensus, and involving every member—are necessary for small groups to function effectively and must be taught and practiced before groups initiate a learning task.

5. **Group processing.** Group members reflect on their collaborative efforts and decide on ways to improve effectiveness.

task, an evaluation, and a conclusion. Some templates for the WebQuest model may also include credits and references or a page providing information for teachers. The current WebQuest model combines process and resources into a single component and is usually organized as a Web page with multiple sections or as a set of linked Web pages.

- *Introduction.* The introduction page or section of a WebQuest addresses the student and introduces the activity or lesson. The introduction is intended to be a hook that motivates the student to learn more by providing a real-world context for the learning activity. The introduction also includes the guiding or central question of the WebQuest. Although the introduction can provide an overview of the learning activity, its primary purpose is to engage the learner.

- *The task.* The task page or section clearly describes what the result of the WebQuest will be, usually a product that students will create, such as a PowerPoint presentation or a database of information. The task is a creative work of some kind that requires students to transform the information they collect and synthesize into useful knowledge.

- *The process.* The process page or section is a list of recommended or suggested steps that students should undertake to accomplish the task. This section would also include the Web-based resources that students should use. In addition, it might address specific skills needed for the lesson—such as brainstorming, teamwork, or role-playing—and might describe how to organize the information collected.

- *Evaluation.* The evaluation section of a WebQuest clearly describes how student performance will be evaluated. Usually a rubric is used to examine different aspects of the students' product and process. The rubric should establish benchmarks for multiple levels of performance or accomplishment and should specify how grading will relate to both group and individual performance on the task.

- *Conclusion.* The conclusion page or section summarizes what students have accomplished or learned by completing the WebQuest. The conclusion can present questions about the task to stimulate whole-class discussion or to debrief the class on the WebQuest. The conclusion can also include reflective questions and additional links to encourage students to extend their learning.

- *Credits and references.* The credits and references page or section contains a description of sources used in the creation of the WebQuest. It should list both online and off-line sources of images, music, text, or other content and should provide links back to the original source when appropriate. This section can also acknowledge anyone who helped create the WebQuest.

## Building Your Toolkit:
## Searching The WebQuest Portal

The best way to start using WebQuests is to find a good one in the WebQuest portal (**http://www.webquest.org**) of the WebQuest site (**http://webquest.sdsu.edu**). The WebQuest portal is basically an index to hundreds of WebQuests that have been developed by teachers and students. It allows you to search, rate, and comment on WebQuests and see the newest submissions. To help you become familiar with what WebQuests look like and how they work, the following activity has you locate two or three WebQuests for your curriculum area or grade level, review them, and then use the online rating form to rate them.

### STEP   PROCEDURE

**1.**   Open your Web browser and then the WebQuest portal site at **http://www.webquest.org**. On the left side of the screen you should see links for Top, Middling, and New. These are the quality categories, based on user ratings, of the WebQuests indexed on this site.

- *Top* refers to WebQuests that have been evaluated and found to be good examples of the WebQuest model. Thus, they may not require any modifications.
- *Middling* refers to WebQuests that have been evaluated and found to have a number of good features. They may need some modifications or adaptations to be effective.
- *New* refers to newly submitted WebQuests that have not yet been evaluated.

**2.**   Select the **Search** link from the menu to perform a search of the WebQuest index. The search form looks similar to that in Figure 8–2. Read the suggestions below the examples.

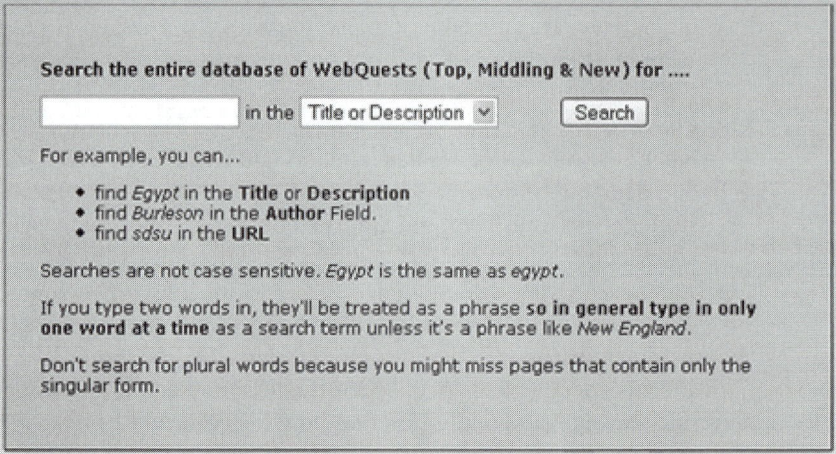

**Search the entire database of WebQuests (Top, Middling & New) for ....**

[        ] in the [ Title or Description ▼ ]   [ Search ]

For example, you can...

- find *Egypt* in the **Title** or **Description**
- find *Burleson* in the **Author** Field.
- find *sdsu* in the **URL**

Searches are not case sensitive. *Egypt* is the same as *egypt*.

If you type two words in, they'll be treated as a phrase **so in general type in only one word at a time** as a search term unless it's a phrase like *New England*.

Don't search for plural words because you might miss pages that contain only the singular form.

**FIGURE 8–2:   The WebQuest Search Form**
*Source:* Retrieved from http://www.webquest.org. Reproduced with permission.

**3.**   Enter search criteria (i.e., keywords) that represent a topic or curriculum area appropriate for the grade level or subject you teach. Perform the search of the keywords in the **Title or Description option,** and click the **Search** button.

**4.**   On the hit list find a WebQuest that would be appropriate, and review it by clicking through its pages. Notice the following features, which are rated with the WebQuest Rating Form:

- The *overall aesthetics* are appropriate, and thematic graphic elements are used to make visual connections that contribute to the understanding of concepts, ideas, and relationships. Differences in type size and/or color are used well and consistently. Navigation is seamless. It is always clear to the learner what all the pieces are and how to get to them. There are no broken links, misspellings, or grammatical errors.

*(Continued)*

### Building Your Toolkit:
## Searching The WebQuest Portal (Continued)

| STEP | PROCEDURE |
|---|---|

- The *introduction* draws the reader into the lesson by relating to the learner's interests or goals and/or engagingly describing a compelling question or problem. It builds on the learner's prior knowledge and effectively prepares the learner by foreshadowing what the lesson is about.

- The *task* is referenced to standards and is clearly connected to what students must know and be able to do to achieve proficiency. The task is doable and engaging and elicits thinking that goes beyond rote comprehension. The task requires synthesizing multiple sources of information and/or taking a position and/or going beyond the data given and making a generalization or creative product.

- Every step in the WebQuest learning *process* is clearly stated so that most students would know exactly where they were at each step of the process and what to do next. The process provides students coming in at different entry levels with strategies and organizational tools to gain the knowledge needed to complete the task. Activities are clearly related and designed to take students from basic knowledge to higher level thinking. Checks for understanding are built in.

- There is a clear and meaningful connection between all the *resources* and the information needed for students to accomplish the task. Every resource carries its weight. Links make excellent use of the Web's timeliness and colorfulness. Varied resources provide enough meaningful information for students to think deeply.

- *Evaluation* criteria for success are clearly stated in the form of a rubric. Criteria include qualitative as well as quantitative descriptors. The evaluation instrument clearly measures what students must know and be able to do to accomplish the task.

> **Go to the Companion Website and browse *8.1 Building Your Toolkit Enrichment Activity: Using the WebQuest Matrix and Adding a New WebQuest to the Database*. Practice the skills presented in the enrichment activity to submit WebQuests you create to the WebQuest matrix database.**

**5.** You can find a rubric for evaluating WebQuests at **http://webquest.sdsu.edu/webquestrubric.html**. Use this rubric to help you review the WebQuest.

**6.** After you have finished reviewing the WebQuest, close the window in which the WebQuest is displayed to return to the hit list window.
Select the **Rate It** link for the WebQuest you reviewed, complete a WebQuest Rating Form, and submit it.

**7.** Repeat this search, review, and rating process for two or three WebQuests.

## Lesson 8.2 Adapting Existing WebQuests for the Classroom

### FOCUS QUESTIONS

- When should you adapt an existing WebQuest, and when should you create a new WebQuest?
- What is the process for adapting an existing WebQuest to meet classroom or curriculum learning goals?

### ■ A PROCESS FOR ADAPTING AND ENHANCING WEBQUESTS

Before trying to create a new WebQuest for a particular lesson, you should search through the thousands of WebQuests already available on the World Wide Web to see whether any existing ones are appropriate for your purposes. For example, Ms. Allison and Mr. Chang were able to locate numerous WebQuests on researching events in American history to help with their Back to America's Future project.

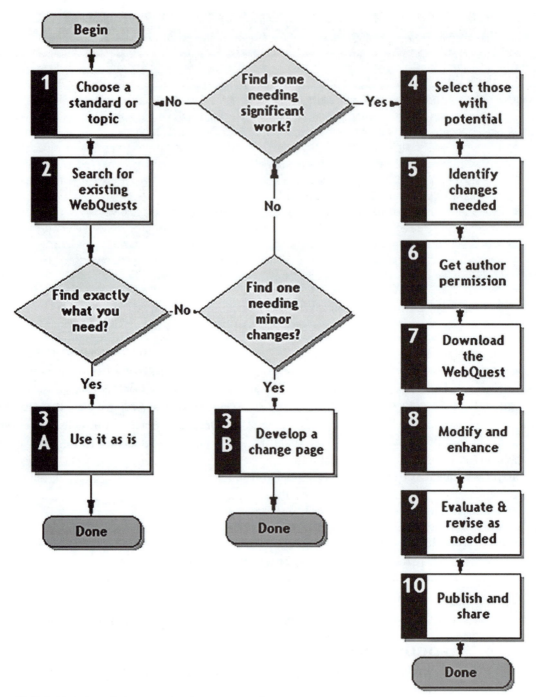

**FIGURE 8–3:    A Process for Adapting or Enhancing WebQuests**

*Source:* Retrieved from http://webquest.sdsu.edu.adapting. Reproduced with permission.

When searching for existing WebQuests for your classroom use, remember that a Web page or a website that calls itself a WebQuest may not have been created with WebQuest design principles. For that reason, the WebQuest site recommends a process for adapting existing WebQuests to your particular curriculum priorities and learning goals (http://webquest.sdsu.edu/adapting/). The diagram in Figure 8–3 illustrates the steps, which are described here by Dodge (2002). This simple process is also applicable to the design and development of other kinds of Web-enhanced learning activities.

### *Step 1: Choose a standard or topic*

Designing and developing lessons usually begins with identifying a curriculum standard. What do you want your students to know and/or do at the end of the learning activity? Thus, before you start searching for resources, you need to establish your learning goals and objectives, choosing goals that can be facilitated by the rich reserve of information on the Web. The WebQuest model should be used for learning activities that will require critical-thinking skills, such as analysis, synthesis, problem solving, decision making, and creativity.

### *Step 2: Search for existing WebQuests*

Finding existing WebQuests is not a problem; finding one that matches the learning goals you defined in Step 1 may be a little more difficult. However, the first place to look is the WebQuest portal (http://www.webquest.org). Many of these WebQuests have been selectively chosen from submissions and other sites on the Web, but many have not been recently updated, and some (or many) of the links contained in them may be out-of-date. You can use the search engine in the WebQuest portal or simply browse through the appropriate subject and grade level in the WebQuest matrix.

### *Step 3: Determine whether a WebQuest can be used as presented*

Because many WebQuests are created by highly talented and skilled educators, it is possible that you will find a WebQuest on your chosen topic that is educationally sound. It may be well developed and need no adaptation to your identified goals and objectives. In that case, if you can use a WebQuest without changing anything, you can skip the next seven steps. On the other hand, if you find a WebQuest that needs minor changes—perhaps classroom resources are different, or the WebQuest is a few years old and many of the Internet resources are no longer available (or the URLs have changed)—then you can create a change page. A change page is simply a Web or printed document created to accompany the existing WebQuest and provide information on how to modify the lesson for your classroom setting.

However, if you find an existing WebQuest that presents the information you need but is not quite right for your situation, you will need to continue to Step 4. If you are unable to locate a WebQuest that even comes close to your specified goals, you will learn to create original WebQuests later in this chapter.

### *Step 4: Select high-quality WebQuests*

When adapting a WebQuest, it is best to work with one that is educationally sound. A high-quality WebQuest contains several important features:

- The links all work and are up-to-date.
- The Web pages or printed documents are visually appealing and free of spelling, grammatical, and technical errors.
- The task is engaging and requires higher-level thinking.
- What is learned from the WebQuest aligns well with your learning goals and objectives.
- The readability level and the manner of presentation are appropriate for your class.

If three out of five of these features are found in the WebQuest, it is probably worth the effort to adapt it for your classroom.

### *Step 5: Identify changes to the WebQuest*

You should examine each of your WebQuest selections in detail, using the WebQuest evaluation rubric (http://webquest.sdsu.edu/webquestrubric.html). You can assign a score to each and then select the WebQuest with the highest score to adapt. You should generate a to-do list for each component of the WebQuest that you choose to adapt.

### *Step 6: Get author permission*

Just because information can be easily accessed on the Internet does not mean that it is legal or free to copy it. Unless the author of a WebQuest has explicitly given permission for others to modify and repost the work, you should ask the author for permission to use it or parts of it.

Tracking down WebQuest authors is generally a simple task; they usually put their e-mail addresses on the WebQuest document. If, however, the WebQuest was written by a university student who has since graduated, you can try contacting the faculty member who taught the course.

In your e-mail to request permission, you should tell who you are and how you plan to use the WebQuest, in addition to giving a general description of your planned adaptations. You should tell the author that you would like to include the following statement with your version of the WebQuest and thank the author in the credits section:

> *Permission is hereby granted for other educators to copy this WebQuest, update or otherwise modify it, and post it elsewhere, provided that the original author's name is retained along with a link to the original URL of this WebQuest.*

If you cannot locate the author, the best approach is to pick another WebQuest to adapt. However, it is implicit in the submission process to a reviewed site, such as the WebQuest portal, that a WebQuest is available for use by others. Therefore, you can proceed with caution to use such a WebQuest but should include a statement that you were unable to locate the author to obtain formal permission and will retract the page if the author objects. You should include the original author's name in the credits section, just as you would if you had obtained formal permission.

### Step 7: Download the WebQuest

It is easy to retrieve a simple one-page WebQuest. With the page displayed in your browser, you should select **File > Save As,** enter a file name, and select a location to save the file on your computer. You will usually get the Web page file and all associated graphics. Another approach is to copy and paste the Web page and graphics into a word processing document.

### Step 8: Modify and enhance

As you begin making modifications to the WebQuest, you can use the to-do list you created in Step 5. Additional resources are available on the WebQuest site to help you modify and enhance an existing WebQuest:

- **Fine Points** (http://webquest.sdsu.edu/finepoints/) is a set of 14 small changes that can make a big difference in how professional your WebQuest pages appear.
- **Sources of Graphics** (http://webquest.sdsu.edu/graphics.html) provides links to a number of clip art resources that are available for free.

### Step 9: Evaluate and revise as needed

You should have a colleague review your WebQuest pages or documents for language mechanics and for appropriateness and accuracy of content and presentation. In addition, it is always good to try out your WebQuest with real learners in a real learning environment. (This is called *beta testing*.) You should observe them using the WebQuest and also allow them to provide written or oral feedback. After testing is complete, you can review the feedback and determine what changes need to be made. When all revisions are in place, you can evaluate your new version with the WebQuest evaluation rubric.

### Step 10: Publish and share

You can showcase the new and improved WebQuest by submitting it to the WebQuest portal so that others can use it or adapt it. You can also showcase it on your school or classroom website.

## Building Your Toolkit: Adapting a WebQuest

Go to the Companion Website and browse *8.2 Building Your Toolkit Enrichment Activity: The WebQuest Taxonomy.* Use the information in the enrichment activity to write appropriate tasks for WebQuests you adapt for use in your classroom.

The best way to start using WebQuests is to find a good WebQuest in the WebQuest portal. In the 8.1 toolkit exercise you searched the WebQuest portal and identified two or three WebQuests that you would like to adapt for your classroom. Now, pick one of these WebQuests and follow the steps for adapting and enhancing a WebQuest in order to create a WebQuest that is appropriate for the grade level and/or subject you teach. You can create the WebQuest as a word processing document.

## Lesson 8.3    Creating Original WebQuests for the Classroom

### FOCUS QUESTIONS

- What is the design process for creating new WebQuests?
- What questions should you ask when deciding to create new WebQuests?

### ■ USING THE WEBQUEST DESIGN PROCESS

Tina Simpson has been using WebQuests with her third graders for several years. In one of her most popular WebQuests, Virtual Bug Hunt, her third graders use the Internet to locate information on various kinds of insects and then create a multimedia virtual insect collection. To complete the WebQuest, her students read articles or reports and use Internet and classroom resources to identify each insect species and then complete data worksheets about all the bugs in their collections. Finally, students use a graphics program to invent and name an insect of their own. Ms. Simpson then links the virtual insect collections to her classroom website for parents and other students to see.

When you are unable to locate an appropriate WebQuest to adapt to your curricular goals, you may want to design and develop your own. Dr. Alice Christie (2002), a professor of technology and education at Arizona State University, has extensive experience teaching her students how to create WebQuests. On her website she offers this advice about designing WebQuests:

> A WebQuest is not much different from creating any kind of lesson. It requires getting your learners oriented, giving them an interesting and doable task, giving them the resources they need and guidance to complete the task, telling them how they'll be evaluated, and then summarizing and extending the lesson.

In creating the Virtual Bug Hunt WebQuest, Ms. Simpson was able to locate a number of WebQuests on researching information about insects, but none really accomplished all of the specific curricular goals she had set for the project. So she decided to create her own WebQuest. Tom March (1998a) says that developing a WebQuest is not necessarily a linear activity. On his website (see http://www.ozline.com/webquests/design1.html) he recommends a process for designing and developing WebQuests that includes choosing the topic and clustering it in its logical components, identifying learning gaps in the curriculum that can be addressed with WebQuests, and acquiring appropriate Web resources.

- *Choose and chunk the topic.* The best WebQuests address complex issues or problems or require students to perform a complex task. March (1998a) suggests that you ask the following questions about your topic to determine whether it is appropriate for a WebQuest.
  - Is the topic worth the time and effort needed to build this WebQuest?
  - Is the level of potential student learning worth the effort?
  - Is a WebQuest the right teaching and learning strategy?
  - Are you excited by the available resources (both online and off-line)?
  - Does the Web offer enough information to warrant its use?
  - Does the question ask something important?
  - Is the answer to the question open to interpretation or argument or hypothesis?

The most important aspect of a WebQuest is its question. Answering the question should require students to employ higher order thinking skills. To uncover the main question and devise roles for learners, you should chunk the topic into its component parts and cluster these parts into subcategories.

- *Identify learning gaps.* You should look for learning gaps in the curriculum and then use these as questions in stating the task for the WebQuest. WebQuests are best used when the learning goals include critical-thinking skills, problem-solving abilities, or team building and cooperative learning.
- *Inventory resources.* You can find related websites and build a hotlist by searching or browsing other hotlists. For example, you can look through the hotlist category in Blue Web'n (http://www.kn.pacbell.com/wired/bluewebn/) or use a search engine to find someone else's hotlist on the topic. The hotlist feature of Filamentality (http://www.filamentality.com/wired/fil/) is useful for gathering websites. You can also use the clusters you identified earlier as search terms.

You can adapt the WEL lesson plan for use in WebQuest projects by adding the components of the WebQuest model. Figure 8–4 gives a template that you can use in planning and creating WebQuest projects.

| **FIGURE 8–1** | **Lesson Plan Template for WebQuest Projects** |
|---|---|
| Title/topic | *State an interesting, attention-getting title.* |
| Author information | *State author's name, school or organization, and e-mail address.* |
| Curriculum area | *State the curriculum subject area to which the learning activity relates.* |
| Grade level | *State the grade level or range for which the learning task is appropriate.* |
| Standards of learning | *State subject-specific standards and grade-specific technology standards to be addressed by the project.* |
| Objectives | *State the learning goals, objectives, or purpose of the project relative to the curriculum and technology standards.* |
| Introduction | *Describe the context of the project in a way that will generate learner interest. Include the guiding or central question.* |
| Task | *Describe the problem or task learners will solve or perform and the creative work learners will produce to demonstrate that they have transformed collected information into useful knowledge.* |

*(Continued)*

| FIGURE 8–4 | Lesson Plan Template for WebQuest Projects (Continued) |
|---|---|
| Process | *Describe the steps the learner should follow to complete the project, including procedures for interaction among participants. State what Web resources are available, what learning strategies are needed—such as brainstorming, teamwork, or role-playing—and how collected information should be organized.* |
| Evaluation | *Describe how learner performance will be evaluated. State what assessment process (i.e., rubrics) will be used to determine whether learners have understood the lesson. State the person(s) who will perform the assessment, the format for the assessment, the assessment deadline, and distribution of assessment results.* |
| Conclusion | *Summarize what learners have accomplished, and present questions about the task to stimulate whole-class discussion or to use for debriefing. Include reflective questions and additional links to encourage learners to extend their learning.* |
| Credits and references | *List both online and off-line sources of images, music, text, or other content that were used, and provide links to the original source when appropriate. Acknowledge anyone who helped create the WebQuest.* |

## Building Your Toolkit:
### Building WebQuests with Filamentality

To create a WebQuest using Filamentality, you should first complete a WEL lesson plan for a WebQuest project. (You can download the template file, **WELWebQuestProject.doc,** from the Companion Website and save it on your computer.) Use the information in the project lesson plan in Figure 8–5 to build a WebQuest with Filamentality in the tutorial that follows.

| FIGURE 8–5 | Project Lesson Plan for a WebQuest |
|---|---|
| Title/topic | Who's the Greatest President of All? |
| Author information | Enter your name and school/college. |
| Curriculum area | Social Studies |
| Grade level | 4–6 |
| Standards of learning | • Students understand the shared ideals and the diversity of American society and political culture.<br>• Students explain the principles and ideals of the American republican system.<br>• Students recognize important founding fathers and their contributions. |
| Objectives | State the learning goals, objectives, or purpose of the project relative to the curriculum and technology standards. |
| Introduction | Remember in the fairy tale *Sleeping Beauty* that the wicked witch would ask her magic mirror, "Mirror, mirror on the wall, who's the fairest of them all?" You are going to look at some of the presidents of the United States and ask, "Who's the greatest president of all?" In the following WebQuest, you will work in groups using information you find on the Internet to learn all about U.S. presidents. Each person on your team will learn one piece of the puzzle, and then you will come together to get a better understanding of the topic. |

*(Continued)*

*Building Your Toolkit:*
**Building WebQuests with Filamentality (Continued)**

| FIGURE 8–5 | Project Lesson Plan for a WebQuest (Continued) |
|---|---|
| Task | Select a president of the United States, locate information about him, and prepare a written and oral report in which you try to convince the whole class that your president is the greatest of them all. |
| Process | As a member of a group you will explore Web pages that provide information about U.S. presidents. Because these are real Web pages and not just pages made up for schools, the reading level may challenge you. You can use a dictionary or an encyclopedia to help you.<br><br>From the information you find about your selected president, each team member should provide two or more reasons why this is the greatest president. You will need factual or historical information to support each reason.<br><br>Use the Internet links that follow to answer the basic questions of who? what? where? when? why? and how? Be creative in exploring the information so that you answer these questions as fully and insightfully as you can.<br><br>• Presidents of the United States at http://www.whitehouse.gov/history/presidents/: the White House history of the presidents of the United States<br>• American Presidents Life Portraits at http://www.americanpresidents.org/: CSPAN's portraits of American presidents<br>• President—Linking America's Past to Her Future at http://www.ibiblio.org/lia/president/: presidential libraries IDEA network<br><br>Remember to write down or copy/paste the URL of any Web page you use to support your reasons so that you can quickly go back to it if you need to prove your point.<br><br>When group members come back together as a WebQuest team, you must all now agree on the best reasons for your selected president being the greatest president. Use information from the Web pages you explored to convince your teammates that your reasons are important and should be part of your team's answer to the question. Your WebQuest team should write out an answer and explanation that everyone on the team can accept. |
| Evaluation | 1. Each person in your group should write a paragraph for each of the reasons you agreed that your selected president is the greatest president. Be specific in both the information (include where you got it on the Web) and the reasoning.<br>2. Prepare your report using word processing. Have each person on the team proofread the report, and e-mail the final version to the teacher.<br>3. Present an oral report to the class. Try to convince the whole class that your selected president is the greatest president. You should allow class members to state why they agree or disagree with you. |
| Conclusion | Is your president the greatest of them all? When you are focusing on just one president, it is easy to come up with an answer that might not be completely right. Now that you know a lot more, what other U.S. presidents and parts of American history would you like to explore? |
| Credits or references | |

| STEP | PROCEDURE |
|---|---|
| 1. | Open your Web browser and then the WebQuest portal site at http://www.kn.sbc.com/wired/fil/. |
| 2. | Select **Start a New Page** from the Filamentality home page. You will be prompted to enter the following information:<br>■ **What's the topic you're making a page for?**<br>Enter **U.S. Presidents.**<br>■ **Type your name as you want it to appear on your finished product:**<br>Enter your first and last name. |

*(Continued)*

## Building Your Toolkit:
## Building WebQuests with Filamentality (Continued)

| STEP | PROCEDURE |
|------|-----------|
| | ▪ **Type a password. Each topic needs a different password, so pick something you'll remember.** Enter a password to use for Filamentality. |
| | ▪ **Enter your e-mail address:** Enter your e-mail address. |
| | ▪ **What's your school or library name?** Enter the name of your school or library. |
| | ▪ **Your school's Internet location:** Enter your school or library URL. |
| | ▪ **Your Personal Homepage location:** Enter URL for your home page if you have one. Click the **Spin This Thing** icon to create a WebQuest. |
| 3. | Click on **Add Links** at the bottom of the page. To create a WebQuest, Filamentality begins with a hotlist. Scroll down to add your first links, or read the Mentality Tips. You can use the links to the search engines at the bottom of the page to locate links. |
| | ▪ Location: **http://www.whitehouse.gov/history/presidents/** Title: **Presidents of the United States** Description: **The White House history of the presidents of the United States** |
| | ▪ Location: **http://www.americanpresidents.org/** Title: **American Presidents Life Portraits** Description: **CSPAN's portraits of American presidents** |
| | ▪ Location: **http://www.ibiblio.org/lia/president/** Title: **President—Linking America's Past to Her Future** Description: **Presidential libraries IDEA network** |
| 4. | Click on **Hotlist** on the Navigation menu at the bottom of the page to create a hotlist online activity. To use your hotlist as a part of a WebQuest, click **WebQuest** on that menu. |
| 5. | On the **Let's Spin a WebQuest** page, under **Create Category Names** delete the default information in all the fields. Under **Link to the World with an E-Mail Contact,** enter your name and e-mail address. Under **Doing More with Your WebQuest,** click on **2. Customize** under **WebQuest** on the menu at the bottom of the page. |
| 6. | Under **Customizing Your WebQuest** and **Add Your Title,** enter **Who's the Greatest President of All?** |
| 7. | To customize your WebQuest, you will need to remove the default information for most of the following fields and replace it with the information indicated: |
| | ▪ **Add Your Introduction:** Enter the introduction from the WebQuest lesson plan in Figure 8–5. |
| | ▪ **Add Your Question or Task:** Enter the task from the WebQuest lesson plan in Figure 8–5. |
| | ▪ **Adding Instructions:** Enter the first two paragraphs of process information from the WebQuest lesson plan in Figure 8–5. (The links have already been added in the hotlist.) |
| | ▪ **Phase 1—Background: Something for Everyone:** Keep the default information that is displayed in this field. |
| | ▪ **Phase 2—Looking Deeper: Different Perspectives on the Topic:** Enter the fourth paragraph of process information from the WebQuest lesson plan in Figure 8–5. Then delete the default information that is displayed in each of the **Instructions & Links for** fields. |
| | ▪ **Phase 3—Debating, Discussing, and Reaching Consensus:** Enter the last paragraph of process information from the WebQuest lesson plan in Figure 8–5. |

*(Continued)*

## Building Your Toolkit:
### Building WebQuests with Filamentality (Continued)

| STEP | PROCEDURE |
|------|-----------|

■ **Real-World Assessment:**
Enter the evaluation information from the WebQuest lesson plan in Figure 8–5.

■ **Conclusion:**
Enter the conclusion from the WebQuest lesson plan in Figure 8–5.

**9.**    To post your Web page on the Internet, click **Post** on the menu at the bottom of the page (under WebQuest). When the confirmation page is displayed that your WebQuest has been posted on the Web, write down the URL or add it to your Favorites.

**Go** to the Companion Website and browse *8.3 Building Your Toolkit Enrichment Activity: Using WebQuest Design Patterns for Creating WebQuests.* Use the information in the enrichment activity to create WebQuests using WebQuest design patterns.

## REFLECTIONS

WebQuests are a widely used method of integrating the Internet into teaching and learning. They have the potential to maximize and motivate student learning because they guide students through a sequence of steps that organize the learning process. Because almost all WebQuests are created by teachers for their own classroom use, WebQuests can easily be adapted for other classroom environments. A multitude of WebQuests are available on the Internet.

Although WebQuests represent a simple way to begin using Internet technology in the classroom, the pedagogical changes teachers must make to support WebQuests—that is, inquiry-oriented, problem-solving, group-based teaching and learning strategies—are not so easy. WebQuests require teachers to spend more time with planning and designing instruction and researching information resources. The trade-off is that teachers are less involved in the delivery of instruction as students work in cooperative groups and learn from one another and from the Internet resources. WebQuests help students become more responsible for their own learning by establishing a process for conducting research and working with others to accomplish a task or solve a problem that they can then transfer to other experiences.

## EXERCISES TO REVIEW AND EXPAND YOUR SKILLS

### Set 1: Reflecting on Practice

■ *Closing the Case.* Ms. Allison, a high-school English teacher, and Mr. Chang, a high-school history teacher, created a multidisciplinary WebQuest. What would be the classroom complications in collaborating with a teacher from another discipline? Locate examples of multidisciplinary WebQuests; many links are to schools and classrooms. What are the pros and cons of working on projects across disciplines? or even collaborating within the same discipline?

■ *Closing the Case.* Ms. Simpson, an elementary teacher, created a WebQuest in which her students build a virtual insect collection. Search the Internet and locate classroom projects that create virtual collections. Do you think student learning is as good with a virtual collection as with a real collection? Why or why not?

### Set 2: Expanding Your Skills

By definition WebQuests are inquiry-oriented activities, and most are designed to support introductory levels of inquiry that are well structured and defined. **Web inquiry projects**

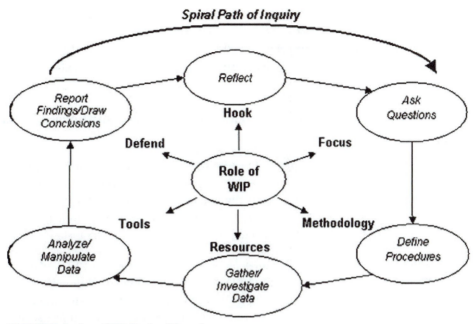

**FIGURE 8–6:    WIP Path of Inquiry**

*Source:* Used with permission from the Association for the Advancement of Computing in Education, Norfolk, VA. SITE: Society for Information Technology & Teacher Education, 2002, Vol. 1, pp. 67–72. *Promoting Student Inquiry: WebQuests to Web Inquiry Projects (WIPs)* by Philip Molebash, Bernie Dodge, Cheryl Mason, and Randy Bell. www.aace.org. Reproduced with permission.

(WIPs) use Internet technologies and resources for higher levels of inquiry, such as guided or open inquiry (see http://edweb.sdsu.edu/wip/). With *guided inquiry* students investigate a teacher-presented question but use their own investigative procedures; with *open inquiry* students investigate questions they have formulated and also use their own investigative procedures (Herron, 1971). WIPs are open-inquiry learning activities that use uninterpreted online information; they are designed to help teachers promote inquiry in their classrooms (Molebash, Dodge, Bell, Mason, & Irving, 2002). Chapter 9 of this text addresses inquiry-based learning.

Because it can be difficult for students to ask their own inquiry-oriented questions and define appropriate procedures for answering those questions, WIPs help teachers scaffold student inquiry (Molebash et al., 2002). They can be used as a road map to guide students through inquiry-oriented activities derived from student interest. WIPs use a six-stage spiral path of inquiry (see Figure 8–6), which can begin at any of the stages but is designed to initiate student inquiry at the Reflect stage (Molebash et al., 2002).

1. *Reflect.* Teachers build on previous activities or start anew by sparking students' interest in a topical area. Teachers are to provide a hook, causing students to reflect on the topic.

2. *Ask questions.* Responding to students' interests, the teacher leads students to ask questions related to the topic.

3. *Define procedures.* After students have asked questions, the teacher assists them in defining the procedures for investigation, including the type(s) of data to be used.

4. *Gather/investigate data.* Students seek online data that will be used to answer their questions, while the teacher provides guidance on the relevancy and reliability of the data.

5. *Analyze/manipulate data.* When data is found, the teacher must ensure that students can manipulate the data to aid in analysis. If numerical data must be manipulated, students will likely need facility with a spreadsheet application. If data is nonnumerical, concept mapping or database software might be required.

6. *Report findings/draw conclusions.* No conclusion is meaningful unless it is communicated appropriately. Students report their findings, draw conclusions, and support

these conclusions with data. The teacher must support students' efforts to present their results through writing, graphic presentations, and rhetoric. At this point, new questions might be asked as students reflect on their results, restarting the process.

Find out more about WIPs as an extension of WebQuests by viewing examples of WIPs at http://edweb.sdsu.edu/wip/.

### Set 3: Using Productivity and Web-Authoring Tools

- *WebQuest PowerPoint Presentations.* Create the WebQuest in the 8.3 toolkit exercise using a multimedia presentation program, such as PowerPoint. Place each component of the WebQuest on a different slide(s). Insert hyperlinks for the Web resources so that students can link to the website directly from the presentation program.

- *Develop Your Own WebQuest Matrix.* Search for WebQuests for the grade level and/or subject you teach, and create a spreadsheet document to keep a hotlist of the WebQuests you may want to use or adapt. Your spreadsheet should have columns for title, curriculum area or subject, rating, URL, and description. Insert hyperlinks for each of the URLS so that you can link to it directly from the spreadsheet document.

- *Create a Web Page.* On the WebQuest site there are templates for creating a WebQuest using Web pages (http://webquest.sdsu.edu/LessonTemplate.html). Download a set of templates, and then use a Web page authoring program to create Web pages for the WebQuest you created in the 8.3 toolkit exercise.

### Set 4: Creating Your Own Web-Enhanced Project

- *Develop a WebQuest Project.* Use WebQuest design patterns to develop a plan for an original WebQuest project that is appropriate for the grade level and/or subject that you teach. Document your plan using the WEL lesson plan for WebQuest projects.

- *Develop a WebQuest Rubric.* Create an evaluation rubric for the WebQuest developed in the 8.3 toolkit exercise.

## REFERENCES

Christie, A. A. (2002). *What is a WebQuest?* Retrieved October 5, 2003, from http://www. west.asu.edu/achristie/675wq.html

Dodge, B. (1997). *Some thoughts about WebQuests.* Retrieved October 2, 2003, from http:// webquest.sdsu.edu/about_webquests.html

Dodge, B. (2002). *Adapting and enhancing WebQuests.* Retrieved October 14, 2003, from http:// webquest.sdsu.edu/adapting/

Herron, M. D. (1971). The nature of scientific enquiry. *School Review, 79*(2), 171–212.

Johnson, D., & Johnson, R. (1999). *Learning together and alone: Cooperative, competitive, and individualistic learning.* Boston: Allyn & Bacon.

Johnson, D. W., Johnson, R., & Holubec, E. (1990). *Circles of learning: Cooperation in the classroom.* Edina, MN: Interaction Book.

March, T. (1998a). *The WebQuest design process.* Retrieved October 3, 2003, from http://www. ozline.com/webquests/design1.html

March, T. (1998b). *Why Webquests? An introduction.* Retrieved October 3, 2003, from http:// www. ozline.com/webquests/intro.html

Molebash, P. E., Dodge, B., Mason, C. L., & Bell, R. L. (2002). *Promoting student inquiry: WebQuests to Web inquiry projects (WIPs).* Society for Information Technology in Teacher Education, 2002 [CD ROM]. Charlottesville, VA: Association for the Advancement of Computing in Education.

Roblyer, M. D. (2003). *Integrating educational technology into teaching.* Upper Saddle River, NJ: Prentice Hall.

# CHAPTER 9

# Using the Internet for Inquiry and Discovery

Kyle Warner has over 10 years of experience teaching high-school science. A few years ago his school was connected to the Internet, and each teacher was provided with a classroom computer. When Mr. Warner discovered the vast resources available on the Internet, he told his principal about the possibilities for science learning using the Internet and was able to acquire four more computers in his classroom.

Now Mr. Warner uses Internet resources to support inquiry teaching methods in his science classes. His students work in pairs or small groups to search for solutions to science questions; their research often leads different groups in different directions of inquiry. To encourage his students to pursue their own questions, Mr. Warner reserves time for student-generated questioning during each project and makes it a part of the total project grade. Mr. Warner has observed that inquiry methods allow students to make connections with their topic and increase their interest in science learning.

## NEW TERMS

cases
discovery learning
inquiry-based learning
microworld

scenario
simulation
virtual reality
Web essay

| National Educational Technology Standards for Teachers | National Educational Technology Standards for Students |
|---|---|
| The following NETS•T are addressed by the lesson content and learning activities in this chapter: | The following NETS•S are addressed by the lesson content and learning activities in this chapter: |

**National Educational Technology Standards for Teachers**

The following NETS•T are addressed by the lesson content and learning activities in this chapter:

**II. Planning and Designing**

  **A.** Design technology-enhanced learning opportunities to support diverse needs

  **B.** Apply current research on teaching and learning with technology

  **C.** Identify, locate, and evaluate technology resources

  **D.** Plan for the management of technology resources

  **E.** Manage student learning in a technology-enhanced environment

**III. Teaching, Learning, and the Curriculum**

  **A.** Facilitate technology-enhanced experiences to address standards

  **B.** Use technology to support learner-centered strategies

  **C.** Apply technology to develop students' higher order skills

  **D.** Manage student learning activities

**National Educational Technology Standards for Students**

The following NETS•S are addressed by the lesson content and learning activities in this chapter:

**3. Technology Productivity Tools**

  • Use technology to enhance learning, increase productivity, and promote creativity

  • Use tools to collaborate, prepare publications, and produce creative works

**4. Technology Communications Tools**

  • Use telecommunications to collaborate, publish, and interact with others

  • Use varied media and formats to communicate information and ideas

**5. Technology Research Tools**

  • Use technology to locate, evaluate, and collect information

  • Use technology tools to process data and report results

  • Evaluate and select new information resources and technology

**6. Technology Problem-Solving and Decision-Making Tools**

  • Use technology to solve problems and make decisions

  • Employ technology to develop real-world problem-solving strategies

# OVERVIEW

Inquiry-based learning challenges students to investigate real-world or relevant questions and focus their attention on creating solutions. Student-generated questions stimulate a desire to understand the problem or concept. Inquiry is not so much a method of teaching as it is an approach to learning by posing real questions whenever they occur. Thus, inquiry becomes the organizing principle of student learning activities and the teacher's approach to participation.

Discovery learning is an inquiry-based learning method that generally takes place in problem-solving situations in which students draw on their own experience and prior knowledge to discover the rules, relations, or concepts about something. Simulations are technology tools that can be used to support discovery learning. They are easy to use and rich in feedback, and they provide students with learning experiences unavailable in real life. Various simulations are available on the Internet that can support curriculum-related learning activities.

Case-based learning uses cases based on real-world situations, actual or imagined, which students analyze, explore, and critique, and about which they inquire, make judgments, speculate, reason, and reflect. Cases promote active learning, team-based activities, and the ability to deal with complex, open-ended problems. The World Wide Web can provide a suitable platform for the presentation of case studies; multimedia case studies have been developed for a number of curriculum areas and professions.

## Lesson 9.1  Using Inquiry and Discovery Learning in the Classroom

### FOCUS QUESTIONS

- What are inquiry-based learning and discovery learning? How are they similar? How are they different?
- How can inquiry and discovery learning be used to provide Web-enhanced learning activities?
- What learning strategies and Web-based resources can be used to implement inquiry and discovery learning in the classroom?

## ■ UNDERSTANDING INQUIRY AND DISCOVERY LEARNING

In a geography lesson many of Ms. Loewen's sixth graders were struggling to understand the concept of time zones. One of her students, Arlo, asked why his father, who was working in London, was always in bed asleep when Arlo called him after dinner from Trenton, New Jersey. Ms. Loewen helped Arlo prepare a demonstration about time zones for the class. She assembled two small sun dials and attached them to a large globe where Greenwich, England, and Trenton, New Jersey, were located. With a powerful flashlight to represent the sun, Ms. Loewen asked Arlo to hold the flashlight above the globe's equator in a position due south of Greenwich. When the sun dial at Greenwich registered 12:00 noon, the sun dial at Trenton showed 7:00 A.M. Then Ms. Loewen asked Arlo to rotate the globe until the flashlight sun was due south of Trenton. The time displayed on the sun dial at Trenton became 12:00 noon, whereas at Greenwich it moved to 5:00 P.M. Ms. Loewen explained to the class that the time in Trenton was 5 hours behind the Greenwich mean time because it takes 5 hours for the earth to make that part of its daily rotation, that is, the distance between Greenwich and Trenton. This demonstration made it easy for Arlo and the other students in Ms. Loewen's class to see that when Arlo called his father at 7:00 P.M. from Trenton, New Jersey, it was actually midnight in London.

Any discussion about inquiry learning must recognize that it is difficult to improve on the ideas put forward by John Dewey in *Experience and Education* (1938), which said that learning starts with first-hand exploration of familiar aspects of a student's experience. Dewey proposed starting with ordinary experience and emphasized the importance of selecting "the kind of present experiences that live fruitfully and creatively in future experiences" (p. 28) and involving students in "the formation of the purposes which direct [their] activities" (p. 67).

In some modern classrooms educational researchers have joined Dewey in emphasizing exploration and inquiry (see Brown & Campione, 1994; Gardner, 1989; Palincsar & Magnusson, 2001; and Scardamalia, Bereiter, & Lamon, 1994). Each of these school-based projects attempted to develop a classroom culture predisposed toward systematic inquiry into questions or topics of interest.

Classroom inquiry is as much about trying to construct and test explanations as it is about mastering a particular body of information. Thus, learning is an outcome that occurs when students create answers or solutions to questions or investigations. They extend their understanding through action, often through the construction of exhibits that present their explanations or solutions.

### Inquiry Learning

**Inquiry-based learning** challenges and motivates students to investigate and learn, using real-world or relevant questions and focusing attention on creating solutions. For inquiry to work, investigative questions must be based on something that students really care about or that stimulates their curiosity or interest so that they become engaged in the learning process. The teacher should not only propose topics for investigation and ensure that time and resources are used productively, but also should be involved as a coinquirer with the students.

Inquiry-based learning experiences must be open-ended and flexible enough to allow for alternative paths of investigation. Even though inquiry may start with a clearly formulated question, some of the most absorbing questions that arouse student interest may occur spontaneously or arise after some preliminary work has been carried out or even develop as a by-product of trying to answer some other question (Wells, 2000). Because inquiry learning requires that more time be appropriated for a topic than would be needed with more directed teaching approaches, teachers may encounter some difficulty completing a prescribed curriculum using only an inquiry-based approach.

The advantage of inquiry learning is that it permits students to investigate engaging and authentic topics and generate new knowledge and understandings. It moves students toward deeper understanding of a topic by allowing them to organize, analyze, synthesize, and assimilate information using higher order thinking skills. They can then generate new ideas about the topic and present these ideas for further scrutiny by peers, teachers, or experts. The ability to inquire and utilize appropriate resources also helps students learn to solve unstructured or ambiguous problems or questions.

With inquiry methods the teacher supports students by questioning and guiding them in their investigations. Refinement of ideas takes place through discussion and debate. Thus, the questioning and facilitating skills of the teacher are important to the success of the inquiry approach. Teachers must challenge students to form their ideas and explanations precisely, basing them on legitimate and credible facts and information.

### Discovery Learning

**Discovery learning** is an inquiry-based learning method that encourages students to discover for themselves the rules, relations, or concepts about something. The premise is that students are more likely to remember concepts they discover on their own. **Jerome Bruner's** connection with the curriculum development projects of the National Science Foundation in the 1960s and 1970s was instrumental in developing approaches to science learning that fostered problem-solving skills through inquiry and discovery. Bruner believed that students learn best by discovery and that the learner is a problem solver who interacts with the environment by testing hypotheses and developing generalizations. Thus, discovery learning encourages students to ask questions and formulate their own tentative answers, deducing general principles from practical examples or experience (Bruner, 1960, 1966).

*Go to the Companion Website and browse Chapter 9 Lesson Links: Jerome Bruner and Discovery Learning to learn more about this topic.*

Although discovery is one of the oldest and most common methods of learning, it is not widely used in classrooms today. With conventional classroom resources discovery learning is not efficient or productive. When it is used in the classroom, teachers are more successful if students have prerequisite knowledge accompanied by structured learning experiences (Roblyer, 2003). Without adequate preparation or constructive coaching, students may not discover anything worth learning.

### ■ USING THE WEB FOR INQUIRY

Using Internet technologies to promote inquiry-based learning encourages the development of independent learners capable of processing and developing solutions to problems in an information-centered society. A Web-enhanced inquiry approach maximizes information seeking, evaluating, and applying. Jakes, Pennington, and Knodle (2003) suggest an eight-step process for inquiry-based learning using the World Wide Web (see Figure 9–1):

1.  Students begin by generating an essential question for the inquiry. An essential question requires students to make a decision or plan a course of action.

2.  After the essential question has been framed, students write foundation questions, which give structure to the investigation so that students know what they need to research. Foundation questions and answers provide a factual basis for developing

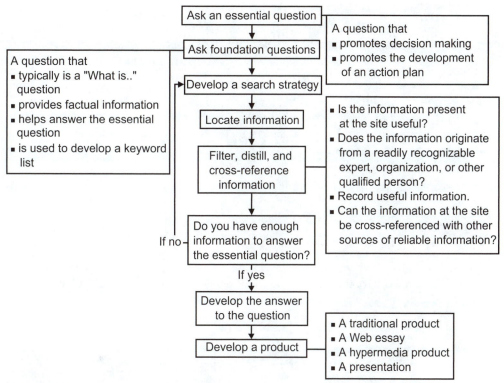

**FIGURE 9–1:   An Inquiry-based Learning Process**

*Source:* From *Using the Internet to Promote Inquiry-Based Learning* by D. S. Jakes, M. E. Pennington, and H. A. Knodle. Retrieved March 23, 2002, from http://www.biopoint.com/inquiry/ibr.html. Adapted with permission.

an answer to the essential question. Answers to foundation questions are integrated into an answer to the essential question.

**3.** Students use keywords from foundation questions to develop a search strategy to locate Web information.

**4.** Students are then ready to locate information on the Web. They can start by using a single search engine, such as Google, and then moving on if necessary to a metasearch engine or other search tools.

**5.** Students evaluate the Web resources they have collected, a critical process skill that students must learn. Information quality is assessed using a three-part process:

- *Information Applicability*—Students determine whether the information is related to their essential question and useful for answering their foundation questions.

- *Information Authority*—Students determine whether the information originates from a readily recognizable expert, organization, or other qualified person or group.

- *Information Reliability*—Students cross-reference information among websites to ensure that information is reliable.

**6.** Students evaluate the quantity of information to determine whether there are sufficient answers to each of the foundation questions. If not, students return to the search strategy to locate new sites.

**7.** Students develop the answer to the question. At this point students must organize and synthesize.

**8.** Students develop a product to represent the answer, that is, their knowledge about the essential question. The product can take many forms, including a Web essay. **Web essays** are living documents that contain multiple information types, such as text, sounds, graphics, pictures, and movies that are published on the Web. Students can produce Web essays as a Web log or a Web page.

## Building Your Toolkit:
## Using Project Pages To Support Inquiry Learning

Project pages are online documents that guide learners through inquiry-based learning activities. They are composed of five distinct components: the scenario, the task, the resources, the product, and the assessment. Each component has a particular structure and function that promote inquiry-based learning; the World Wide Web is the primary information resource.

The Jakes, Pennington, and Knodle research model described previously is embedded within the project page tool to provide pedagogical support. The purpose of the tool is to introduce to students both inquiry-based learning and use of the Web as a learning tool. Because of the complexity of the inquiry approach, students should not be asked to do too much until their process skills are developed, many of which are needed initially.

Myprojectpages.com is a design environment for creating project pages; it uses a wizard interface so that you do not have to know HTML programming. In addition, myprojectpages.com hosts your project pages so that you do not need another place to publish them. Project pages can take some time to design, depending on the complexity of the content.

### STEP  PROCEDURE

1.  Open your Web browser and then the website at **http://myprojectpages.com/**. A Web page similar to the screen shot in Figure 9–2 should be displayed. You can download a user guide by selecting the link on the right side of the home page—download the **Project Page** tutorial.

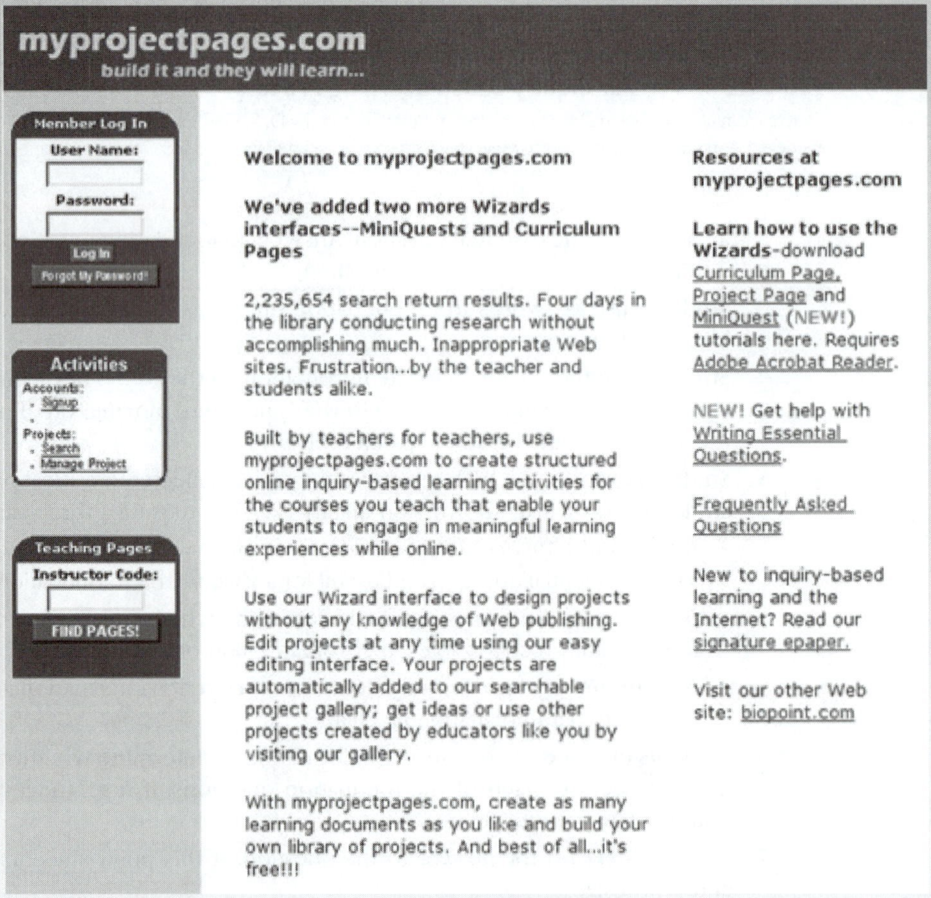

**myprojectpages.com**
build it and they will learn...

**Member Log In**
**User Name:**
**Password:**
Log In
Forgot My Password?

**Activities**
Accounts:
• Signup
Projects:
• Search
• Manage Project

**Teaching Pages**
**Instructor Code:**
FIND PAGES!

**Welcome to myprojectpages.com**

**We've added two more Wizards interfaces--MiniQuests and Curriculum Pages**

2,235,654 search return results. Four days in the library conducting research without accomplishing much. Inappropriate Web sites. Frustration...by the teacher and students alike.

Built by teachers for teachers, use myprojectpages.com to create structured online inquiry-based learning activities for the courses you teach that enable your students to engage in meaningful learning experiences while online.

Use our Wizard interface to design projects without any knowledge of Web publishing. Edit projects at any time using our easy editing interface. Your projects are automatically added to our searchable project gallery; get ideas or use other projects created by educators like you by visiting our gallery.

With myprojectpages.com, create as many learning documents as you like and build your own library of projects. And best of all...it's free!!!

**Resources at myprojectpages.com**

**Learn how to use the Wizards**-download Curriculum Page, Project Page and MiniQuest (NEW!) tutorials here. Requires Adobe Acrobat Reader.

NEW! Get help with Writing Essential Questions.

Frequently Asked Questions

New to inquiry-based learning and the Internet? Read our signature epaper.

Visit our other Web site: biopoint.com

**FIGURE 9–2:  The website for myprojectpages.com**

*Source:* Retrieved from http://www.myprojectpages.com. Reproduced with permission.

*(Continued)*

### Building Your Toolkit:
### Using Project Pages To Support Inquiry Learning (Continued)

| STEP | PROCEDURE |
|---|---|
| **2.** | To use the project page tool, you will need to register and get an account. Select the **Signup** link in the Activities box, enter your registration information, and click the **Signup** button to save your registration information. Use of the website tools is free, and you can create as many projects as you wish. When you register, your personal information is held confidentially and myprojectspages.com will send you an occasional e-mail when improvements are made to the website. |
| **3.** | Once you have registered, the Project Manager screen will be displayed. Notice the Instructor Code that is assigned to your account. Your students will use this code to access your projects. Select the link for **Start New Project,** and on the following screen select the link for **Build a Project Page.** |
| **4.** | Select a curriculum topic that is appropriate for the subject and grade level you teach. You can view or download the Web page **AnasaziProj.htm** from the Companion Website to see what information is needed. You can use that information or your own topic for this exercise. Your finished project page should look similar to that in Figure 9–3. |

**FIGURE 9–3:    The Anasazi project page**

| STEP | PROCEDURE |
|---|---|
| **5.** | The project page wizard will guide you in entering the information for your learning project. On your first attempt to create a project page, you may not have the appropriate information for all fields in the wizard. You can enter minimal information or even skip a field and go back and edit it later. |

- **Project Title.** Use a short, attention-getting title.
- **Project Subtitle.** Provide more descriptive information, as well as keywords.
- **Author Information.** Enter your name, school, city, and state or any combination of information.
- **Scenario.** Review the directions and then enter a description that frames the essential question in an authentic, real-world context, placing students in a real-world situation and a real-world role.
- **Essential Question.** State the essential question directly so that there is no confusion about what students are required to answer.

*(Continued)*

## Building Your Toolkit:
## Using Project Pages To Support Inquiry Learning (Continued)

**STEP    PROCEDURE**

- **Foundation Questions.** List the foundation questions to structure the research. Foundation questions ask for discrete information needed to answer the essential question. On the Web display of your project, both the essential question and the foundation questions will be listed under the task heading.

- **Resources.** Include links to websites that provide the factual information necessary to answer the foundation questions. Specifying websites ensures that students use appropriate Web resources for the research process and eliminates the time required for them to locate their own sites. Enter a title, a URL, and a description for each resource. Click the **New** button one more time after the last resource to ensure that all entries are properly saved in the database.

- **Product.** Define what the students will produce to represent their answer to the essential question. Typical products include essays or papers or multimedia presentations. The project page tool recommends using Web essays, which contain hyperlinks to supportive Web resources, along with graphics and even sounds or movies. You can view an example of a Web essay at **http://www.biopoint.com/rustywebpage/ rusty webpage.html/**.

- **Copyright** (optional). As the original author, you hold the copyright for your project. Adding a copyright statement helps you maintain the intellectual property rights of your project.

- **Images** (optional). You can download graphic images to specific pages of your project by specifying the file name and location of the image, the size of the image, and the page of the project on which you want it displayed.

- **Rubric.** Focus on only the product or on both product and process. Process skills could include developing an Internet search strategy or working as a group member in completing the project. Specify the skill or competency and the behaviors that represent various levels for that skill.

**Go to the Companion Website** and browse *9.1 Building Your Toolkit Enrichment Activity: Using Curriculum Pages to Support Inquiry Learning with the Web.* Practice the skills presented in the enrichment activity to learn how to create curriculum pages using **myprojectpages.com.**

6.    After you have entered all information, select the link to view the final page.

7.    Once you have entered a project page, you can edit it by logging in to the website and selecting the link for **Manage Project** on the left side of the home page.

## Lesson 9.2   Using the Case Method for Inquiry and Discovery Learning

### FOCUS QUESTIONS

- How does the case method support inquiry and discovery learning?
- How can case-based approaches support Web-enhanced learning?
- What are some educational strategies for writing case scenarios?
- How can online simulations be used to support curriculum-based learning activities?
- What are some examples of online simulations?

## ■ CASE-BASED LEARNING

**Cases** are narratives, situations, data samplings, or statements that present unresolved and provocative issues or questions in a form that is intended to educate. Cases can be brief for classroom discussions or comprehensive for extended projects. To be effective, they must relate to curriculum objectives. Cases can be worked independently but are typically worked in teams so that students can brainstorm solutions and share the workload. The case method is not focused on the acquisition of knowledge but is primarily useful for developing problem-solving skills. Case-based learning is widely used in medical, law, and business schools, where entire courses often use a case-study format.

Case-based and problem-based learning are similar learning methods. With problem-based learning, students are presented with an unstructured problem that mirrors a real-world problem. With case-based learning, students analyze a problem in the form of a case study, share views and perspectives with their peers, propose problem solutions, and develop a plan of action for case resolution.

Cases are designed to confront students with a specific problem that does not have a simple solution. They provide a context to focus discussion and help students learn to define and recognize appropriate criteria for solving problems. Cases also expose students to multiple perspectives and require them to develop multiple solutions. Cases are open-ended, requiring students to analyze data as well as choose appropriate analytic techniques in order to reach a conclusion.

The case method is characterized by real-world situations, actual or imagined. Case studies involve students with real-world data and provide opportunities for students to insert themselves into the role of a decision maker. In addition, case studies allow students to see the relevance of their curriculum to the real world outside the classroom and to understand the complexity and ambiguity of many problems or situations.

## Types of Case Studies

Case studies can be of several varieties. Finished cases indicate a solution(s) and are presented for analysis to help students develop appropriate inquiry skills. Unfinished cases are open-ended cases, for which results or solutions have not been derived or are not yet clear. Fictional cases created by the teacher can be open-ended or finished and are useful for adherence to the curriculum.

The Teaching and Learning with Technology (TLT) website at Pennsylvania State University has published a series of Web pages to provide teachers with some basic information about cases, such as the nature of a case, tips for writing a case, and links to additional resources and case repositories (http://tlt.its.psu.edu/suggestions/cases/). A basic case includes a scenario, a statement of the issue, and an assignment, but there are several variations that support different types of learning. The TLT provides a list and explanations of cases, as well as suggestions to help teachers choose case studies based on their teaching objectives. No one type of case study is best for all situations.

- *Role play*—In this type of case students are assigned roles to play in a scenario, such as developing a business plan or staging a mock trial. Role-playing allows students to express diverse views in a relatively safe classroom climate.

- *Background*—Here students are exposed to a real-world scenario to learn basic facts about a subject or a topic. This type of case is useful for students who relate better to content when it is contextualized.

- *Diagnose the problem*—In this case students diagnose an underlying problem based on case data, both relevant and irrelevant. A variant of the diagnosis case is the in-tray diagnosis, in which students are presented with a number of documents that might be found in their in-trays, or in-boxes. Students have a limited amount of time to determine and record their actions for each of the documents provided. This type of case study is intended to approximate real-life job functions and can be adapted to a number of professions. It is useful for improving analytical skills, promoting creative thinking, and practicing decision making.

- *Jigsaw*—Here students are assigned a section of a larger topic or case and are responsible for researching it and presenting their results to the team or class.

- *Live*—The information provided for a live case study comes from current events, usually a newspaper article. The teacher provides up-to-date factual information and questions for thought to begin the discussion of the case but no known solutions. Over time student conclusions can be compared with the actual decisions made. A good summary exercise is to compare and evaluate a variety of solutions for the problem.

- *Pause the action*—This case study is similar to the live case study, but an ongoing scenario is paused in midaction and students are asked to predict the outcome or suggest solutions. This case study is also known as a *sequential case*.
- *Create a case*—Here students develop and present a case study to the group, thus increasing their responsibility to research and contribute materials for the learning experience. This type of case study is useful as a final class exercise that uses the information presented during an entire course or unit.

## Instructional Strategies

Case studies are usually designed for small groups to promote discussion, which should be structured by the teacher. A sequence of written questions can guide students into making observations about the facts of the case, comparing and contrasting competing hypotheses, taking a position or offering a solution, and reaching consensus. However, groups should work with limited teacher intervention. Case studies should then be debriefed with the whole class to compare group responses and interpret the implications of group solutions.

Case studies can be supported in the classroom with several commonly used teaching and learning strategies. Whole-class discussion allows students to actively participate and interact with one another. Thereafter students can be asked to create a short summary, which organizes and structures the facts and concepts of the case and makes generalizations based on the class discussion. Or small groups can present their findings to the whole class, perhaps accompanied by written reports prepared by individuals or the small groups. The written report should identify the issues and problems represented by the case; a thorough examination, analysis, and evaluation of the case; and recommendations for resolution. Students should commit to a particular position or solution and explain why they have chosen this position.

Case-based learning is a powerful educational approach that permits students to apply higher order learning processes. Internet technologies support this approach by providing pedagogical tools and resources, such as search capabilities, collaborative work spaces, and publication capabilities. In addition, the Web provides multimedia case studies already developed for a number of curriculum areas and professions.

## ■ DEVELOPING SCENARIOS

Scenarios are the most important aspect of the case study; they set the stage for student learning by making connections between the classroom subject and the real world. **Scenarios** should describe a real-world problem, which may be open-ended, complex, and unstructured and may have multiple solutions. The problem can be actual or imagined, but it must be realistic and believable. The description of the problem must be rich enough to make the situation credible, but not so complete as to close off discussion or exploration. In role-playing cases, the descriptions of fictional characters, organizations, locales, and other elements should be adequate to interpret the tasks of particular roles.

The following suggestions will help you create effective case study scenarios:

- *Connection to the curriculum*—The scenario should connect to curriculum objectives. It should be structured to support the learning objectives for the activity in a way that students will understand.
- *Use of narrative*—The scenario should be written in a format that is appropriate for the case and builds student interest. A narrative format, similar to the style of a short story, is usually appropriate (Herreid, 1999). Some case studies, however, may require the presentation of facts and information such as clinical reports or official documents.

- *Elicit student response*—The scenario should be stated in such a way that students are required to give a decision, recommendation, prediction, or other specific conclusion.
- *Appropriate in length*—Case studies should be well focused so that the learning activity is doable within the amount of time available. Sometimes a scenario can be stated in a paragraph or two, whereas more complex case studies may even include links to other sources of additional information. Although the length of the scenario will vary according to the complexity of the case or problem, enough background information and facts should be included so that students feel empowered to solve the case.
- *Supporting data, documents, and resources*—Supporting data, documents, and links to resources can be embedded in the scenario narrative and sequenced to correspond to the logical progression of the case. In some cases, however, a random presentation of supportive information may be part of the instructional strategy. The information can include excerpts from newspaper or magazine articles, statistical reports, historical writings, and literary works, as well as clips from video and audio recordings.
- *Designing case study questions*—The questions asked or implied in the scenario can direct the students' line of inquiry and clarify teacher expectations. Such questions can be embedded in the scenario at different points or included at the end. Some questions that you may want to consider include the following:
  - What are the big issues?
  - What questions do you have?
  - What problems need to be solved?
  - What information do you need?
  - What are the underlying assumptions?
  - What are all the possible alternatives?
  - What are the pros and cons of each alternative?
  - What criteria will you use to select an alternative?
  - What assumptions are you making in selecting an alternative?

Scenarios are an important aspect of Web-enhanced learning projects because they provide a context for the project and motivate students to learn more about the topic. The case scenario should be incorporated into the scenario section of the WEL lesson plan.

---

## Building Your Toolkit:
### Case-Based Learning Resources and Examples

Discover more about case-based learning by browsing the following websites. Note how cases are structured and especially how scenarios and settings are developed for cases.

| STEP | PROCEDURE |
|---|---|
| **1.** | Clyde Herreid has been working with faculty at the University of Buffalo on case-based science learning. The website of the National Center for Case Study Teaching in Science at **http://ublib.buffalo.edu/libraries/ projects/cases/case.html** provides links to theory, educational practices, and other projects, as well as faculty working with cases across several disciplines. |
| **2.** | The BioQUEST Curriculum Consortium has been working on connecting cases to open-ended student investigations. Browse the tutorials and example cases of investigative case-based learning (ICBL) at **http://serc.carleton.edu/introgeo/icbl/index.html**. |
| **3.** | The Teaching and Learning with Technology (TLT) website at Pennsylvania State University has published a series of Web pages to provide basic information about cases and links to additional resources and case repositories at **http://tlt.its.psu.edu/suggestions/cases/**. |

*(Continued)*

---

*Building Your Toolkit:*
**Case-Based Learning Resources and Examples (Continued)**

| STEP | PROCEDURE |
|------|-----------|
| 4. | Case study websites include these: |

- Lizzie Borden Murder Case **http://ccbit.cs.umass.edu/ lizzie/ intro/home.html**, where students can explore authentic historic documents, maps, and testimony to determine the guilt or innocence of Lizzie Borden
- Earthquake Safe Zones **http://sd67.bc.ca/schools/sss/ Science/webquest/frontmenu.htm**, where students can research geologic maps and data to determine how and where to build earthquake resistant areas in Turkey

| STEP | PROCEDURE |
|------|-----------|
| 5. | The University of Delaware at **http://www.udel.edu/pbl/** is using problem-based learning for an institutionwide reform of science teaching and learning. |

**Go to the Companion Website and browse** *9.2 Building Your Toolkit Enrichment Activity: Writing Scenarios for Web-Enhanced Learning Activities.* **Use the information in the enrichment activity to practice writing scenarios for Web-enhanced learning activities.**

---

## ■ USING ONLINE SIMULATIONS TO EXPLORE REAL-LIFE PROBLEMS

Over the past several years many of the students in Joe Wyatt's 10th-grade biology class have refused to do the frog dissection project. This year Mr. Wyatt is giving his students the option of using a computer program that simulates the experience. With the simulation, students use the mouse to make virtual incisions and are then asked to locate and identify organs inside their virtual specimen.

The virtual approach to dissection eliminates the mess and objections. In addition, virtual dissections are far more cost-effective, and mistakes are easily correctable. Some proponents also claim that students who use the computer simulations test better on the material than those who do the actual dissection.

Many science teachers, however, object to the use of simulation programs as substitutes for hands-on dissections. The National Association of Biology Teachers (NABT) in Reston, Virginia, endorses hands-on dissection over technological alternatives. But Mr. Wyatt believes that the benefits of the computer experience outweigh those of actual dissection. "It is more important to me that the students understand the anatomical systems than that they know how to perform a dissection" says Mr. Wyatt.

An attempt to model a real-life problem or situation in an educational context is called a **simulation.** Simulations are based on the premise that certain interesting aspects of the real world can be copied or duplicated and virtually experienced on computers. Thus, a simulation is a computer program that is based on an underlying computational model that recreates a somewhat simplified version of a complex phenomenon, environment, or experience.

Online simulations are a form of discovery learning that promotes inquiry and discussion as students learn concepts, interpret, and make inferences or predictions. Simple online simulations allow users to enter and reenter multiple criteria and then model the reality in charts and graphs. More complex simulations permit collaborators at multiple sites to interact visually and verbally.

### Implications for Teaching and Learning

Because a simulation is interactive and is usually grounded in some objective reality, it can provide students with a new level of understanding and can be highly motivating, providing a learning experience unavailable in real life. Simulations are rich in feedback and can be used in the classroom in several ways:

- ■ To demonstrate or explain a concept(s)
- ■ To practice a skill(s)

- To help students visualize models or theories
- To assess or examine student understanding or skills
- To supplement or follow-up on real laboratory experiences

The educational goal of most simulations is to uncover the rules underlying the simulation. It should include guided activities, such as hints, questions, exercises, and games. And to be effective in the classroom, it should always be accompanied by one or more of the following supports:

- Preparation for or instruction on the topic prior to the simulation
- An embedded help system that provides information on request
- Tutorials embedded in the simulation or running parallel with it
- An intelligent tutoring system that adapts to the knowledge and skills demonstrated by the simulation user
- Adaptive testing or questioning that provides students with feedback

It is important that students have a context for the questions they may be asking and the data they will use. Consequently, teachers should be sure that resources are available to provide sufficient background information. They should also be certain that students have a clear understanding of the differences between the simulations and the real events.

## Examples for Classroom Use

The Internet is a great resource for simulated educational activities. A **microworld** is a form of simulation that is a tiny world, or virtual space, inside which students can explore alternatives, test hypotheses, and discover facts that are true about that world. Students are encouraged to think about the microworld as a real world, not simply a simulation of another reality. **Virtual reality** is a sophisticated form of simulation that includes props—such as goggles, helmets, and special gloves—to create the sense of an immersive environment. However, most computer simulations available as computer programs or on the World Wide Web model realities that rely primarily on visual experiences.

*Go to the Companion Website and browse Chapter 9 Lesson Links: Microworlds to learn more about this topic.*

According to Robert Morgan (2003), the use of simulated activities is becoming an important tool in education. He notes that simulation programs such as Flight Simulator or The Sims run from an individual computer, whereas Web-based simulations like The Stock Market Game run from the Internet. A number of interesting online simulations can be found on the World Wide Web; the following discussion considers three examples.

### The Stock Market Game

The Stock Market Game (http://www.stockmarketgame.org/) gives students a chance to learn economic and financial concepts by investing a hypothetical $100,000 in an online portfolio. The Stock Market Game is a computer-assisted classroom simulation of Wall Street trading, following stocks listed on the NYSE, AMEX, and NASDAQ (see Figure 9-4). On average, trading sessions last for 10 weeks. The game is available to all grade levels, postsecondary and college students, adults, and organizations. It makes extensive lesson plan activities available to teachers of math, reading, social studies, and business. The game is closely tied to educational requirements and curriculum standards, and correlations are available in the Teacher Support Center.

The Stock Market Game is designed to develop higher level thinking skills by challenging students to combine knowledge learned in school with an awareness of current events, a curiosity about the business and economic environment, and an interest in managing money. Students learn how financial markets work and how capital is raised to fund business growth. The game is a rich educational experience that enhances academic and life skills.

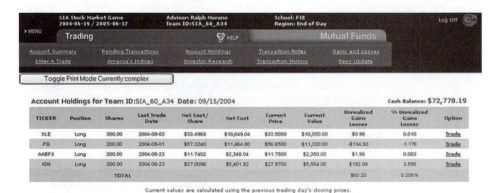

**FIGURE 9–4:    Account Holdings Screen from the Stock Market Game**

*Source:* The Stock Market Game. © Copyright SEA games. Reproduced with permission.

### U.S. Oil Policy Simulation

Another economics simulation is the U.S. Oil Policy Simulation, developed by Forio Corporation (http://www.forio.com/). Forio creates management training simulations and sells simulation development software to corporations, universities, and government agencies around the world. The U.S. Oil Policy Simulation (http://broadcast.forio.com/pro/oil/) can

## U.S. Oil Policy Simulation

**What would it take to reduce U.S. dependence on foreign oil?**

Start the Simulation >>

After Saudi Arabia, the U.S. is the second largest oil producer in the world. But the United States also happens to be the largest consumer of oil. Oil consumption in the United States and Canada is almost three gallons per person per day, twice as high as in Europe. As a consequence more than 50% of U.S. oil must be imported. These oil imports are expensive and have complex political and security consequences.

What would it take to reduce United States dependence on foreign oil?

In this simulation, you are elected President of the United States on a platform of reducing U.S. dependence on oil imports. How will you achieve your goals? You decide on initiatives that include everything from opening oil fields in Alaska to mandating improved fuel efficiency of new vehicles. Then you write a speech to the American people outlining your policies. The simulation shows if you were able to achieve your goals by 2020.

Good luck!

**FIGURE 9–5:    U.S. Oil Policy Simulation Beginning**

*Source:* Retrieved December 6, 2004, from http://broadcast.forio.com/pro/oil. Developed by forio Corporation. Reproduced with permission.

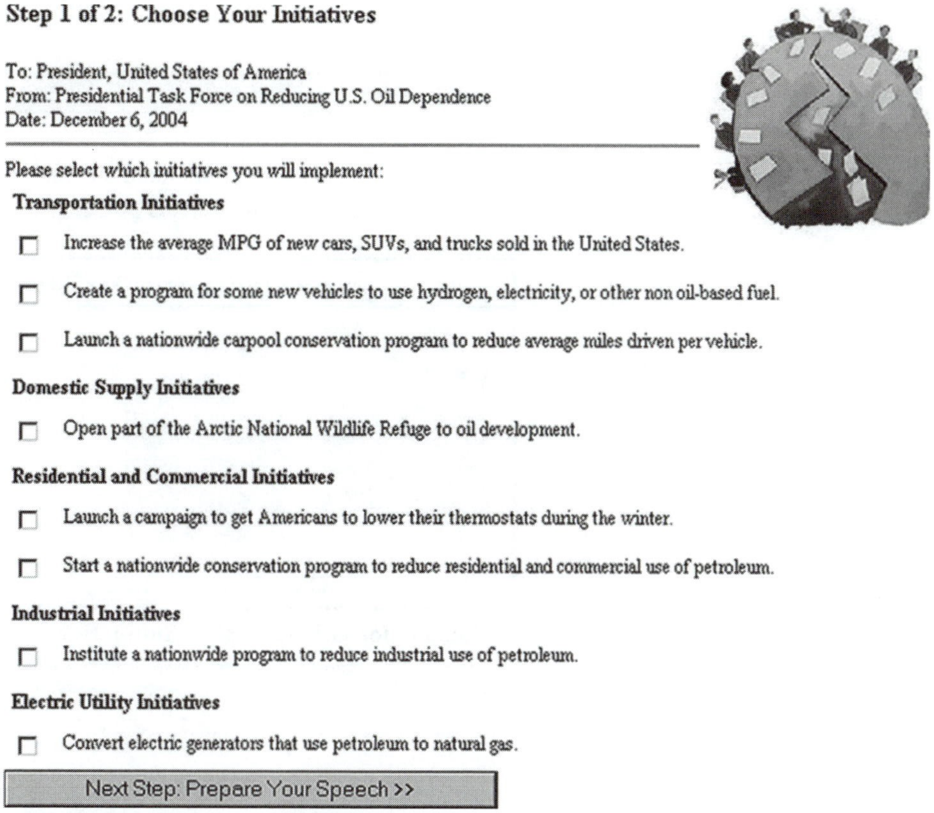

**Step 1 of 2: Choose Your Initiatives**

To: President, United States of America
From: Presidential Task Force on Reducing U.S. Oil Dependence
Date: December 6, 2004

Please select which initiatives you will implement:

**Transportation Initiatives**

☐  Increase the average MPG of new cars, SUVs, and trucks sold in the United States.

☐  Create a program for some new vehicles to use hydrogen, electricity, or other non oil-based fuel.

☐  Launch a nationwide carpool conservation program to reduce average miles driven per vehicle.

**Domestic Supply Initiatives**

☐  Open part of the Arctic National Wildlife Refuge to oil development.

**Residential and Commercial Initiatives**

☐  Launch a campaign to get Americans to lower their thermostats during the winter.

☐  Start a nationwide conservation program to reduce residential and commercial use of petroleum.

**Industrial Initiatives**

☐  Institute a nationwide program to reduce industrial use of petroleum.

**Electric Utility Initiatives**

☐  Convert electric generators that use petroleum to natural gas.

`Next Step: Prepare Your Speech >>`

**FIGURE 9–6:   Policy Initiatives for U. S. Oil Policy Simulation**

*Source:* Retrieved December 6, 2004, from http://broadcast.forio.com/pro/oil. Developed by Forio Corporation. Reproduced with permission.

help students discover the complex economic and political policies and principles behind the production and consumption of oil on a national level.

The simulation allows students to pretend that they are the president of the United States (see Figure 9-5) and must set a number of economic policies to reduce the consumption of oil imported from other countries. The simulation begins by explaining how the simulation works and providing links to related information about the topic.

The first part of the discovery process is the selection of a set of policy initiatives. Students can select any combination of initiatives that they want (see Figure 9-6). Thereafter, they will set specific objectives to be communicated in a presidential speech. The specific objectives for each initiative consist of a start year, a target value (amount of increase or decrease), and the number of years to reach the target value.

The final screen of the simulation displays the calculated results of the policies submitted by the students (see Figure 9-7). If the energy goals have not been achieved, students have the opportunity to try again and again (hence, discovery), setting different objectives until the goals are achieved.

### NASA's Virtual Skies

Virtual Skies (http://virtualskies.arc.nasa.gov/) was developed by NASA Ames Education Division for use by high-school and homeschool teachers and students in Grades 9-12, as well as aviation enthusiasts—pilots and passengers alike. The website allows students to explore the world of air traffic management and learn more about NASA research in aviation operations and safety (see Figure 9-8).

**You did not achieve your goal of a 40% reduction in imported oil by 2020.**

US oil imports increased by 36%, from 11.44 million barrels per day in 2002 to 15.56 million barrels per day in 2020.

| << Try Again | Where did these numbers come from? | Exit Simulation >> |

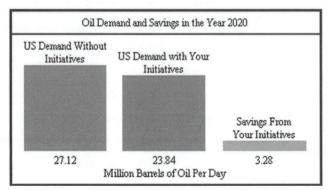

**However, your initiatives reduced oil consumption by 3.28 million barrels per day.**

**FIGURE 9–7:   Results for U.S. Oil Policy Simulation**

*Source:* Retrieved December 6, 2004, from http://broadcast.forio.com/pro/oil. Developed by Forio Corporation. Reproduced with permission.

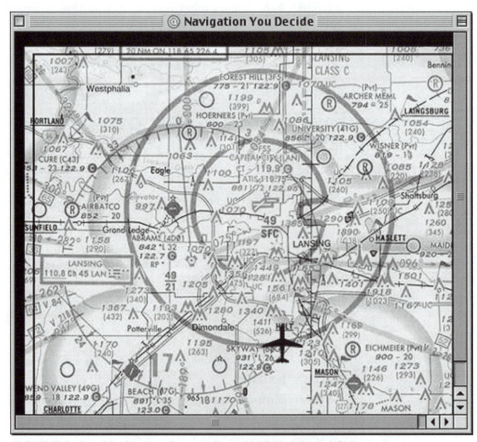

**FIGURE 9–8:   Navigation Screen from NASA's Virtual Skies**

*Source:* Retrieved from http://virtualskies.arc.nasa.gov. Reproduced with permission.

Each of the seven content sections of the website allows students to use principles of algebra, geometry, and calculus and apply decision-making and collaborative skills. The sections include aeronautics, airport design, air traffic management, communication, navigation, research, and weather. Each section includes online activities, complemented by downloadable print materials that can be used in the classroom to supplement the geography, mathematics, and science concepts. And all activities are correlated with national standards in mathematics, science, geography, and technology.

## *Building Your Toolkit:*
### DESIGNING AND CREATING A SIMULATION

Forio (**http://www.forio.com**) has an online software tool for developing simulations. Forio's Broadcast Express is a free, entry-level service that provides everything you need to get a simulation running on the Web. Broadcast Express provides free simulation hosting, a URL for your simulation, an easy-to-use control panel to set it up, import models from other simulation software products, and instant site setup. With Broadcast Express anyone is able to run your simulation, but only you can view or edit it.

| STEP | PROCEDURE |
|------|-----------|
| 1. | Try out several of the publicly available simulations from Forio Broadcast simulation authors at **http://broadcast.forio.com/sims**. |
| 2. | Complete the tutorial at **http://www.forio.com/broadcast_tutorial.htm** to learn how to use Forio Broadcast to build Web-based simulations. |
| 3. | Work in a small group to create a Web-based simulation or the mathematical model for a simulation. Create a solution to a problem in biology, chemistry, earth science, physics, mathematics, or business and economics. Use Forio Broadcast Express or a spreadsheet application like Microsoft Excel to create a mathematical model. Or simply create a paper design for your simulation, using a word processing application or Inspiration. |
| 4. | Review the other two simulations presented in this chapter: The Stock Market Game at **http://www.smg2000.org/** and Virtual Skies at **http://virtualskies.arc.nasa.gov/**. |

Go to the Companion Website and browse *9.2 Building Your Toolkit Enrichment Activity: Downloading and Installing an Educational Simulation.* Use the information in the enrichment activity to access Web-based simulations or simulation software that can be used for Web-enhanced discovery learning activities.

# REFLECTIONS

The Internet facilitates the use of multiple learning environments within a single classroom. Today's classrooms can be places where students are doing things and thinking about what they are doing. When classrooms are organized to promote and support the interactive involvement of students in learning, students are motivated toward further learning, they learn to apply information in new settings, and they develop thinking skills.

Active learning approaches—such as inquiry learning, discovery learning, and case-based learning—are based on the involvement of students working independently or in groups to complete projects or solve problems. Although these learning approaches may seem impractical in a conventional classroom, the information and communication resources of the Internet make these useful and effective approaches to teaching and learning.

The educational philosophy behind inquiry and discovery is similar to that of a scientific laboratory. Students explore the online environment independently and then come back to the teacher when they have questions. Guided discovery can take advantage of particular Internet resources, such as online simulations, and permit the teacher to introduce questions or concepts that can be enriched by online material. Sometimes, however, students should be provided with opportunities for unguided discovery to freely browse the Web and find their own resources from which questions and concepts can emerge. The imagination and inventiveness of teachers and students can create unlimited learning opportunities for inquiry and discovery.

# EXERCISES TO REVIEW AND EXPAND YOUR SKILLS

## Set 1: Reflecting on Practice

- *Closing the Case.* Mr. Warner used Internet technologies to facilitate inquiry and discovery in his science classes. Student inquiries often led a class in many different directions and allowed students to ask questions or solve problems that were not necessarily the ones they had been assigned. Would you encourage students to pursue off-topic or related inquiries in the classroom? Why or why not? If so, how would you manage off-topic inquiries initiated by students?

- *Closing the Case.* Ms. Loewen's sixth graders were struggling to understand the concept of time zones. Although Ms. Loewen had explained it and her students had read about it in their textbooks, they finally understood it when one of her students performed a demonstration for the class. What does this story demonstrate about learning? Based on the discussion presented in this and previous chapters, what techniques or strategies would you use in the classroom to ensure that student learning extended to understanding concepts? How can Web-enhanced learning support and promote true understanding?

- *Closing the Case.* Mr. Wyatt's biology class uses a computer program that simulates the experience of dissecting an actual frog. Many science teachers object to the use of simulation programs as substitutes for hands-on dissections, but Mr. Wyatt believes that the benefits of the computer experience outweigh those of actual dissection. Do you think that students can create knowledge and transfer learning from simulations? Why or why not? Mr. Wyatt said, "It is more important to me that the students understand the anatomical systems than that they know how to perform a dissection." What does this statement tell us about Mr. Wyatt's philosophy of teaching and learning? Is this statement consistent with inquiry and discovery learning approaches? Why or why not?

- *Inquiry-Based Learning.* Consider the inquiry-based learning model presented in this chapter. How would you modify it to be appropriate for the subject and/or grade level you teach? Draw a diagram of the adapted model you would propose for use in your classroom.

- *Discovery Learning.* Some educators think that discovery learning approaches are impractical for use in the regular classroom. Devise a chart listing the strengths (i.e., practicalities) and weaknesses (i.e., impracticalities) of discovery learning in the classroom. Summarize how Internet and information technologies might make discovery learning a more usable approach.

- *Microworlds.* Find examples of microworlds on the Web and try them out. How could microworlds be used in the classroom to support inquiry-based learning and problem solving? What curriculum topics would benefit from microworld exploration?

## Set 2: Expanding Your Skills

Myprojectpages.com allows members to design three different types of online learning documents: project pages, curriculum pages, and miniquests. A miniquest is an online learning activity that has inquiry-based learning as its pedagogical foundation. The instructional model begins with a scenario, which includes an essential question and assigns an authentic task and role for the student. The miniquest continues with a task section, which defines a question set that students need to answer to obtain the raw information necessary to answer the essential question. In the task section questions are directly associated with Web resources; in general, one or two resources will be sufficient per question. After the task questions are answered, a product section describes what students will do with the information they have obtained. The product should require a synthesis of information into a new, personal insight.

You can create several types of miniquests:

- *Discovery miniquests* occur at the beginning of a curriculum unit and are designed to introduce students to it.

- *Exploratory miniquests* occur within the curriculum unit and address the acquisition of content required for the understanding of a particular concept or curricular objective. Exploratory miniquests can be used in conjunction with discovery miniquests or as stand-alones.

- *Culminating miniquests* occur at the end of a curriculum unit and require the use of content information obtained from other types of miniquests or from other instructional methods. Because students have a larger knowledge base as a result of prior learning, they can address a more in-depth question.

| Step | Procedure |
|------|-----------|
| 1. | To begin building a miniquest, open the website **http://myprojectpages.com**. You can download a user guide by selecting the link on the right side of the home page—download the **MiniQuest** tutorial. |
| 2. | Log in to the myprojectpages.com website. When the project manager is displayed, select the link for **MiniQuests** and then the link for **Start New Project.** On the following screen select the link for **Build a MiniQuest.** |
| 3. | Build your miniquest with the same information you used for the 9.1 toolkit exercise. The miniquests wizard will require you to enter this information: scenario, task, and product. If you do not have the appropriate information for all fields, you can record minimal information or even skip a field and go back and edit it later. |
| 4. | After you have entered all the information, select the link to view the final page. |
| 5. | Once you have entered a miniquest, you can edit it by logging in to the website and selecting the link for **Manage Project** on the left side of the home page. |

## Set 3: Using Productivity and Web-Authoring Tools

- *Develop a Project Scenario.* Use a word processing program or Web page authoring program to create a document that provides a detailed scenario for a case-based learning project. Your scenario can be used as a student handout and can include links to Web resources for supplemental contextual information for the case.

- *WebQuest PowerPoint Presentations.* Create the Anasazi project in the 9.1 toolkit exercise, using a multimedia presentation program such as PowerPoint. Place each component of the project on a different slide.

## Set 4: Creating Your Own Web-Enhanced Project

- *Develop an Inquiry-Based, Web-Enhanced Learning Project.* Develop a Web-enhanced learning project based on inquiry or discovery learning. Create a project similar to the one in the 9.1 toolkit exercise that is appropriate for the grade level and/or subject you teach. Document your plan using the WEL lesson plan template or the template for WebQuest projects.

# REFERENCES

Brown, A. L., & Campione, J. C. (1994). Guided discovery in a community of learners. In K. McGilly (Ed.), *Integrating cognitive theory and classroom practice: Classroom lessons*. Cambridge, MA: MIT Press/Bradford Books.

Bruner, J. S. (1960). *The process of education*. Cambridge, MA: Harvard University Press.

Bruner, J. S. (1966). *Toward a theory of instruction*. Cambridge, MA: Harvard University Press. (Quoted in N. Entwistle. (1988). *Styles of learning and teaching: An integrated outline of educational psychology*. London: David Fulton.

Dewey, J. (1938). *Experience and education*. New York: Collier Macmillan.

Gardner, H. (1989). *Art, mind, and education: Research from Project Zero*. Urbana: University of Illinois Press.

Herreid, C. F. (1999). Cooking with Betty Crocker: A recipe for case writing. *Journal of College Science Teaching, 29*(3), 156–158.

Jakes, D. S., Pennington, M. E., & Knodle, H. A. (2003). *Using the Internet to promote inquiry-based learning: An epaper about a structured approach for effective student Web research*. Retrieved May 8, 2003, from http://www.biopoint.com/inquiry/ibr.html

Morgan, R. (2003). Educational simulation website at http://www.creativeteachingsite.com/edusims.html

Palincsar, A. S., & Magnusson, S. J. (2001). The interplay of first-hand and second-hand investigations to model and support the development of scientific knowledge and reasoning. In S. M. Carver & D. Klahr (Eds.), *Cognition and instruction: Twenty-five years of progress* (pp. 151–193). Mahway, NJ: Erlbaum.

Roblyer, M. D. (2003). *Integrating educational technology into teaching*. Upper Saddle River, NJ: Prentice Hall.

Scardamalia, M., Bereiter, C., & Lamon, M. (1994). The CSILE project: Trying to bring the classroom into World 3. In K. McGilley (Ed.), *Classroom lessons: Integrating cognitive theory and classroom practice* (pp. 201–228). Cambridge, MA: MIT Press/Bradford Press.

Wells, G. (2000). Dialogic inquiry in education: Building on Vygotsky's legacy. In C. D. Lee & P. Smagorinsky (Eds.), *Vygotskian perspectives on literacy research*. Cambridge, England: Cambridge University Press.

# CHAPTER 10

# Using the Internet for Online Collaborations

Abiodun Adeferati is a secondary-school teacher in Nigeria. Because he wants his students to have a better understanding of the election process in democracies around the world, he publishes a collaborative project, Global Democracies in Action, on the Internet, seeking 100 other classrooms around the world to participate. Participation requires completion of an easy-to-use Web form, summarizing the election process for a selected official. Sofia Santoro is a middle-school teacher in a large, urban U.S. school district. Although her inner-city school does not have new computer equipment, it recently acquired Internet access on some of the computers in the library. While browsing the Web for learning activities, Ms. Santoro discovers Mr. Adeferati's project and decides that it would be a great learning opportunity for her seventh-grade civics class.

## NEW TERMS

| | |
|---|---|
| avatar | MUD |
| collaborative learning | MUVE |
| learning community | Tapped In |
| MOO | Wiki |

## National Educational Technology Standards for Teachers

The following NETS•T are addressed by the lesson content and learning activities in this chapter:

**II. Planning and Designing**

  **A.** Design technology-enhanced learning opportunities to support diverse needs
  **B.** Apply current research on teaching and learning with technology
  **C.** Identify, locate, and evaluate technology resources
  **D.** Plan for the management of technology resources
  **E.** Manage student learning in a technology-enhanced environment

**III. Teaching, Learning, and the Curriculum**

  **A.** Facilitate technology-enhanced experiences to address standards
  **B.** Use technology to support learner-centered strategies
  **C.** Apply technology to develop students' higher order skills
  **D.** Manage student learning activities

## National Educational Technology Standards for Students

The following NETS•S are addressed by the lesson content and learning activities in this chapter:

**3. Technology Productivity Tools**

  • Use technology to enhance learning, increase productivity, and promote creativity
  • Use tools to collaborate, prepare publications, and produce creative works

**4. Technology Communications Tools**

  • Use telecommunications to collaborate, publish, and interact with others
  • Use varied media and formats to communicate information and ideas

**5. Technology Research Tools**

  • Use technology to locate, evaluate, and collect information
  • Use technology tools to process data and report results
  • Evaluate and select new information resources and technology

**6. Technology Problem-Solving and Decision-Making Tools**

  • Use technology resources to solve problems and make decisions
  • Employ technology to develop real-world problem-solving strategies

## OVERVIEW

Internet technologies make it possible to transform classrooms into virtual learning communities by connecting students with peers, experts, and other resources beyond the classroom. This chapter focuses on implementing learning environments that promote effective online collaboration through synchronous and asynchronous communication. Collaborative learning generates dialogue and interaction as students construct collective knowledge or shared understanding about a concept, case, or problem.

Forming effective groups is an important aspect of using online communication to increase student participation and to develop a learning community in the classroom. Groups can be formed either within a classroom or across classrooms. Collaboration in small groups involves shared problem solving, interpersonal feedback, and social support and encouragement. The process can be facilitative, providing scaffolding for various types of learning activities.

One approach to Internet collaboration is the use of online projects, which allow students to participate with peers in classrooms around the world in completing educational activities or tasks.

Another approach is multiuser virtual worlds (MUVEs), which are two- or three-dimensional text-based or graphic environments that allow people to meet and communicate in a virtual space. They are immersive environments that are usually based on a room metaphor. Participants issue simple commands to navigate through the rooms and to interact with other characters and objects in the space.

## Lesson 10.1    Online Collaborative Projects

### FOCUS QUESTIONS

- What is collaborative learning, and how is it used in the classroom?
- How can online collaborations support Web-enhanced learning?
- How do online collaborations transform classrooms into learning communities?
- What are online collaborative learning projects?

## ■ UNDERSTANDING COLLABORATIVE LEARNING

When students work in groups, they can encourage each other, ask questions of one another, require each other to justify opinions and reasoning, and reflect on the group's collective knowledge. When students work in groups, they bring different abilities and expertise to bear on the task. Research in education has demonstrated that collaborative and cooperative learning can promote academic achievement (Brown & Palincsar, 1989; Cohen, 1994; Johnson & Johnson, 1994), as well as improved behavior and attendance and positive attitudes about school (Slavin, 1987). In addition, collaborative and cooperative learning are easy and inexpensive to implement.

With Web-based collaborative activities, students meet online to discuss topics and solve problems jointly. And even though online collaboration usually involves teams or groups of students in multiple locations, it can be structured to work within one classroom, too.

### Learning as a Social Process

Whereas cooperative learning uses small groups to accomplish a learning task, collaborative learning uses group interactions to create a shared understanding among group members (Schrage, 1990). **Collaborative learning** encompasses a variety of educational approaches that involve shared intellectual effort by two or more peers or by peers and experts. Such activities can range from classroom discussions that might include short lectures to participation on research teams and can involve subject matter at varying levels. Collaborative learning is better suited to complex and ambiguous problems because it can facilitate the construction of complex knowledge process (Feltovich, Spiro, Coulson, & Feltovich, 1996).

Collaborative learning generates dialogue and interaction among peers as they search for a mutual understanding or solution and create a product of their shared learning experience. With collaborative learning, peers are responsible for each other's learning as well as their own; thus, teamwork can be facilitative and can provide scaffolding for the construction of knowledge. Collaborative learning also builds student awareness of different perspectives. And by justifying and defending their ideas to peers, students build deeper knowledge and understanding of a topic.

In addition, group work develops social skills useful for later working environments. Small groups learn team-building skills and goal-setting strategies that are needed to be productive in the workplace. Group collaboration takes advantage of learner-learner interactions rather than learner-content interactions. Small groups can also improve student satisfaction and learning (Doran, 2001) and can decrease a teacher's time administering and structuring a program or other unit of instruction, because teams are self-monitoring.

| **FIGURE 10–1** | **Suggestions for effective use of small groups (Doran, 2001)** |
|---|---|

- At the beginning of a course or school year discuss with students the basic principles of small group work, and include the benefits and challenges it poses.
- At the beginning of a course or school year incorporate team-building activities that encourage communication and trust among group members and that facilitate the development of collaborative skills.
- Provide groups with a systematic appraisal system for giving supportive feedback to one another.
- Require dyads or groups to periodically report progress by e-mail.
- Require students to engage in and report ongoing evaluation of group experiences.
- Use multiple instructional strategies with group work, including panel discussions, role-playing, group investigations, and case studies.
- Model collaboration by encouraging pairs or groups to collaborate with you.

## Forming Effective Groups

Doran (2001) offers a number of suggestions for forming and using groups effectively for collaborative learning (see Figure 10-1). Although group work is not an easy process to implement, teachers can start with pairs, or dyads, and then advance to small groups or teams. Because dyads are simpler to operate and easier to manage than groups, they are a good way to begin Web-enhanced activities. For example, you might divide your class into dyads and have partners use e-mail to interview each other. Then they could send their interviews to a distribution list consisting of the whole class to help all students in the class get to know one another better. Small groups formed within a classroom may work best with asynchronous communication tools, whereas online groups may work best with synchronous communication. As students become more comfortable with partnerships and Internet communication tools, you can form groups comprised of four to six students to work collaboratively on problems or projects.

## Creating Communities of Learning

A **learning community** is a group of people who share a common interest in a topic or a subject and who employ a shared set of practices to build their collective knowledge. Collaborative learning is concerned with building learning communities. In fact, learning communities provide an organizing structure and delivery system for the practice of collaborative learning; they frequently provide more time and space for collaborative learning and other more complicated educational approaches.

Internet technologies make it possible to transform classrooms into virtual learning communities by connecting students with peers, experts, and resources beyond the classroom. Classrooms then can create collective knowledge as students share learning objectives, information, and interests via the Internet.

In a collaborative classroom teachers and students take on more complex roles as the classroom becomes more of an interdependent and interactive community of learners. As students work in teams, the accomplishment of the team becomes the primary concern, and each team member contributes in some way. Student control of learning develops as the classroom learning community works together to create collective knowledge.

## ■ SUPPORTING COLLABORATIVE LEARNING WITH THE INTERNET

### Using Online Projects

One simple approach to collaborative learning and collective knowledge building is the use of online collaborative projects. With online collaborative projects, students work together in teams, use the Internet to research a topic, and publish their findings as an educational website for peers and classrooms around the world. Online collaborations allow students to learn about Internet research, asynchronous project management, and Web communication while they think critically about their selected subject and organize their research into a format that will educate and engage their audience.

Even though an e-mail account is usually all that is needed to participate, most online projects use sophisticated programs, such as elaborated e-mail systems and Internet-based conferencing systems. Internet conferencing is similar to other forms of computer-mediated communication, such as e-mail lists, but it has special features—for example, user control, document structures, shared databases, and interaction management—which make it an especially effective form of educational interaction (Bonk, Malikowski, Angeli, & East, 1998).

The classroom conference is a meeting conducted over the Internet in which the participants can see and hear each other, even though the attendees may be in different places. Students can use live conferencing to share research results, interact with experts, and practice speaking different languages. Group communications technologies, such as CUSeeMe and NetMeeting, which were mentioned in Chapter 3, can connect classrooms around the world so that students can collaborate and learn together.

Online collaborative projects can utilize the publishing features of the Internet as well as the communication features. A collaborative Web publishing tool similar to a Web log is a **Wiki**, which actually permits editing of original posts. Wikis can be used for collaborative publication of Web projects.

*Go to the Companion Website and browse Chapter 10 Lesson Links: Wikis to learn more about this topic.*

## Planning an Online Project

The Internet offers a number of ways for teachers and students around the world to collaborate. Telecollaborate (http://www.telecollaborate.net) is a website that offers the choice of participating in an existing telecollaboration project or starting your own (see Figure 10–2).

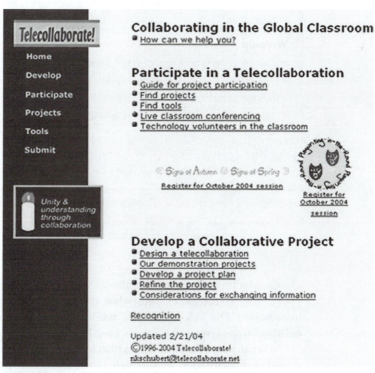

**FIGURE 10–2:   A telecollaboration website**

*Source:* Retrieved from http://www.telecollaborate.net. Reproduced with permission.

| FIGURE 10–3 | Suggestions for managing online collaborative learning projects |

**Project planning**

- Know your specific hardware and software needs.
- Work out the bugs ahead of time.
- Test your project on a different computer before soliciting participants.

**Recruiting participants**

- Clearly state specifics in the call for participants, including dates, deadlines, hardware/software requirements, and project requirements.
- Select enough participants to complete project goals.
- If there are too many participants, offer to provide names to someone interested in running a second group.

**Training participants**

- Make sure participants can do what the project requires before you start. Provide clearly outlined requirements and procedures.
- Practice data-exchange procedures. Learning the tasks ahead of time makes the project more enjoyable for everyone.

**Conducting the project**

- Meet the deadlines set for the project.
- Remind participants about long-term deadlines.
- Provide encouragement and support to participants, and always acknowledge extra efforts.
- Offer a helping hand when you can because education on the Internet is new for many people.
- Be flexible to the needs of participants because technological limitations may arise after the project begins.
- Be ready to go the extra mile by answering a wide variety of questions and searching for solutions to problems.

**Wrap-up**

- Complete the project regardless of complications or setbacks.
- Thank everyone; student thank-yous from classroom to classroom are a nice touch and a good practice to teach.
- Distribute outcomes to all. Be sure everyone gets copies of any information you compile or deduce from the project.
- Keep in touch because participants may want to know about future projects. Make a mailing list.
- Most important of all, have fun. The world is now your classroom.

*Source:* Retrieved from http://www.telecollaborate.net/education/eddevelop.html. Reproduced with permission.

Conducting an online collaborative project is similar to teaching a class: You must plan a lesson and determine what instructional strategies you will use to deliver the information. The Telecollaborate website offers teachers a number of tips for managing collaborative classroom projects (see Figure 10-3).

You can adapt the WEL lesson plan tool for use with telecollaborative projects. Figure 10-4 provides an adaptation that includes information for posting your project on the Internet. This document is intended to be an instructional design tool for planning and creating telecollaboration projects.

| **FIGURE 10–4** | **Lesson plan template for telecollaborative projects** |
|---|---|
| Title/topic | State an interesting, attention-getting title. |
| Author information | State author's name, school or organization, and e-mail address. |
| Project summary | Describe the problem or task the learner needs to solve or perform. |
| Curriculum area | State the curriculum subject area to which the learning activity relates. |
| Participant information | State the grade level or range for which the learning task is appropriate, the maximum number of participants and/or classes, the desired locations of participants, and any other important characteristics. |
| Posting information | State the website (URL) for the project, the posting date, and the deadline for participating. |
| Contact information | State the project coordinator's name, e-mail address, Web page (if available), school or organization, phone number, and postal address. |
| Registration information | Describe how to register for participation in the project, including where (URL or e-mail), when (deadline), and what information to include when registering. |
| Standards of learning | State subject-specific standards and grade-specific technology standards to be addressed by the project. |
| Objectives | State the learning goals, objectives, or purpose of the project relative to the curriculum and technology standards. |
| Background information | Provide orienting or organizing information about the project, including facts, concepts, or rules needed to complete the project. |
| Scenario | Develop a context for the project based on a real-world problem or task that will focus attention on the subject matter and generate learner interest in the project. |
| Procedures | Describe the step-by-step procedures the learner should follow to complete the project, including procedures for interactions and exchanges among participants. Describe the time frame for the project; the starting and ending dates and a schedule of activities with deadlines for each. Describe any alternative approaches or adaptations that learners may use. Allow for deviation. |
| Resources | State the telecommunications hardware, software, and other resources needed to complete the project. State what Web resources are available for the learner to appropriately and successfully complete the project's stated goals, objectives, or purpose. Identify other resources that would enhance the learning experience. |
| Teaching learning strategies | Describe the classroom management methods used to complete the project. |
| Assessment | State what the learner will do to demonstrate understanding and mastery of objectives (should be directly tied to the objectives). State what assessment process (i.e., rubrics) will be used to determine whether learners have understood the lesson. State the person(s) who will perform the assessment, the format for the assessment, the assessment deadline, and distribution of assessment results. |

### Building Your Toolkit:
### Finding Collaborative Projects on the Internet

Global SchoolNet (**http://www.globalschoolnet.org/**) is an international network of over 70,000 online educators who engage in online project-based learning activities. Global SchoolNet (GSN) combines teaching ideas with Web publishing, video conferencing, and other online tools that support project-based learning. GSN partners with schools, universities, communities, businesses, and other organizations to develop free or low-cost programs to help students become literate and responsible global citizens and to prepare them for the workforce.

*(Continued)*

## *Building Your Toolkit:*
## Finding Collaborative Projects on the Internet (Continued)

The Projects Registry of GSN is a clearinghouse for collaborative projects from across the globe. It is hosted by the Global SchoolNet Foundation, other reputable organizations, and outstanding partner projects worldwide. You can choose to join an existing project or announce one of your own on the registry. GSN provides a tutorial for understanding and developing collaborative projects on the Internet; it is called "Harnessing the Power of the Web."

| STEP | PROCEDURE |
|------|-----------|
| **1.** | Open your Web browser and then the website Global SchoolNet at **http://www.globalschoolhouse.org/ GSH/pbl/harnessing.html**. Just above the Join the NetPBL options, select the link **Harnessing the Power of the Web** archives. On that page select the link **Introduction to NetPBL: Collaborative Project-Based Learning**. |
| **2.** | Work through each page of the tutorial, reading the Web page and the links. Select the right arrow (→) at the bottom of each page to advance to the next page. |
| **3.** | Return to the Global Schoolhouse home page at **http://www.globalschoolnet.org/** and select from the menu on the left the link for **Partners and Programs**. Then select the link for **Project Registry** to search past, current, and future collaborative projects. |
| **4.** | In the center of the page select the **Search for Projects** link to conduct a search of projects. Enter an age range appropriate for the grade level you teach, and enter a month and a year that will display current or future projects. |
| **5.** | Select several project links that interest you, and review the information that is posted on the Web. What information is posted? Who is sponsoring the project? How do students participate? How do they successfully complete the project? GSN provides some guidelines on evaluating a project at **http://www.globalschoolhouse. org/GSH/pbl/evaluating.html**. |

**Go to the Companion Website and browse 10.1 Building Your Toolkit Enrichment Activity: Project Registries and Examples for Online Collaborative Projects. Use the information in the enrichment activity to learn more about posting online collaborative projects using Telecollaborate and other project registries.**

Now create a plan for a telecollaborative project that is appropriate to the grade level and/or subject matter that you teach, and complete a WEL lesson plan for it. (You can download the template file **WELTelecollaborateProject.doc** from the Companion Website and save it on your computer.) Use information from GSN's GeoGame project to develop the lesson plan. Open the GeoGame website at **http://www.gsn.org/project/gg/**. Click on the **Project Description**, **Helpful Resources**, and **GeoGame Archives** links to understand how GeoGame works and to gather information for the telecollaborative project lesson plan.

## Lesson 10.2  Collaborative Learning in Virtual Environments

### FOCUS QUESTIONS

- What are MUVEs? MUDs? MOOs?
- How can educational MOOs support teaching and learning in the classroom?
- How can MUVEs be used to establish a community of learning in the classroom?
- What is Tapped In and how can it be used to support teaching and learning in the classroom?

# ■ A SHORT HISTORY OF MUVEs

Multiuser virtual environments (MUVEs) are two- or three-dimensional text-based or graphic environments that allow people to meet and communicate in a virtual space. MUVEs refer to a whole genre of interactive, synchronous communication services on the Internet, which provide a great deal of flexibility and creativity in expression and interaction that is not available with other forms of Internet communication. **MUVEs** are immersive online environments that permit multiple participants to log in simultaneously to a central database through a computer connected to the Internet. Elements of that database are presented as a virtual environment of text descriptions and documents. Participants with access to the World Wide Web through a graphic Web browser can use a point-and-click interface and share images as well as text documents.

The design of most MUVEs is based on a room metaphor; rooms are places within the virtual space depicting physical locations. Participants issue simple commands through the client application on their computer (often a Web browser) to navigate through the rooms and to interact with other characters and objects in the space. The vocabulary of MUVE command language is similar to that of English and usually consists of simple verbs followed by modifiers.

MUVEs offer relatively simple and inexpensive ways to support both synchronous and asynchronous forms of interaction among geographically distributed participants accessing shared resources. MUVEs permit a real sense of being present with other people in a common space. And because each room functions as a shared work space, multiple participants in the same room can see and interact with each other and with objects (or resources) created and placed there by other participants.

Virtual environments can trace their roots to the game Dungeons and Dragons, in which players pose as different characters and perform various tasks. In the late 1960s Will Crowther and Don Woods wrote the first version of Dungeons and Dragons as a computer program called Advent (for Adventure). The computer technology at the time permitted only a text-based interface running on large computers. In 1978 two students of the University of Essex, Roy Trubshaw and Richard Bartle, created a networked version of the game and called it Multiuser Dungeon (now known as MUD1). With this version players were able to communicate with each other through large-scale computer networks using Telnet. As players competed in searching for a treasure and exterminating dragons in a maze of dungeons, they all moved through the same space, were in contact with one another, and were rewarded with points for completing different tasks. All subsequent implementations of the game on the Internet were called MUDs, for multiuser dungeons.

## MUDs

Today, a **MUD** is a text-based chat based on a virtual world, or defined environment, in which users, or chatters, interact with one another. A MUD is no longer considered simply a game, and the MUD acronym is now used to mean multiuser dimension or domain.

MUDs have multiple locations, much like an adventure game, and may include combat, traps, puzzles, magic, a simple economic system, and the capability for characters to build more structure onto the database, which represents the existing world. Users can typically define their personal two- or three-dimensional graphic representations, called **avatars**, through which users interact and communicate with each other. Each user takes control of a virtual persona, or avatar, and explores the virtual world, chats with other characters, explores dangerous monster-infested areas, solves puzzles, and even creates personal rooms, descriptions, and items. The administrators, or wizards, of the virtual world define what the world, or game, will be as they create it.

MUDs are usually comprised of several components, including players, rooms, exits, and objects. Players are characters created by users; they can have descriptions, possessions, motivations, and other definable traits. Rooms are spaces in the game world, the main areas in which players and things exist. A room can have a description that conveys its purpose and its appearance. Exits are links between rooms, which allow players and sometimes objects to move between rooms. Exits typically appear at the end of a room description in a list telling players where they can go. Objects within a game can be small pet animals, swords, tables, horses, or almost any other imaginable item. Typically, objects can be moved from location to location.

## MOOs

In 1989 a student at Carnegie Mellon University, James Aspnes, modified the MUD program by removing all the game aspects. He called the program TinyMUD because this new version consisted mainly of clearing out the unwanted functions of the original program. The result of his efforts was a publicly available, compact program that could be modified to serve many purposes.

Today, elaborate virtual worlds are used for social communities, scientific forums, educational environments, and business conferencing systems. As the Internet has evolved, graphic Web interfaces have replaced the Telnet interface of text-based MUD servers. In the mid-1990s graphic MUDs came to be known as **MOOs**—that is, MUDs object oriented. A MOO has become a popular learning environment, providing a richer communication environment than a chat room and a culture populated by teachers and learners. Some examples of educational MOOs include schMOOze University, Diversity University, and MOOse Crossing.

- *schMOOze University*—(http://schmooze.hunter.cuny.edu) opened in July 1994 and was the first networked virtual reality environment designed for students and teachers of English as a Second Language (ESL) or English as a Foreign Language (EFL). Julie Falsetti, an ESL teacher, wanted to expand her teaching into the MUD environment but found that English MUDs were too difficult to use for nonnative speakers. Therefore, she started schMOOze University, which is used as a place for participants to chat and hold classes in a friendly and supportive environment. Its features include language games, a grammar maze, classroom facilities, USENET feed, gopher access, and an online dictionary.

- *Diversity University*—(http://moo.du.org/) is one of the largest and most elaborate academic MUD projects. This MOO has a number of interesting adaptations of academia, including full-credit courses run entirely online. Diversity University also engages in extensive collaboration with other academic MOOs. It has a direct walk-through link room for users to move between academic MOOs. In addition, regular international conferences are held online. Users must be involved in education to apply for permanent accounts.

- *MOOSE Crossing*—(http://www.cc.gatech.edu/elc/moose-crossing/) is an educational MOO where students aged 13 and under can expand their creative writing skills and learn to program at the same time (see Figure 10-5). Students can create objects ranging from magic carpets to virtual pets to even a Pokémon. They can build virtual rooms and cities—such as King Tut's Pyramid, the Emerald City of Oz, or Hogwarts—and can meet and interact with other students from all around the world.

Educational MOOs can be comfortable places for students to learn. Julie Falsetti of schMOOze University and her colleagues (1997) provide several recommendations for using MOOs:

- Provide students with a conceptual picture of what the MOO will be like, using visual media such as screen shots in a PowerPoint presentation or overhead transparencies or simply handouts. Emphasize that students will be talking to people from all over the world. Remind them to be careful to respect the cultures of others.

- Take small groups into the MOO for their first visit so that you can provide all the help students need and they will not be overwhelmed by all the text in a crowded

**FIGURE 10–5:    Moose Crossing home page**

*Source:* Retrieved August 28, 2004, from http://www.cc.gatech.edu/elc/moose-crossing/.
Reproduced with permission.

virtual room. The more familiar students are with the MOO before they log on to begin assignments, the more risks they will probably be willing to take once there.

■ Design MOO assignments as individual or small group efforts. If the entire class is always in the MOO at one time, classmates tend to talk only to each other.

■ Review the Netiquette guidelines for the MOO. Each MOO has different rules regarding courteous behavior, as established by its inhabitants. For example, at schMOOze University it is considered polite to knock on the door of a private room or office before entering.

■ Provide a handout of the basic MOO commands with examples of their uses. At first your students will feel secure knowing that they have a handout for reference, but they will quickly internalize the basic commands and put the handout aside.

■ Students should have a reason for visiting a MOO, such as a task to complete. For example, a nutrition instructor might assign students to compare the cuisine of various countries. Students can get that information by interviewing other users in the MOO.

■ Remember typing speed. Students who have low-level keyboarding skills will be at a disadvantage in a MOO; they will find it difficult to keep up with conversation. Conversing in a MOO may be just the motivation some students need to get their fingers flying.

■ Introduce the lag monster. Prepare students to expect some amount of lag (i.e., temporary freezing of the screen) during MOO sessions. Assure them that others in the same room and all over the MOO are experiencing the same thing so that students do not misinterpret the silence on the screen as being ignored. Tell students that it is considered polite to send out a note letting others know you are lagging.

- Set your cyberlanguage standard. Let students know in advance about the variations in language they may see in the MOO. Be sure they know your guidelines on how formal or informal their cyberlanguage can be.

- Check your institution's lab policy on MOOs and MUDs. Make sure the computer lab or classroom can technically support MOOs and no firewalls will block MOO access. Be aware that, because MOOs began as games, you may have to promote their educational value in order to make them available for your students.

## ■ MUVEs IN EDUCATION

### Benefits for Teachers and Students

MUVEs can form the basis for sophisticated and sustainable communities of learning on the Internet. In a MUVE, teachers from many different schools and classrooms can share experiences and tools and resources. Currently, there are educational MUVEs organized around many themes—for example, teacher collaboration, foreign language, ESL, science, English, and college courses. The success of these communities indicates that MUVEs can overcome many of the limitations of conventional professional development efforts.

Although asynchronous communication tools, such as electronic mail and bulletin boards, permit teachers some degree of interactivity with their professional communities and access to a variety of online information sources, those tools do not support the rich, real-time conversations available through MUVEs. These immersive environments provide a persistent space, rich in resources, where teachers can interact with other educators and students. Together, participants in MUVEs can construct an online library with links to Web documents, for example. Or they can log and distribute meeting transcripts to participants, along with whiteboard entries and copies of presentation slides.

In addition to professional development initiatives, educational MUVEs can provide a resource-based model for student learning. They offer a safe environment in which students can collaborate and can meet after school to work on classroom projects. Students can get help with homework assignments as well as with long-term projects. MUVEs facilitate cooperation among students from distant schools or students in the same school and classroom and offer the potential of obtaining relevant information immediately from MUVE participants.

MUVEs can also be used by teachers to support classroom instruction. Teachers can easily organize a meeting in the MUVE to discuss a topic or issue, and MUVEs can provide students with relevant study materials and links. Moreover, they can permit students to use related tools and resources within the context of the educational MUVE. MUVEs have the potential to impact students' ability to make judgments and decisions. And many students who may not realize their full potential in the classroom may excel in an educational MUVE.

### Tapped In for Teachers

Mr. Capella is an eighth-grade science teacher. He usually logs in to Tapped In over lunch or during his preparation period and enters his virtual office. That office contains file cabinets filled with electronic documents he uses in his classroom. He reads the notes placed in his inbox, announcing upcoming events and meetings. He checks the calendar to see what activities are coming up and notices a presentation he wants to attend later in the week. Mr. Capella also checks to see who else is online, greets a couple of acquaintances, and chats with them for a few minutes. As he eats the last bite of his sandwich, Mr. Capella goes to the After School Online room and downloads a resource that he is going to use in one of his afternoon classes. As the bell rings, Mr. Capella logs off to go teach his fifth-period class.

**FIGURE 10–6:    Tapped In home page**

*Source:* Retrieved from http:www.tappedin.org. Reproduced with permission.

**Tapped In** (http://www.tappedin.org/) is the online workplace of an international community of education professionals (see Figure 10-6). Founded by SRI International in Menlo Park, California, it permits K–12 teachers and librarians, professional development staff, teacher education faculty and students, and researchers to engage in professional development programs and informal collaboration. Tapped In also helps professional development projects, education agencies, and philanthropic and for-profit organizations use the Internet to connect with and support teachers.

The technology that supports the community is a MUVE designed to support large numbers of professionals in a single virtual place. An integrated set of communication mechanisms (e.g., speaking, whispering, paging, using nonverbal actions) and support tools (e.g., virtual whiteboards, sharable text documents, Web page projection, transcript recorders) enable users to be more expressive than they can be with other types of online tools. Tapped In can be accessed with a Web browser.

The Tapped In campus consists of a collection of buildings; including the Tapped In center and a building for each tenant. Most buildings have a ground floor, a groups floor, and an offices floor; all have a reception room on the ground floor and a lobby on all other floors.

Like most MUVEs, Tapped In uses a room metaphor. When you are logged in to Tapped In, you are always in one room or another. The room in which you start is called your home room. If you have chat enabled, anything you say can be heard (i.e., read) by other Tapped In members who are currently in the room with you. There are several types of rooms, including personal offices, reception rooms, and group rooms. The name of the room you are in is always displayed near the top left of the window and at the top of the chat area. When you are in room view, a menu on the left side of the content area shows the different areas of the room. There are various ways to move from one room to another.

While in any room, you can also access certain types of information from the tabs running across the top of the window. Opening a tab does not change the room you are in, but it does replace the window contents with the selected information until you close the tab to go back to the room view. If chat is enabled, the chat area always appears at the bottom of the window.

Other features of Tapped In include file sharing, threaded message board discussions, chat and transcripts automatically e-mailed to you, group rooms with multiple capabilities, whiteboard, an online profile with photo and icon, collaborations with thousands of educators, daily After School Online meetings with a wide variety of K–12 topics, and an online help desk.

## Building Your Toolkit:
### Exploring Tapped In and Creating a Virtual Office Space

Tapped In is specifically aimed at educators, usually has a live person to help you, and has an easy-to-use Web interface gateway. You can use Tapped In with your Web browser if it supports frames, Java, and JavaScript. The following tutorial is adapted from the Tapped In Interface Guide.

| STEP | PROCEDURE |
| --- | --- |
| 1. | Open your Web browser and then the website for Tapped In, **http://www.tappedin.org/**. If you are not a Tapped In member, you will need to **Sign up for free membership**. Then log in. To learn more about the features of Tapped In or tips for holding meetings, conversations, or training sessions, click on the **Tapped In Interface Guide** link under **Featured Items** in the **Tapped In® Reception** room. |
| 2. | When you first start Tapped In, you enter the Tapped In reception room (see Figure 10–7). Examine the different sections of the screen. To close the chat window at the bottom of the screen, drag the top scroll bar all the way down, and then click the **disable chat** link on the left side of the window. (Click **enable chat** to restart chat.) |

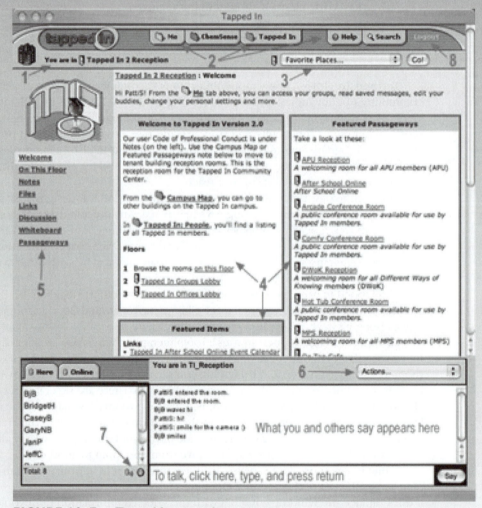

**FIGURE 10–7:   Tapped In reception room**

*Source:* Retrieved from http://www.tappedin.org. Reproduced with permission.

*(Continued)*

**Building Your Toolkit:**
**Exploring Tapped In and Creating a Virtual Office Space (Continued)**

| STEP | PROCEDURE |
|------|-----------|
| **3.** | You can see which room you are in from the **You are in** message near the top left of the window (1) and at the top of the chat area. |
| **4.** | From any room you can also access certain types of information from the tabs across the top of the window (2). Clicking on a tab does not take you out of the room you are in but displays the tab content until you close the tab. Click the **X** in the upper left-hand corner of the tab overlay to close it. Examine each of the following information tabs: |

- **Me tab**—The yellow Me tab is a directory of all of your own personal information about people you know in the community, your favorite places, your links, your notes, your files, groups you are in, and your settings.
- **Tapped In tab**—The blue Tapped In tab provides you with a directory of people, places, and groups in the larger Tapped In community. There is a campus map under this tab that shows you the other buildings and lets you navigate to them.
- **Help tab**—The Help tab provides you with assistance on all topics related to using Tapped In.
- **Search tab**—The Search tab helps you search for people, places, groups, files, and links.

| | |
|------|-----------|
| **5.** | **Favorite Places** (3) is similar to a browser bookmark. It provides a quick way for you to navigate to your favorite Tapped In rooms from anywhere in the environment. Select the pull-down menu in the upper right of the window to view a list of all of your favorite places. Select a room, and then click the **Go** button. You can also add and remove Favorite Places under the Me tab. |
| **6.** | The main area of a room can be filled with notes (4). You can create a note with an image in it to display to people automatically as they enter the room, and you can read notes that others have left. |
| **7.** | Each room has a menu on the left side of the window (5), showing the different areas of the room. At the top of the room window you can see which room you are in as well as which menu item you are viewing. Click on each of the primary menu items to view the different resources of the room: |

- **Welcome**—The Welcome link takes you to the main screen of a room; it is the view you see when you enter a room. Notice that this view contains a Welcome message, Featured Items, and/or Featured Passageways.
- **In this Building**—This view is available from public rooms and provides a building directory and links to each of the floors in the building.
- **On This Floor**—This view is available from public rooms and provides a floor directory and links to each of the rooms on the floor.
- **Notes**—You can create a note in your personal office or in a group room that you own or have joined as a member. You can make both text notes and image notes. Click on the **Notes** link, and review some of the notes posted in the reception area.
- **Files**—Tapped In can be a great way to exchange files with others or a place to start a library of useful documents. You can upload files to rooms that you own or have joined as a member of a group. By default you have 5 MB of file space. Files can be documents, pictures, spreadsheets, or other file types. Once a file is uploaded, anyone who can access the room can see the files. You should use your personal office for files that are of personal interest to you.
- **Links**—This tool is similar to a Web browser's Favorites or Bookmarks tool. The benefit of placing links in Tapped In is that you can access them from any computer, any time, and you can share them with others.
- **Discussion**—Each room in Tapped In has its own threaded discussion board. Any member who can enter a room can post a new topic, read the topics, reply to the topics, and subscribe to the discussion board. Owners of the discussion board have other privileges. Guests may not post to discussion boards.
- **Whiteboard**—This is a simple text board for brainstorming ideas or copying and pasting text from a document.
- **Passageways**—This view shows you all the places you can go directly from this room, as well as information about the rooms that you can enter.

*(Continued)*

**Building Your Toolkit:**
**Exploring Tapped In and Creating a Virtual Office Space (Continued)**

| STEP | PROCEDURE |
|---|---|
| **8.** | The chat area enables you to engage in real-time text-based conversations. For group conversations all group members must be in the same room (i.e., listed under the Here tab). To chat, type what you want to say in the input line at the bottom, and press ENTER (or click **Say**). See what you and others are saying in the larger output area. The **Actions menu** (6) at the top right of the chat area gives you more options. On the left side of the chat area are two awareness tabs labeled Here and Online. Click on each of the tabs: |

- The **Here** tab lets you know who is in the room with you. Below the list of people in the room are two small icons (7):

  - The private message icon allows you to hold a private one-on-one conversation with another user. To send a private message, you would highlight a user name in the list and then click the icon. When a small private message window pops up, you would type your message in the window as you would in the regular chat area. These conversations cannot be seen by other chatters.

  - The information icon shows you the member profile of another user. You would click on a user name in the list and then click the icon. That person's profile would then appear in an overlay.

- The **Online** tab shows you who is currently online and what room they are in, anywhere in the system. Below the list of people are three small icons:

  - As with the Here tab, the private message icon allows you to hold a private one-on-one conversation with another user.

  - As with the Here tab, the information icon shows you the member profile of another user.

  - The open door icon allows you to join another person in whatever room that person is in, provided you have the appropriate permission to enter that room. When you click a user name in the list and then click the door icon, you will be teleported to the room of that user.

| **9.** | To create your office, click the **Me** tab and then in the **Welcome** view click the **Create your office** link. If an information profile appears, fill it out; the information will determine where your office is located. Once you have created your office, a Go to your office link will appear. You can have only one office. |
| **10.** | You can add your office to your favorite places. While in your office, click the **Me** tab and then in the **Places** view click the **Add favorite places** link. |
| **11.** | You can make your office your home room, that is, the room you first appear in when you log in to Tapped In. (Your office must first be added to your favorite places.) While in your office, click the **Me** tab and then in the **Settings** view click the **choose a different home room** link. Select the radio button beside your office, and click the **Use Selected Room as Home Room** button. The Settings view for your office should indicate that your office is set as your home room. |
| **12.** | To obtain a printed guide for using the Tapped In interface, from the **Favorite Places** pull-down menu, select the Tapped In **Reception** room. Then on the **Featured Items** note select the link for Tapped In **Interface Guide,** and print the page from your Web browser. Close the browser window to return to the Tapped In window. |
| **13.** | To obtain more detailed information about navigating Tapped In, click the **Help** tab from the Tapped In window, and then click the **Navigation** link. Review the Help information, and then click the **X** in the upper left-hand corner of the Help tab overlay to close it. |
| **14.** | Click **Logout** (8) in the upper right corner to log out of Tapped In. |

**Go** to the Companion Website and browse *10.2 Building Your Toolkit Enrichment Activity: Creating or Joining Groups in Tapped In.* Practice the skills presented in the enrichment activity to learn how to create your own group or join other groups in Tapped In.

# REFLECTIONS

Although most U.S. schools are connected to the Internet, the use of Internet technologies and resources is still not well integrated into teaching and learning in classrooms. Part of the problem may be that teachers think in limited ways about using online tools and resources in their teaching (Harris, 2002). Many of the Web-enhanced learning activities that have been presented in this textbook are based on students analyzing information and creating work products individually or in small groups, usually within a classroom over a short period of time. By contrast, Web-enhanced learning activities based on online collaborations require interaction among participating classrooms and occur over an extended period of time, with ongoing coordination by teachers and students.

Online collaborative projects are inherently more difficult to conduct because they are more challenging to organize and place more demands on the classroom time of teachers and students. Certainly classrooms are not structured to facilitate high levels of collaboration, especially with participants outside the local classroom. However, online collaborative activities clearly utilize critical-thinking skills and require complex social interactions. Students participating in online collaborations receive numerous educational benefits from having to understand, synthesize, and integrate perspectives different from their own.

A key to the success of online collaboration projects is the willingness of teachers to incorporate collaboration-based tools and resources into classroom learning activities. Even though online collaborative learning can effectively prepare students as productive citizens of the information age, the challenge is for teachers to find creative ways to structure the classroom environment to support that learning.

# EXERCISES TO REVIEW AND EXPAND YOUR SKILLS

### Set 1: Reflecting on Practice

- *Closing the Case.* Mr. Adeferati is a secondary teacher in Nigeria who publishes a collaborative project on the Internet. Ms. Santoro is a middle-school teacher in a large, inner-city urban school district in the United States who decides that joining Mr. Adeferati's project would be a great learning opportunity for her seventh-grade civics class, using the limited computer technology resources in her school. What classroom management problems does participation in a collaborative project on the Internet present?

- *Closing the Case.* Mr. Capella is an eighth-grade science teacher who has a virtual office in Tapped In. Mr. Capella uses Tapped In mainly for professional development and for maintaining and acquiring materials and resources to use in his classes. What are some other ways you could use Tapped In to support teaching and learning? How could you use Tapped In with your students to support a community of learning in your classroom?

- *Educational MUDs and MOOs.* Review several of the MUDs and MOOs referenced in this chapter, and then design a MUD or a MOO for your classroom. Create a map or a drawing of what the virtual space would look like by identifying spaces, tools, and resources in your virtual classroom.

  - What rooms does your MUD or MOO include? What is the purpose of each room?
  - What tools and resources are available in your MUD or MOO? Are there restrictions or limitations on tools and resources?
  - What people are included in your MUD or MOO? Are there restrictions or limitations on who can participate and what they can do?

- *Classrooms as Communities of Learning.* Margaret Riel (1998) says that technology is actually going to increase the need for and access to teachers. She maintains that, as communication technologies transform classrooms into learning communities, teachers will sometimes teach from distant locations.

- If you create a connected classroom, what responsibilities do you have for the learning in classrooms at distant locations?
- If you connect to other classrooms, what learning support should a teacher from a distant classroom provide to your classroom?
- Should teachers be encouraged to provide learning support to other classrooms? Why or why not?
- Should teachers be compensated for providing learning support to other classrooms? Why or why not? If yes, then how?

## Set 2: Expanding Your Skills

If you store documents, links, and notes in Tapped In, then all you have to do is log in to Tapped In from any computer connected to the Internet to make all those resources available to you.

| Step | Procedure |
| --- | --- |
| 1. | Log in to Tapped In at **http://www.tappedin.org**, enter your office, and explore the following tools and resources. |
| 2. | To add After School Online to the Featured Passageways of your office, select **Passageways > Add passageway**. Then enter **After** in the search box, and click the **Find It!** button. Click the selection box beside After School Online, and click the **Continue** button. Then click the selection box beside After School Online again to feature it, and click **Add Passageways**. Click the **Welcome** screen; After School Online has now been added to the Featured Passageways of your office. |
| 3. | Select **After School Online** from your Featured Passageways list. Many of the activities at Tapped In take place in the After School Online (ASO) room, which is equipped with a whiteboard on which everyone can write and read messages and contribute. All ASO sessions are recorded, and the transcript is available for later review by any member. Explore the resources available in ASO by clicking the menu items for **Notes**, **Files**, **Links**, and **Discussion**. |
| 4. | Visit the Tapped In **Reception** room, and check the schedule of events by selecting the link for **Monthly Tapped In® Calendar of Events** on the Featured Items note. |
| 5. | Return to your office. Every Tapped In room has a whiteboard, a simple tool that facilitates unrestricted interactive communication and is especially useful for agendas and brainstorming. Select **Whiteboard** in the room menu of your office, and practice using it. You do not need to have chat enabled to use the whiteboard. Anyone who can enter the room can write on the whiteboard or erase it entirely. Once erased, the contents of the whiteboard cannot be recovered. Any text that you enter on the whiteboard is appended to already-existing text. Links to refresh it, write on it, erase it, edit it, or feature it appear above and below the whiteboard. <br><br> • The whiteboard does not update automatically when someone else writes on it but is refreshed periodically so that new additions become visible. Click the **refresh it** link to force the whiteboard to refresh immediately. The date the whiteboard was last refreshed appears in the upper right-hand corner. <br><br> • If you are in a room where you have permission to create a new note and the whiteboard is not currently blank, a **Print To Note** button appears in the bottom right-hand corner of the whiteboard. Clicking this button copies the current contents of the whiteboard to a new text note in the room titled Whiteboard: Date, Time. <br><br> • If you are the owner of the room or a moderator with whiteboard privileges, you have access to additional features. You can edit the entire contents of the whiteboard just like any other note by clicking the **edit it** link. You can also feature the contents of the whiteboard on the welcome page of the room by clicking **feature it**. Once featured, you can click |

        **unfeature it** to take the whiteboard note off the welcome page again. These links appear beneath the whiteboard.

6.      In Tapped In you can upload files to your office; each member of Tapped In has a default file quota of 10,240 KB. Tapped In reserves the right to remove any files deemed inappropriate, including copyrighted materials, such as movie or music files. Once uploaded to your office, anyone who enters your office can download the files there. From your office select **Files** from the room menu, and browse the hard disk of your computer to locate and select an appropriate file. Enter a **Description** for the file (not the file name), select the check box to make the file appear in your office, and then select the **Upload a File** button.

7.      You can create and maintain links to other websites in Tapped In from your office. Links can be shared in your office or your member profile or created and maintained in a group room. Once created in your office, anyone who enters your office can select any URLs. From your office select **Links** from the room menu. Select the **Add link** button, enter the **URL**, enter a **Title** for the URL, enter a **Description** for the URL, and select the check box to make the file appear in your office.

8.      Select **Passageways** from the room menu of your office, and add a passageway to After School Online.

### Set 3: Using Productivity and Web-Authoring Tools

■ *Create and Upload an Online Resource for Your Tapped In Office.* Use word processing to create a lesson plan document for a telecollaborative project that is appropriate to the grade level and/or subject matter you teach. You can use the information from your 10.1 toolkit project or another topic. Find some websites to support your project (e.g., websites with geography information), and include a hotlist of appropriate websites for your topic.

■ *Online Collaborative Project PowerPoint Presentations.* Use a multimedia presentation program such as PowerPoint to recreate your GeoGame telecollaboration project in the 10.1 toolkit exercise. Place each component of the telecollaboration project on a different slide(s). Insert hyperlinks for the Web resources so that students can link to the website directly from the presentation program.

### Set 4: Creating Your Own Web-Enhanced Project

Develop a WEL lesson plan for a telecollaborative project for a classroom book club. With the book club students can hold debates on the discussion board, or chats and discussions about books can be archived. The discussions can also be used to decide which themes from a book ought to be discussed or which book should be read next. You can develop the project as an online collaborative learning project or use Tapped In. If you create an online collaborative project, you should invite other classrooms to join your book club. If you use Tapped In, you could create a group discussion room for the book club.

## REFERENCES

Bonk, C. J., Malikowski, S., Angeli, C., & East, J. (1998). Web-based case conferencing for preservice teacher education: Electronic discourse from the field. *Journal of Educational Computing Research, 19*(3), 269–306.

Brown, A., & Palincsar, A. (1989). Guided, cooperative learning and individual knowledge acquisition. In L. Resnick (Ed.), *Knowing, learning and instruction* (pp. 307–336). Hillsdale, NJ: Lawrence Erlbaum.

Cohen, E. G. (1994). *Designing groupwork: Strategies for the heterogeneous classroom.* New York: Teachers College Press.

Doran, C. L. (2001). The effective use of learning groups in online education. *New Horizons in Adult Education, 15*(2).

Falsetti, J., Frizler, K., Schweitzer, E., & Younger, G. (1997). Getting started using MOOs: MOO and YOO—What to DOO. In T. Boswood (Ed.), *New ways of using computers in language teaching.* Alexandria, VA: TESOL.

Feltovitch, P. J., Spiro, R. J., Coulson, R. L., & Feltovich, J. (1996). Collaboration within and among minds: Mastering complexity, individually and in groups. In T. Koschmann (Ed.), *CSCL: Theory and practice of an emerging paradigm* (pp. 25–44). Mahwah, NJ: Erlbaum.

Harris, J. (2002, March). Wherefore art thou, telecollaboration? *Learning and Learning with Technology, 29*(6), 54–58.

Johnson, D. W., & Johnson, R. T. (1994). *Learning together and alone: Cooperative, competitive, and individualistic learning* (4th ed.). Edina, MN: Interaction Book.

Riel, M. (1998). *Education in the 21st century: Just-in-time learning or learning communities.* University of California at Irvine, Center for Collaborative Research in Education. Retrieved September 25, 2003, from http://gsep.pepperdine.edu/~mriel/office/papers/jit-learning/index. html

Schrage, M. (1990). *Shared minds.* New York: Random House.

Slavin, R. (1987, March). Cooperative learning: Can students help students learn? *Instructor,* 74–78.

# GLOSSARY

**active learning** Instructional activities that involve students in doing things and thinking about what they are doing. Students learn content by interpreting, processing, and applying it to new ideas and transferring the knowledge they construct to other situations.

**anchored instruction** An instructional method that places students in the context of a problem-based story or activity using multimedia resources.

**asynchronous communication** Communication between computer users that is not in real time; that is, the sender and the receiver of the message do not participate at the same times. E-mail is one example.

**authentic assessment** An evaluation methodology that is intended to correspond to real-world experiences.

**avatar** Two- or three-dimensional graphic representation of a user in a virtual world.

**Big6** An information problem-solving process to guide students through the steps of solving a problem or making a decision.

**blog** See *Web log.*

**blogging** The act of writing and publishing a Web log, which often takes the form of a digital diary.

**cases** Narratives, situations, select data samplings, or statements that present unresolved and provocative issues in a form that is intended to educate.

**chat** Real-time communication between two or more people using computers, usually through the Internet.

**cognitive tools** Mental mechanisms and digital devices that support, guide, and extend the thinking processes of users.

**collaborative learning** A teaching method that generates dialogue and interaction among peers or communities of peers and experts for the purpose of constructing collective knowledge or shared understanding about a concept, case, or problem; tends to be student centered and usually requires participants to reach consensus on a shared solution.

**community of learning** See *learning community.*

**cooperative learning** The instructional use of small groups to maximize individual and group learning; tends to be more teacher directed than collaborative learning.

**course management software** Programs that are used to develop Web-based instruction or courseware; Blackboard and WebCT are examples.

**differentiated classroom** A classroom in which teachers facilitate learning on the premise that learners differ in important ways.

**digital library** Digitized primary source documents, assembled into collections and presented online.

**discovery learning** An inquiry-based learning method that usually takes place in problem-solving situations in which the student draws on personal experience and prior knowledge to discover the rules, relations, or concepts about something.

**e-learning** Also called *online learning* or *Web-based instruction,* a form of distance learning that relies on the Internet for the delivery of instruction.

**electronic portfolios** Living documents that contain multiple information types—such as text, sounds, graphics, pictures, or movies—and that are published on the Web.

**e-mail** An Internet application that allows text messages comprised of text to be sent between computers.

**emoticons** Keyboard characters used to express emotion in online text-based messages.

**e-zines** Journals or magazines that can be delivered and read online.

**flaming** A heated retort of a personally demeaning or derogatory nature, sent in an e-mail message or a newsgroup article.

**generative learning** Learning that occurs when students reorganize facts and information into more flexible knowledge structures, revealing relationships among ideas or identifying gaps in knowledge or conflicts between ideas.

**hotlist** A list of websites that a teacher finds useful in completing a specific learning activity.

**HTML (hypertext markup language)** The language in which Web pages are written.

**information literacy** The skill or ability to locate, evaluate, and use information to create useful knowledge.

**inquiry learning (or instruction)** An instructional methodology that uses questioning strategies to engage students in discovering rules and relationships and generating new knowledge and understandings; similar to discovery learning.

**instant messaging** A form of chat that provides a more personal or private interaction between chatters.

**Internet** A worldwide communications network that provides a common protocol to connect local and wide-area computer networks.

**Internet2** A consortium of more than 200 universities working in partnership with industry and government to develop and deploy networking and other advanced applications for learning and research; joins its members together through many advanced computer networks.

**intranet** A private network within an organization that is not accessible to the public and uses networking hardware and software for communicating, storing, or sharing files.

**invisible Web**   Web content that is often contained in specialized searchable databases and is not or cannot be indexed by search engines.

**keypals**   Penpals that communicate with one another using e-mail.

**learning community (or community of learning)**   A group of people who share a common interest in a topic or a subject and employ a shared set of practices to build their collective knowledge.

**listserv (or discussion group)**   E-mail messages automatically distributed to a large group.

**message board**   A threaded discussion that allows someone to post a message to a common space for others to read at their own convenience.

**metasearch engine**   Utilizes multiple single engines to conduct an information search; has broader Web coverage than a single search.

**microworld**   A type of simulation that is a tiny world, or virtual space, inside which students can explore alternatives, test hypotheses, and discover facts that are true about that world.

**MOO (MUD object-oriented)**   A popular virtual learning environment that is a graphic form of a MUD.

**MUD (multiuser dungeon, dimension, or domain)**   A text-based chat in which users, or chatters, interact with one another in a defined environment, or virtual world.

**MUVE (multiuser virtual environment)**   An immersive online environment that allows multiple participants to log in simultaneously to a central database through a computer connected to the Internet.

**Netiquette**   Network etiquette; the dos and don'ts of online communication.

**plagiarism**   The taking and using of someone else's words or ideas presented as one's own; a dishonest, unethical, and potentially illegal practice.

**plug-in**   A small program that can be inserted into a main program to expand its capability; for example, a plug-in might enable a Web browser to play music or video files.

**portal (or Web portal)**   Websites that provide a structured gateway to the Internet with supporting tools and resources.

**problem-based learning**   An approach to learning that permits learners to investigate engaging and authentic topics and maximizes information seeking, evaluating, and applying.

**RSS (really simple syndication)**   An RSS feed repackages the content of a Web page entry as a list of data items, such as the date of the posting, a summary of the article, and a link to it. An RSS aggregator program, or feed reader, can then check RSS-enabled Web pages and display any updated articles it finds.

**rubrics**   Assessment tools that establish criteria for complex and/or subjective educational activities.

**scaffolding**   Instructional strategies that provide learners with direction and motivation for solving problems or completing learning activities.

**scenario**   A description of a real-world problem that might be open-ended, complex, and unstructured and have multiple solutions.

**simulation**   A computer program based on an underlying computational model that recreates a somewhat simplified version of a complex phenomenon, environment, or experience.

**student-centered learning**   The result of instruction designed to create independent, autonomous learners who assume responsibility for their own learning.

**synchronous communication**   Real-time communication between computer users who are simultaneously present to send and receive messages. Chat is one example.

**task-relevant knowledge**   Information or knowledge that students need to conduct an information search efficiently and effectively.

**TEACH Act**   Expands the scope of educators' rights to use copyrighted works for digital distance education.

**thread**   Multiple posts referring to one particular subject, creating a multilayered discussion.

**universal design**   A design concept that is usable by a broad range of people; see also Web accessibility.

**URL**   The Web location of a document or file that resides on a Web server connected to the Internet.

**Usenet**   A network service that propagates messages or articles posted from a newsgroup.

**virtual reality**   A sophisticated form of simulation that includes props—such as goggles, helmets, or special gloves—to create the sense of an immersive cyberenvironment.

**virus**   Self-replicating pieces of computer code that can partially or fully attach themselves to files or applications.

**Web accessibility**   The ability of Web pages to accommodate the needs of a broad range of users, computers, and telecommunication systems.

**Web-based instruction**   A form of distance learning that delivers instruction through a computer using standard Internet technologies, especially the World Wide Web.

**Webcast**   The real-time transmission of encoded video under the control of the server to multiple recipients, who all receive the same content at the same time.

**Web-enhanced learning**   A classroom-based educational model that allows students to use Internet technologies, especially the Web, to access information and other digital resources in ways that are conducive to learning.

**Web essay**   A collection of journal entries and reflective writings, peer reviews, artwork, diagrams, charts and graphs, group reports, student notes and outlines, and rough drafts and polished writing, which document learning over time and teach students the value of self-assessment, editing, and revision.

**Web inquiry projects (WIPs)**   Learning activities that use uninterpreted online information; designed to help teachers use Internet resources to promote inquiry in the classroom.

**Web log**   A Web page made up of short, frequently updated posts, which are arranged chronologically, like a journal.

**Web portal**   A Website or service that offers a broad array of resources and services, such as e-mail, forums, search engines, and related content.

**WebQuest**   Inquiry-oriented activities in which most or all of the information used by learners is acquired from the World Wide Web.

**Wiki**   Collaborative Web logs that permit editing of original posts; used primarily for collaborative Web publication.

**World Wide Web**   An application used to access information resources through the Internet; allows text and graphics to appear in a standard format, regardless of computer hardware or operating system.

# INDEX